MW01627192

THRIFT STORE PAINTINGS

PAINTINGS FOUND IN THRIFT STORES

Edited by

Jim Shaw

HEAVY INDUSTRY PUBLICATIONS
P.O. BOX 85428
HOLLYWOOD, CALIFORNIA 90072

PRINTED IN SINGAPORE

LIBRARY OF CONGRESS NUMBER 90-084442

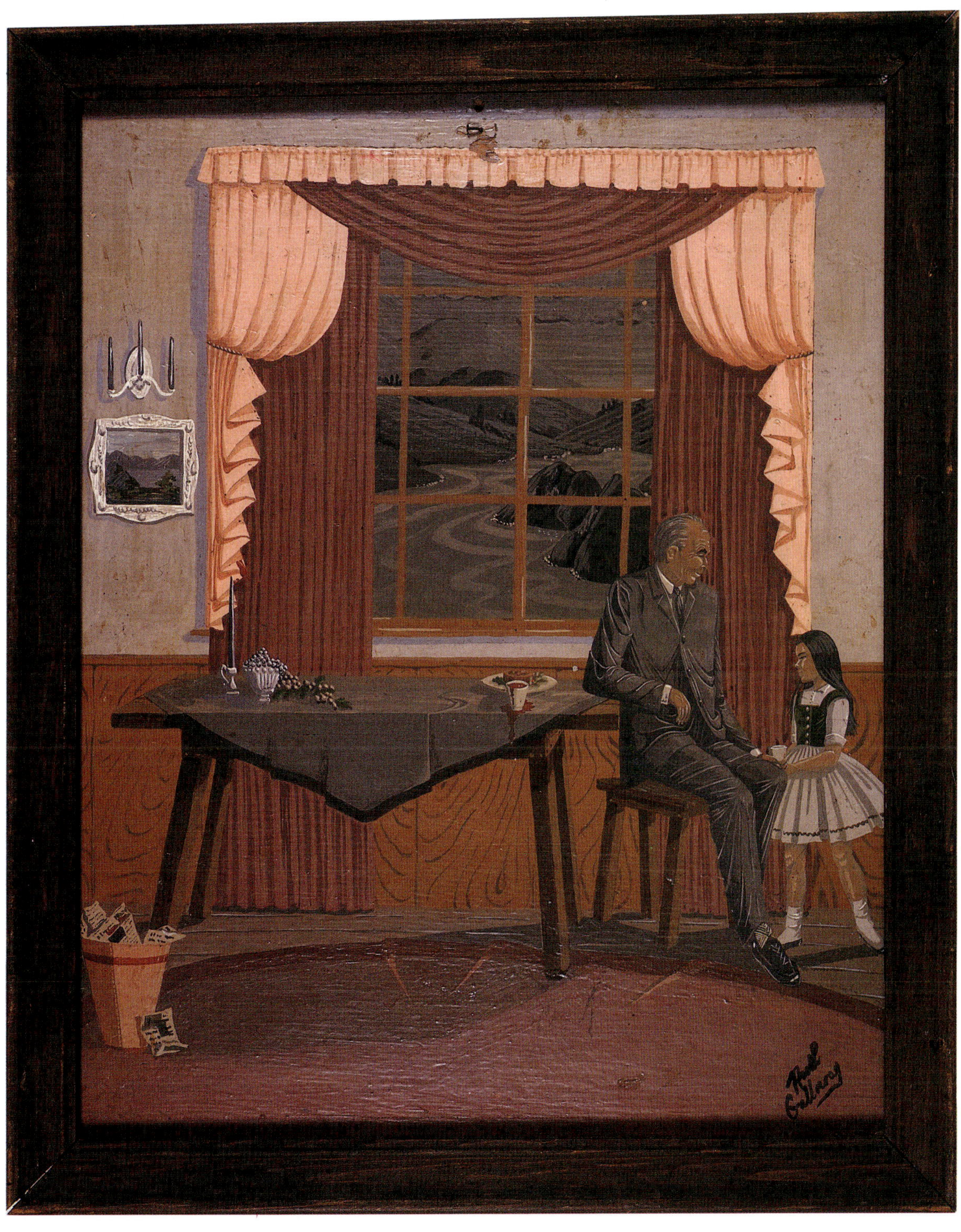

Man and Girl at Table in Gray & Cranberry

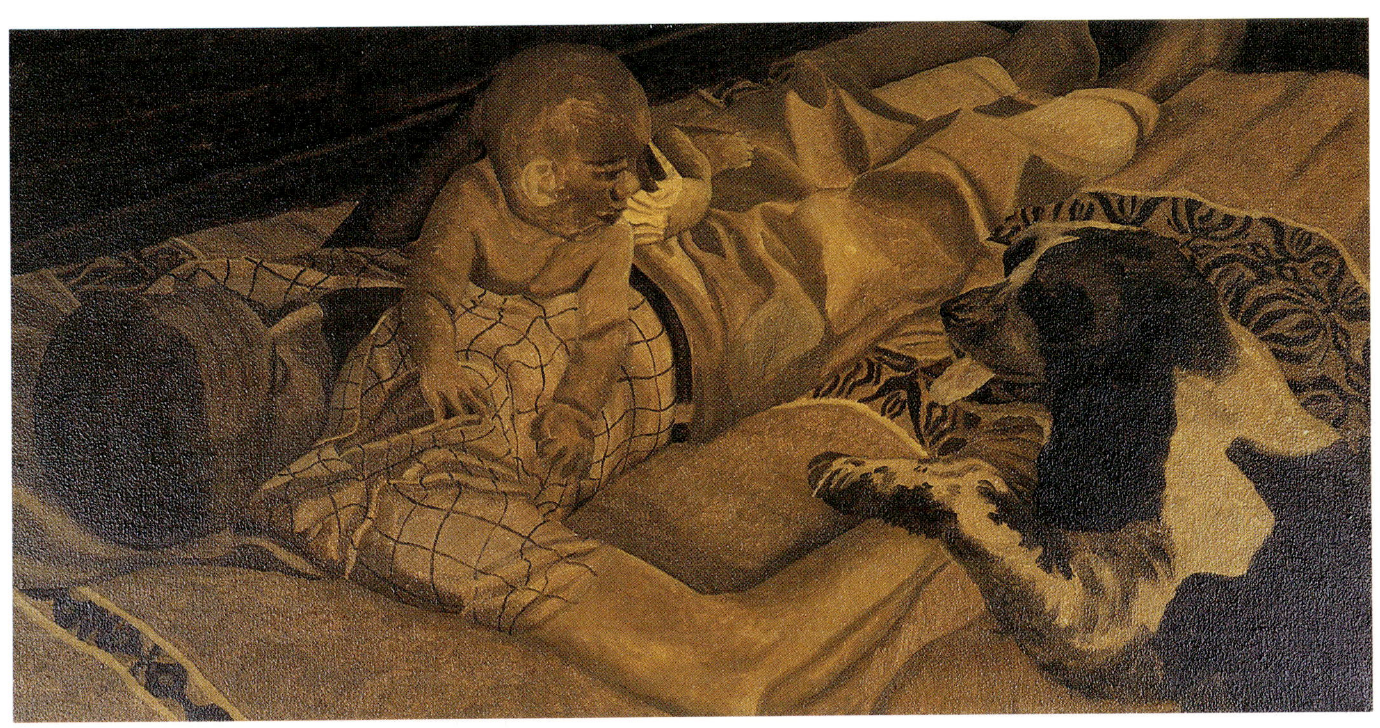

Ochre Baby Crawls on Man's Chest as Dog Looks On

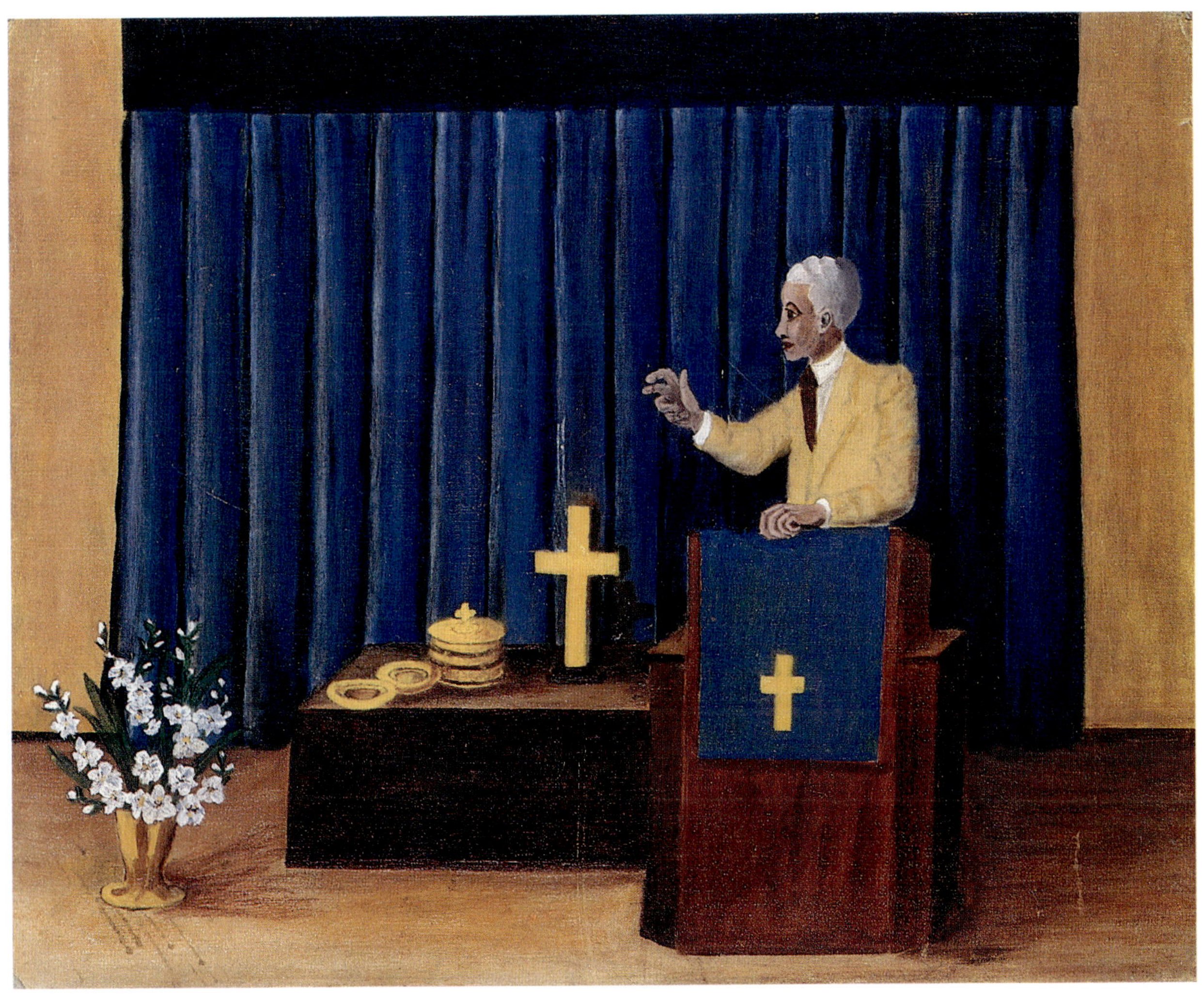

Preacher at Blue Pulpit

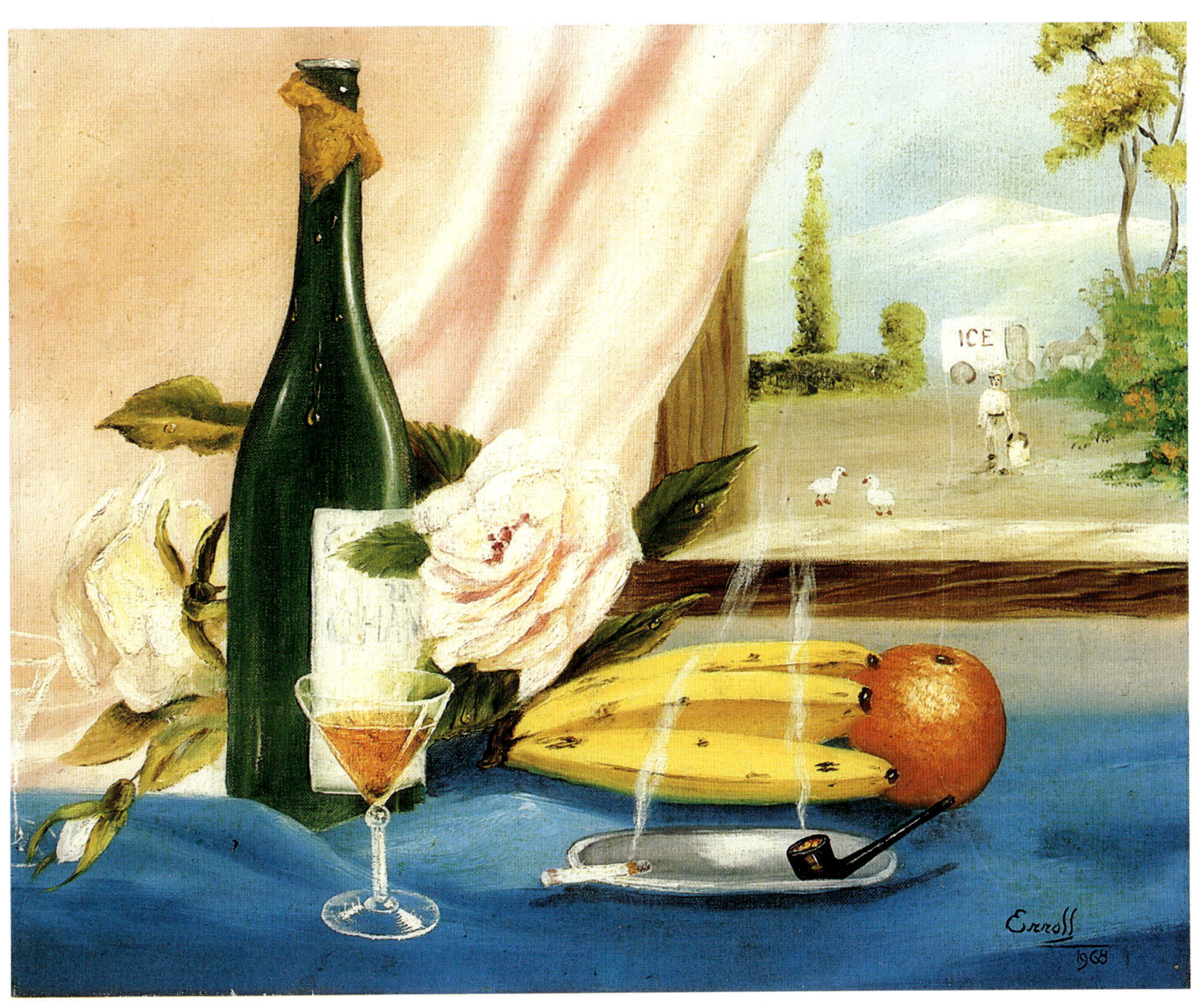

Still Life with Pipe, Cigarette, Banana, Champagne, etc.

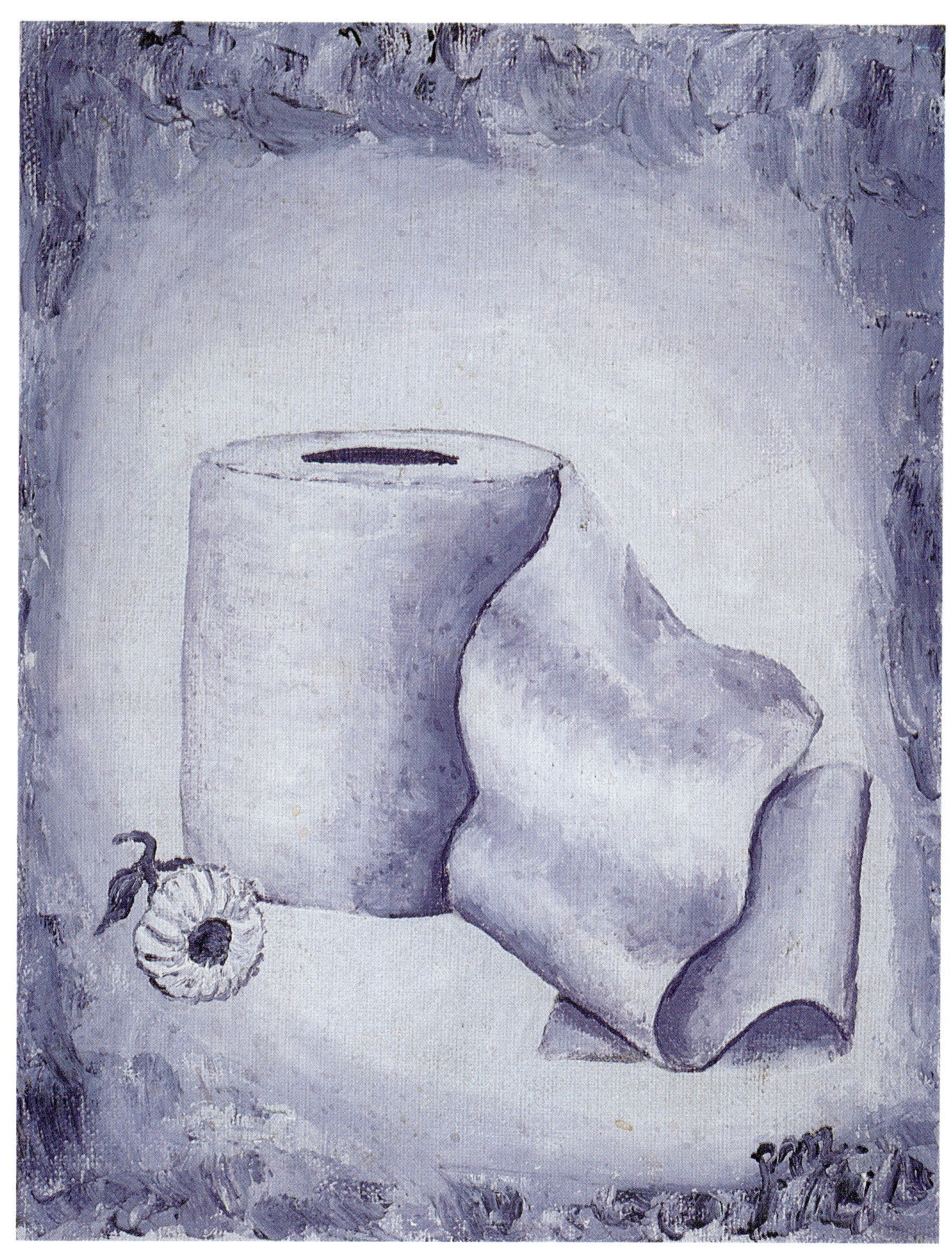

Purple Toilet Paper and Flower

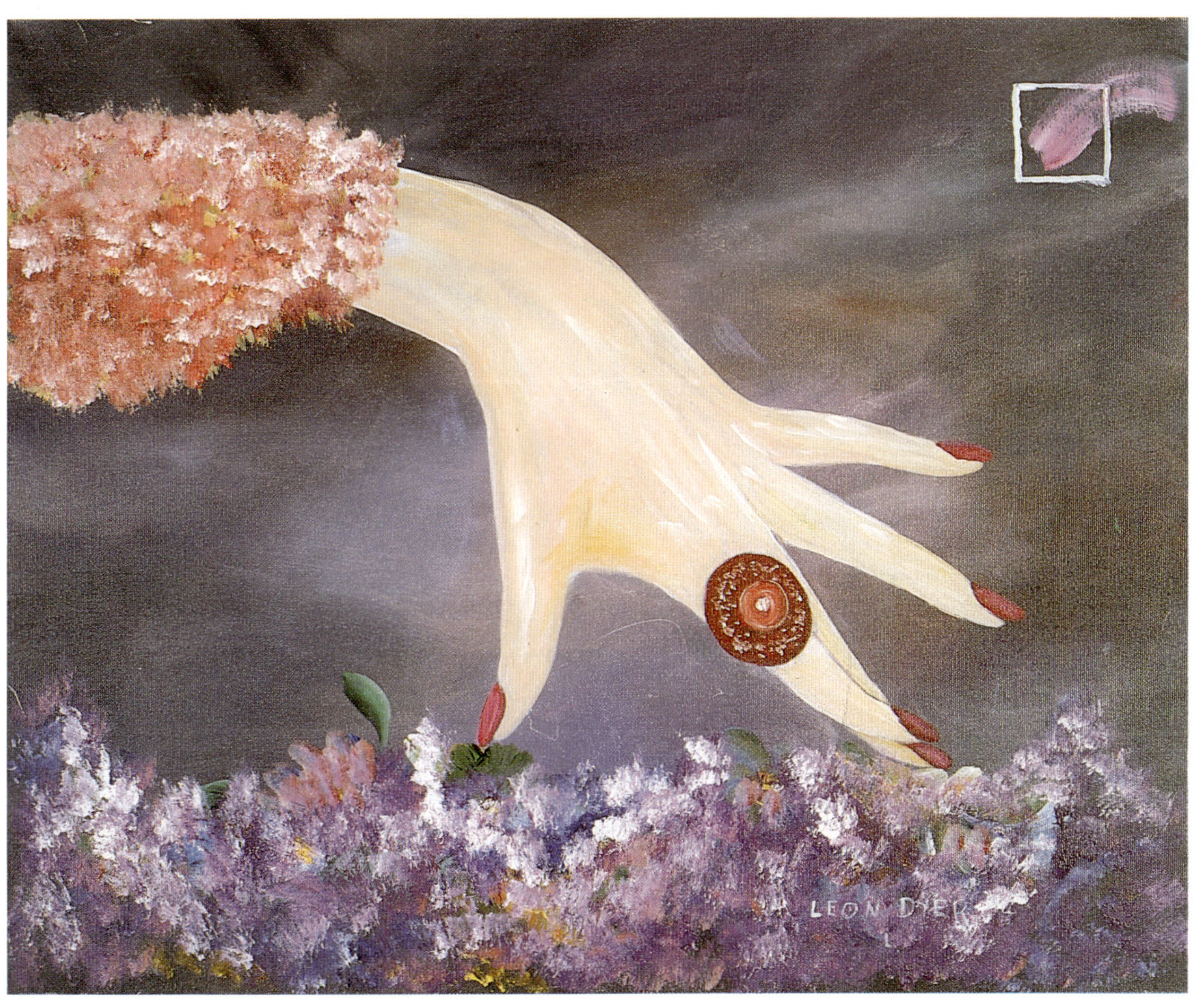

Woman's Hand with Dark Red Ring, Fuzzy Sleeve

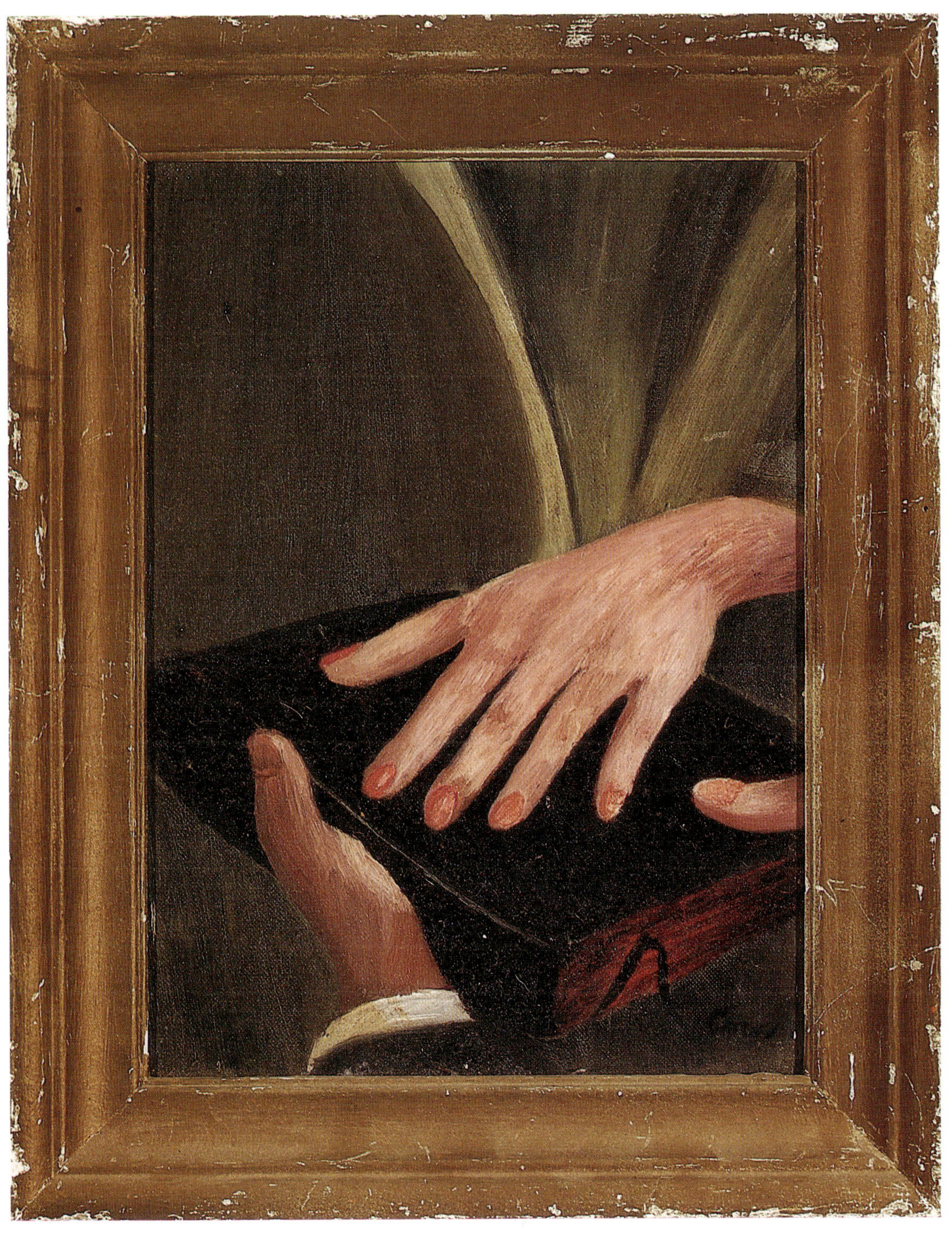

Hand on Bible

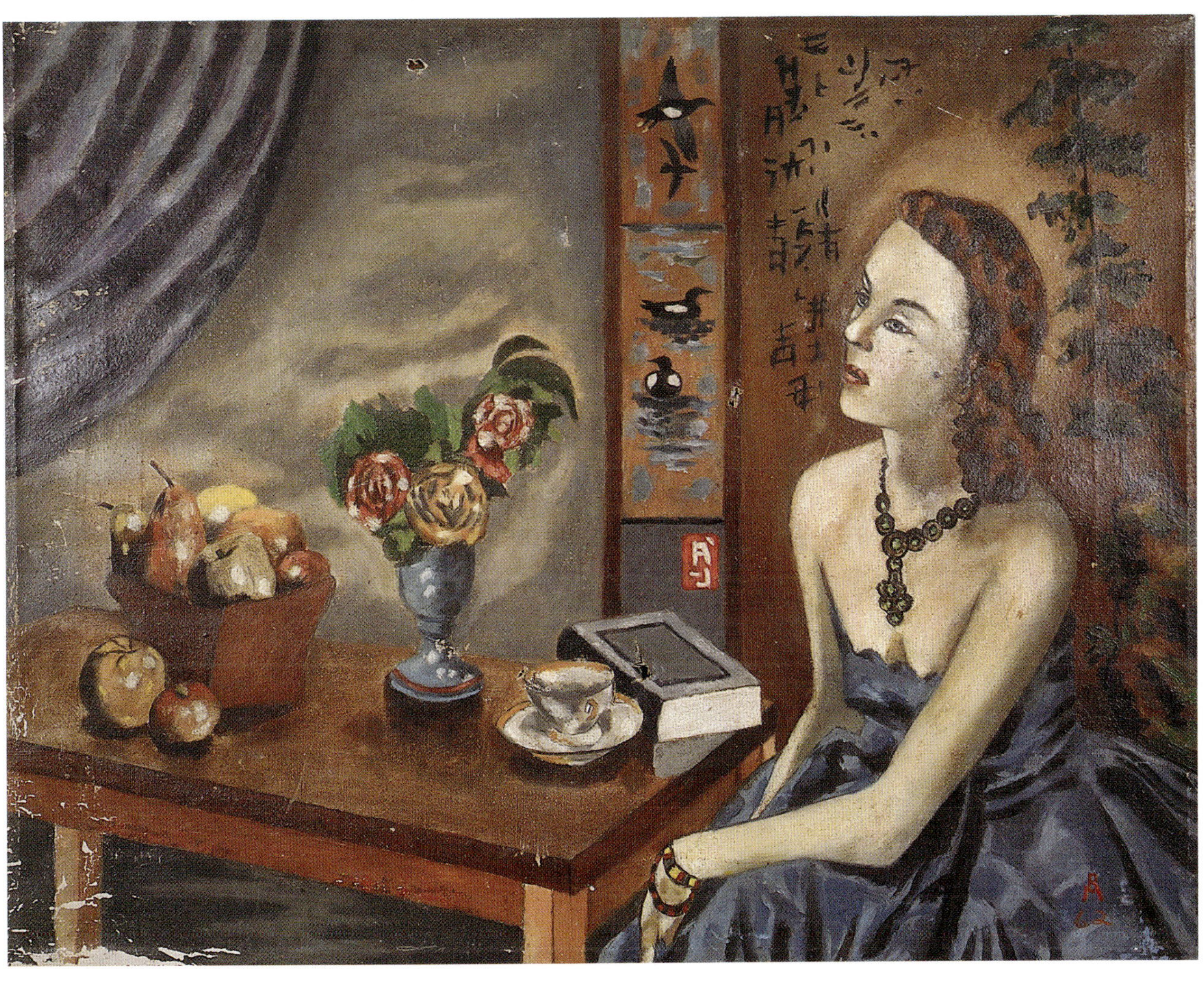

Woman by Table with Chinese Writing

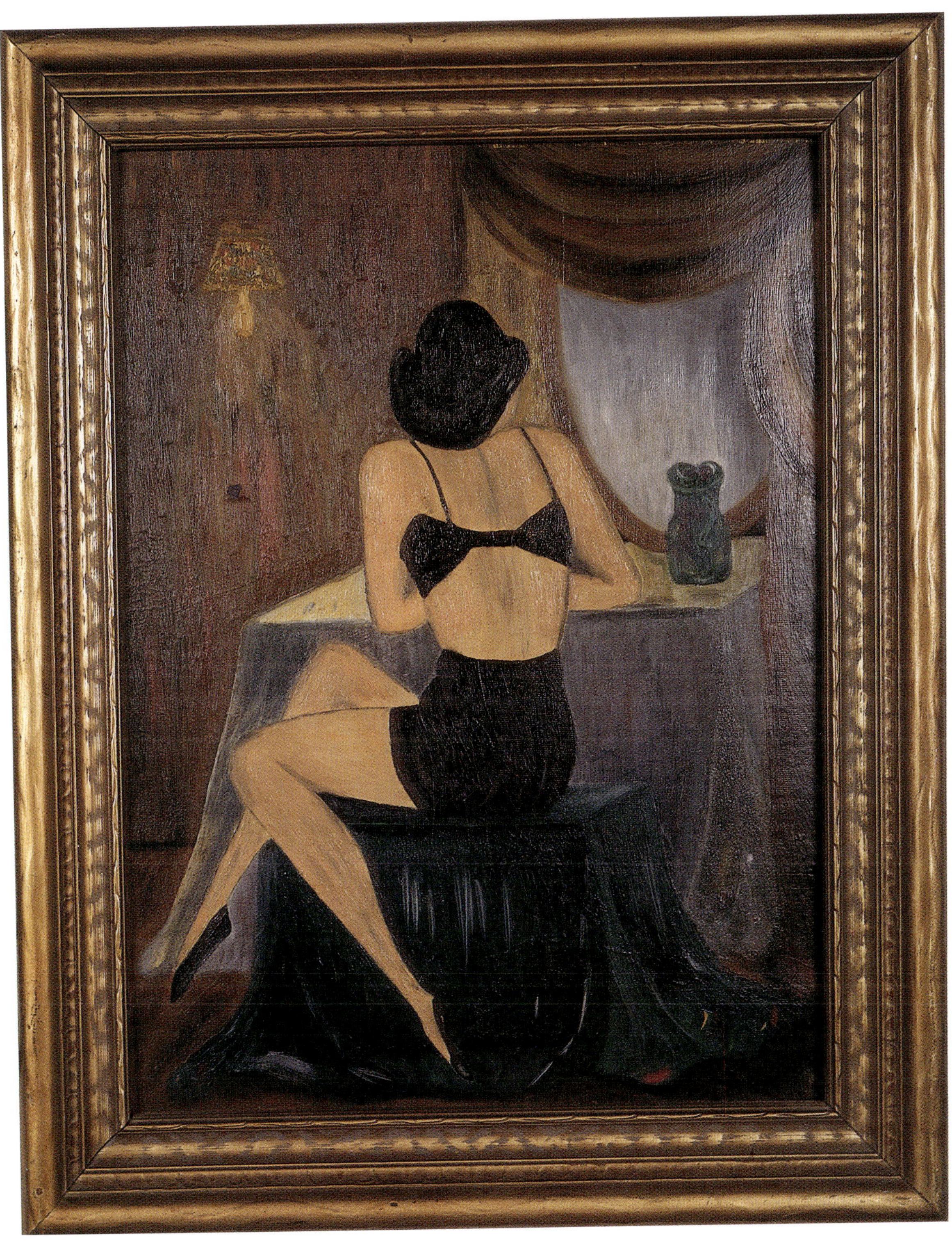

Woman in Black Undies at Vanity Table

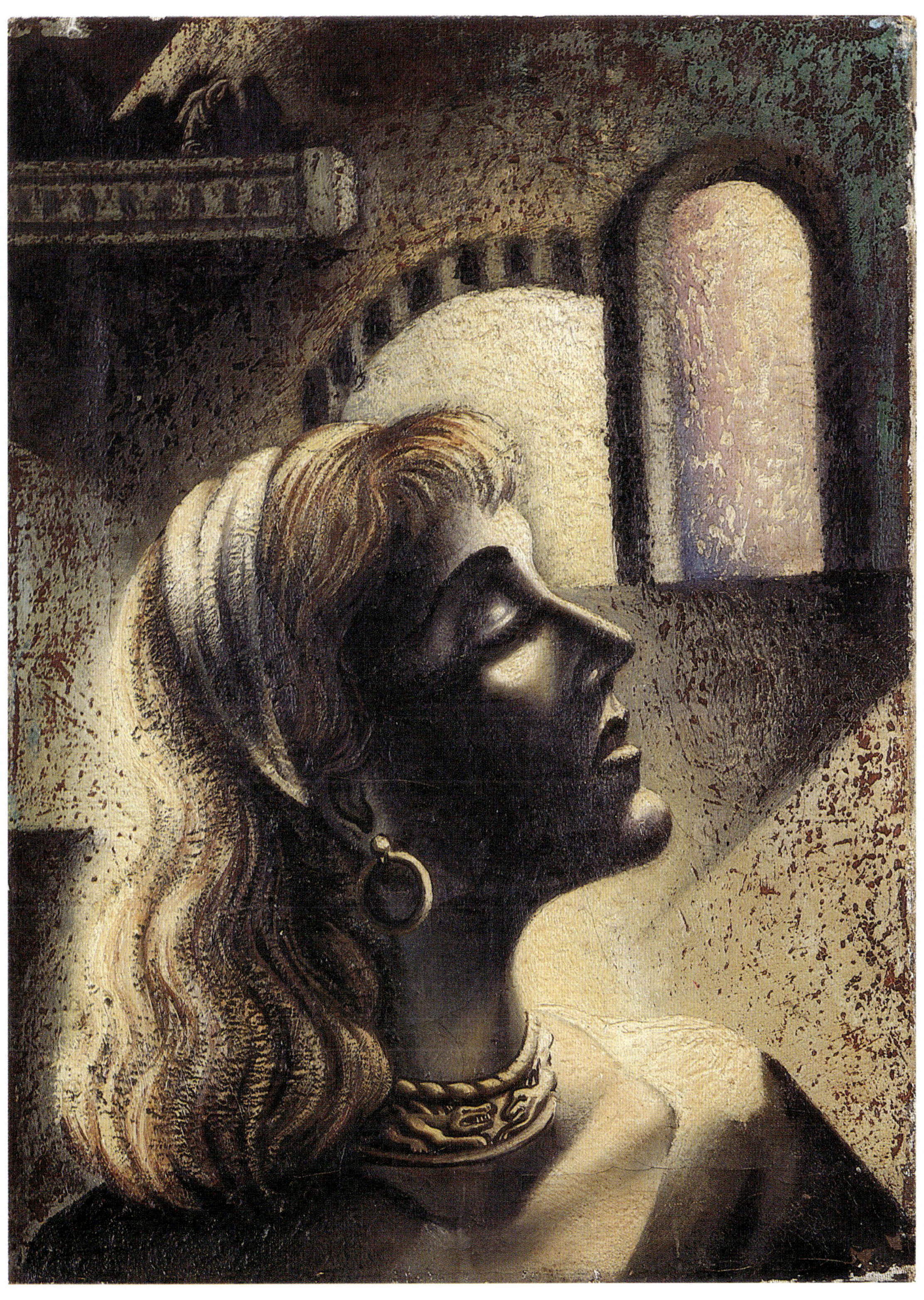

Blonde Woman with Large Necklace in Shadowy Theatre

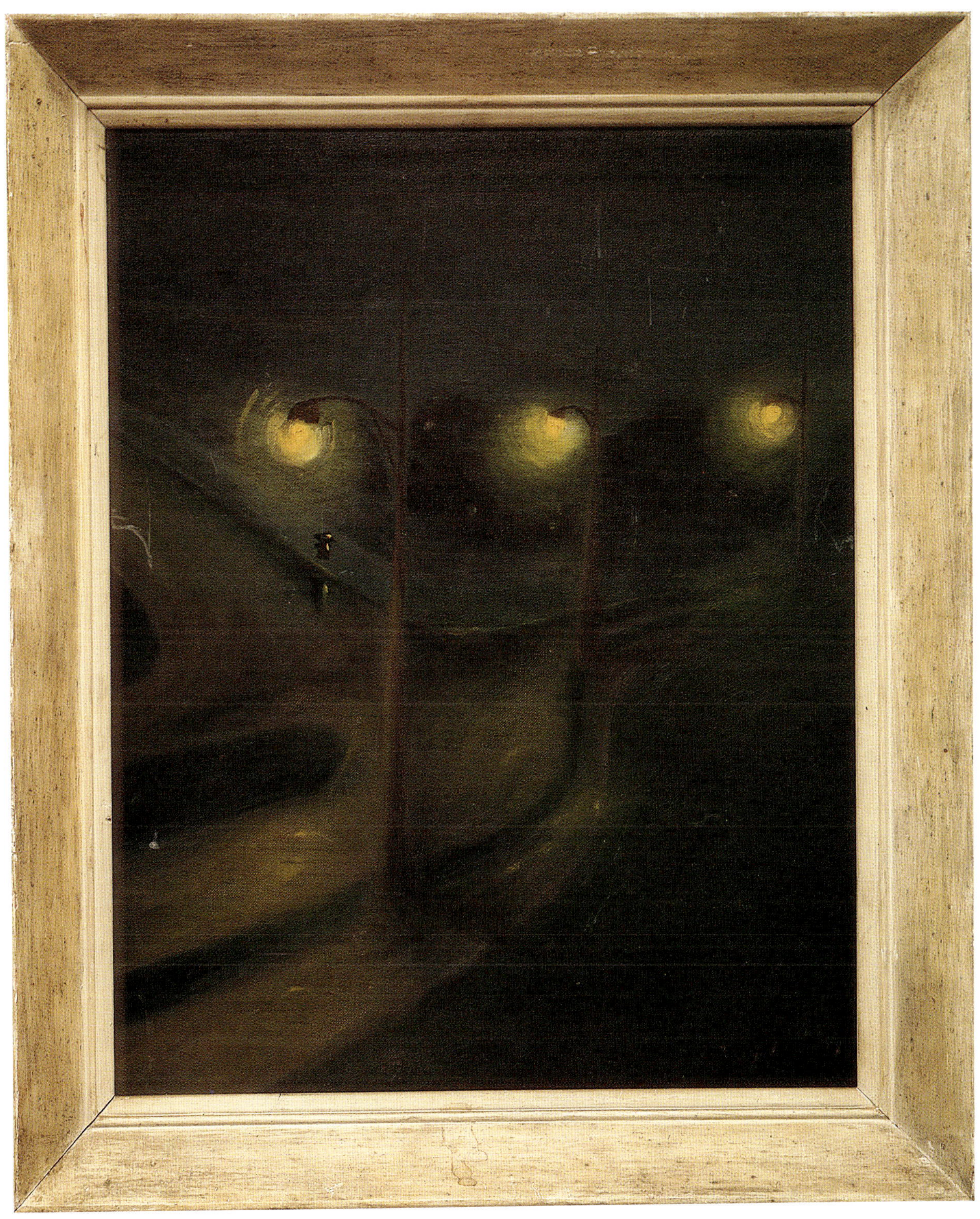

Three Street Lights

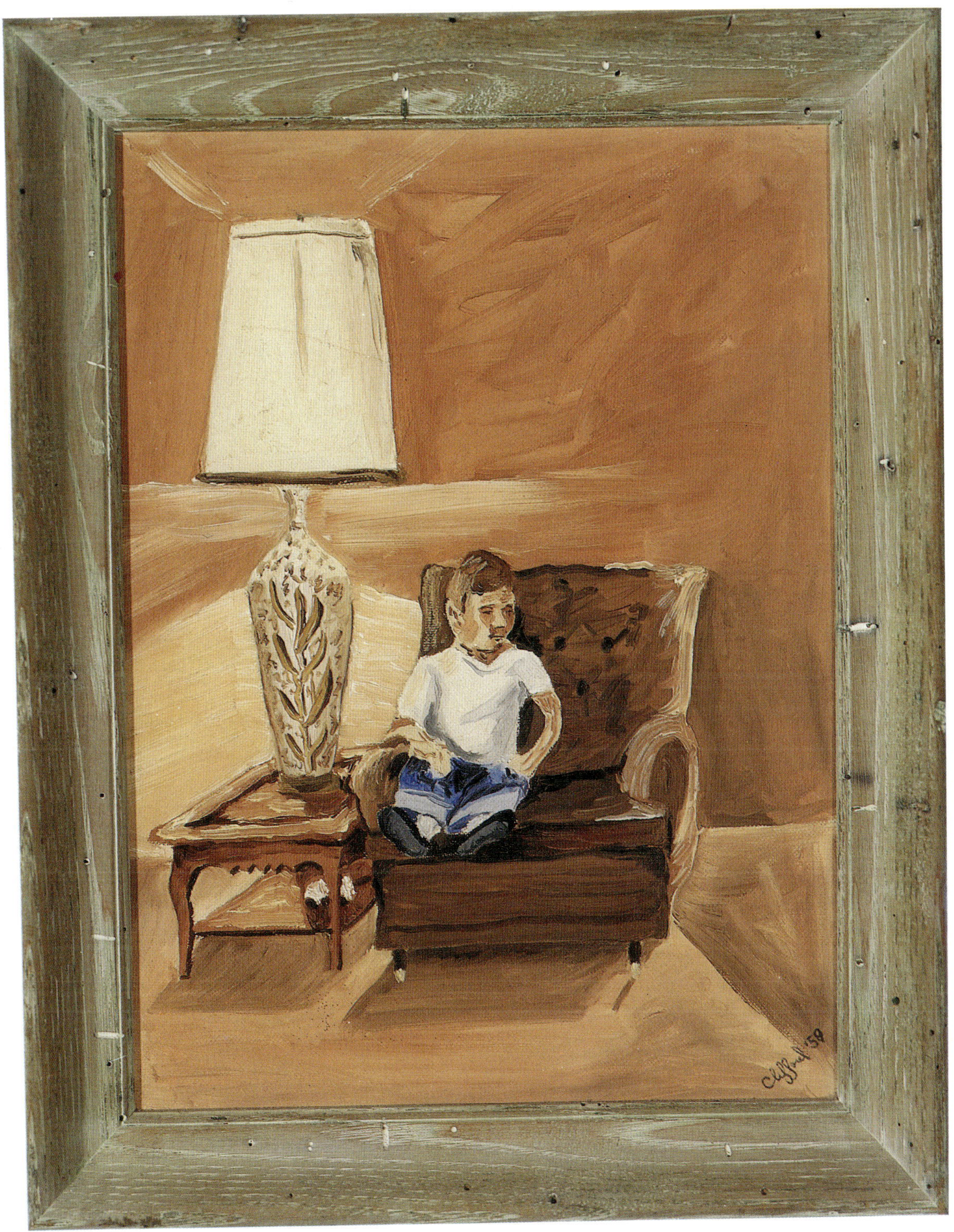

Small Boy in Brown Room

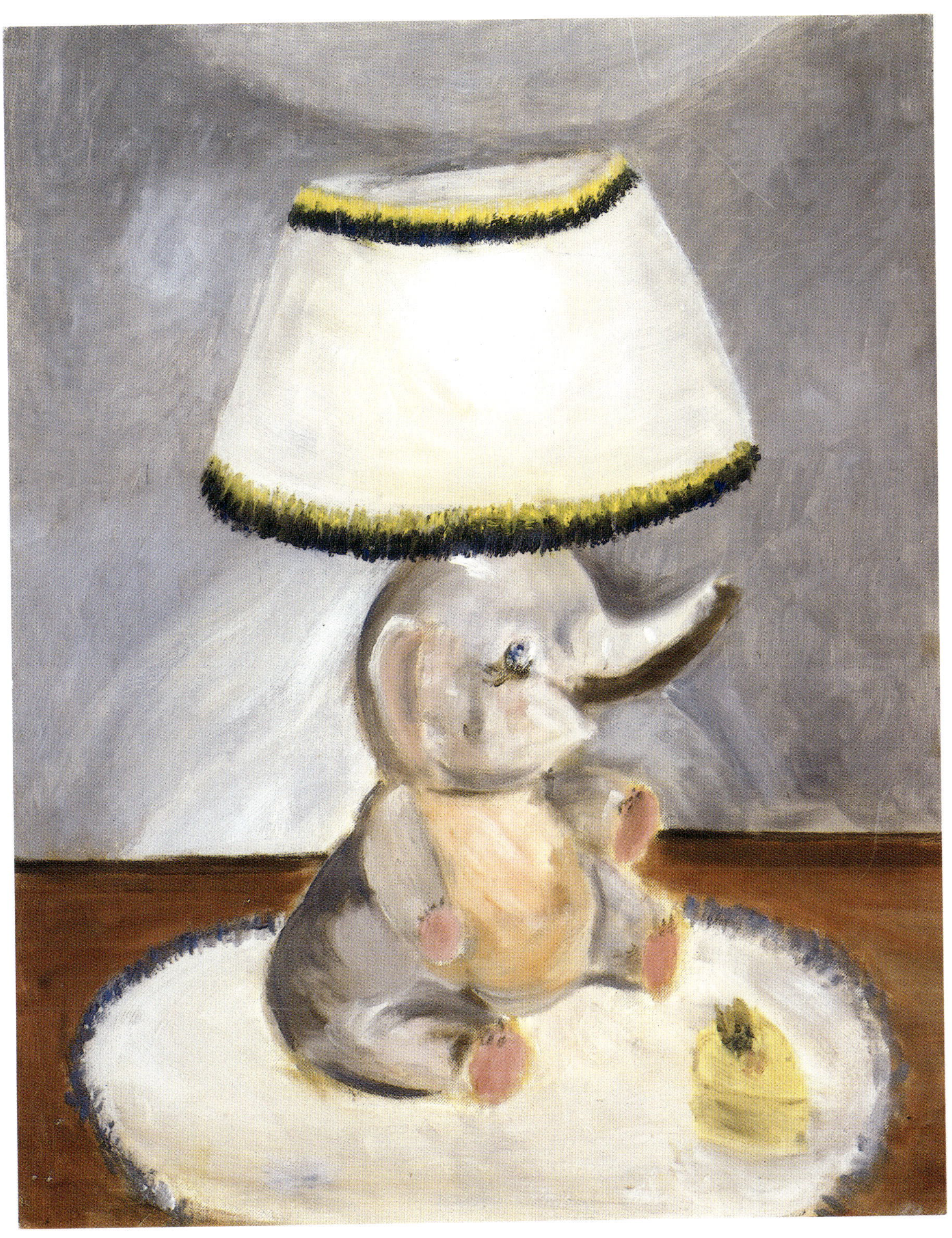

Child's Elephant Lamp

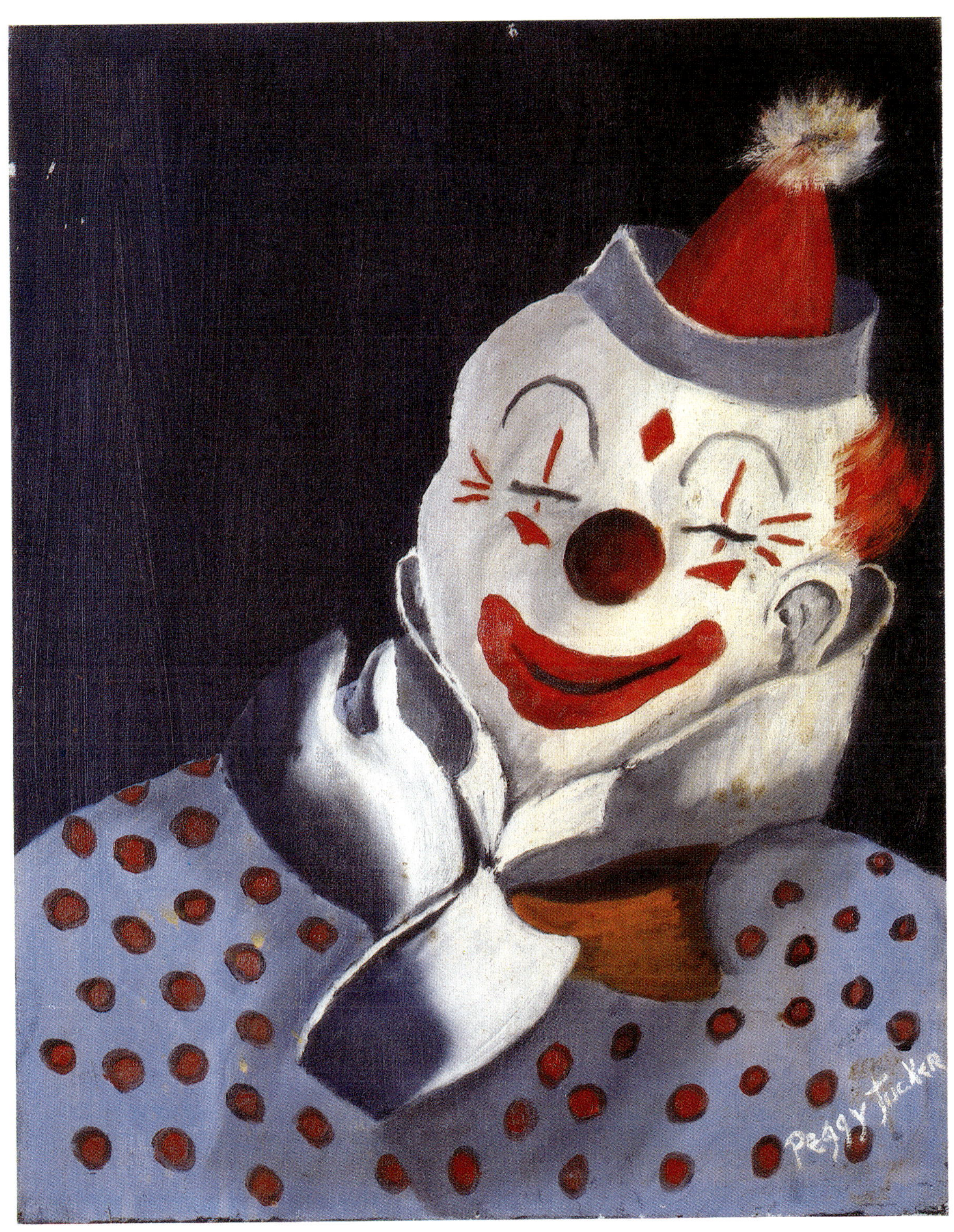

Drunken Clown, Blue with Red Dots

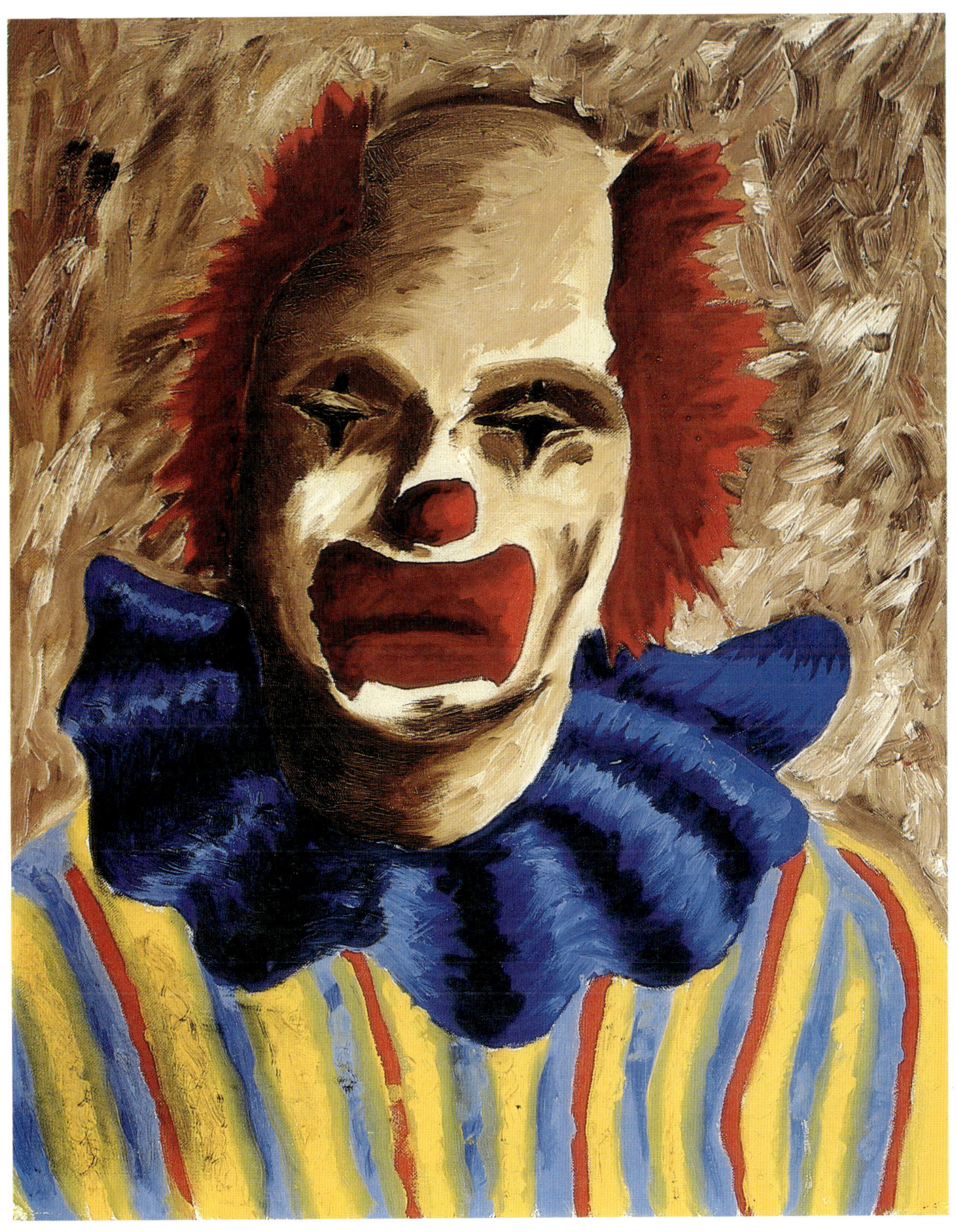

Bitter Clown, Sepia with Red Hair, Blue Collar

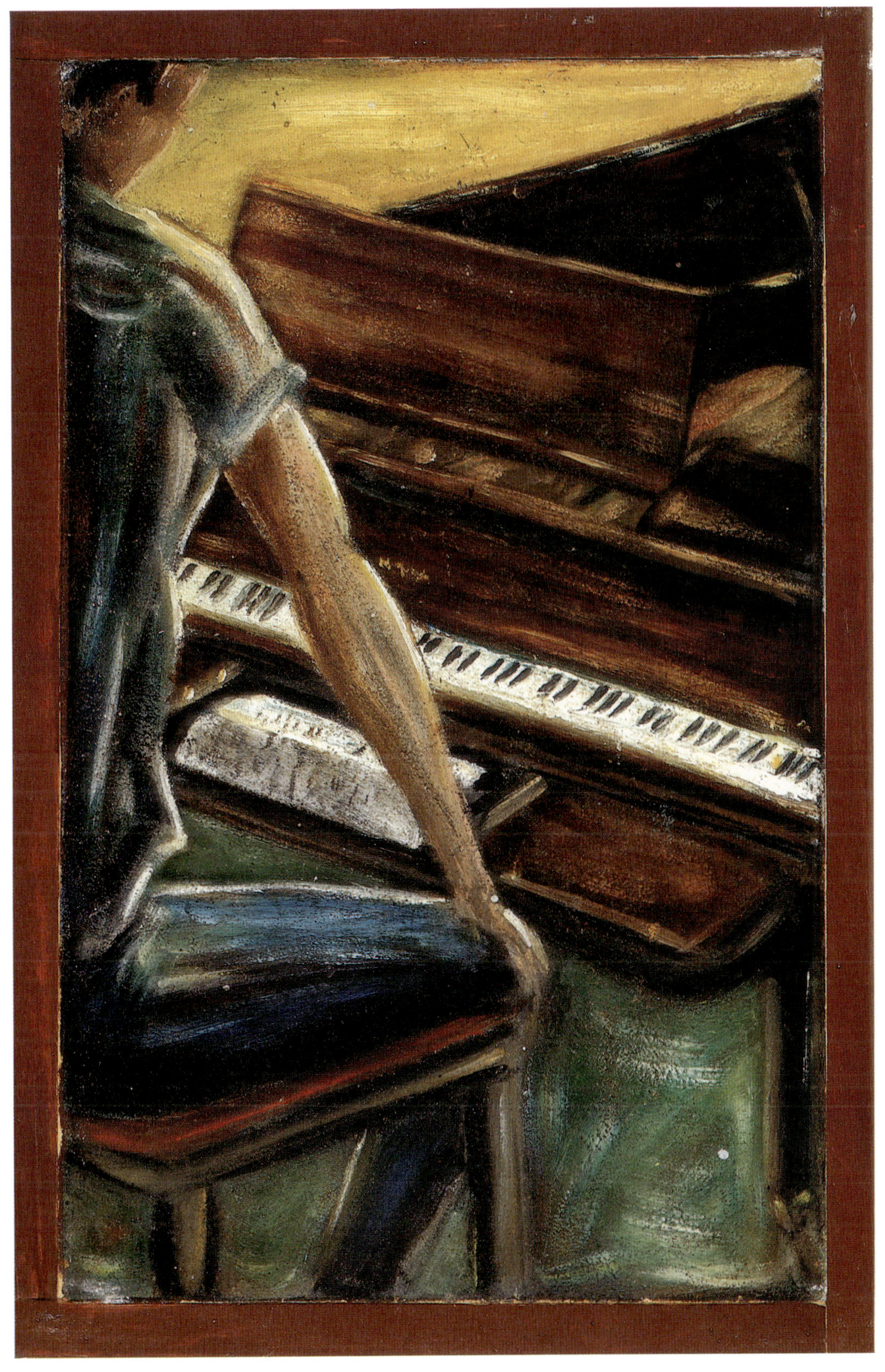

Man at Piano

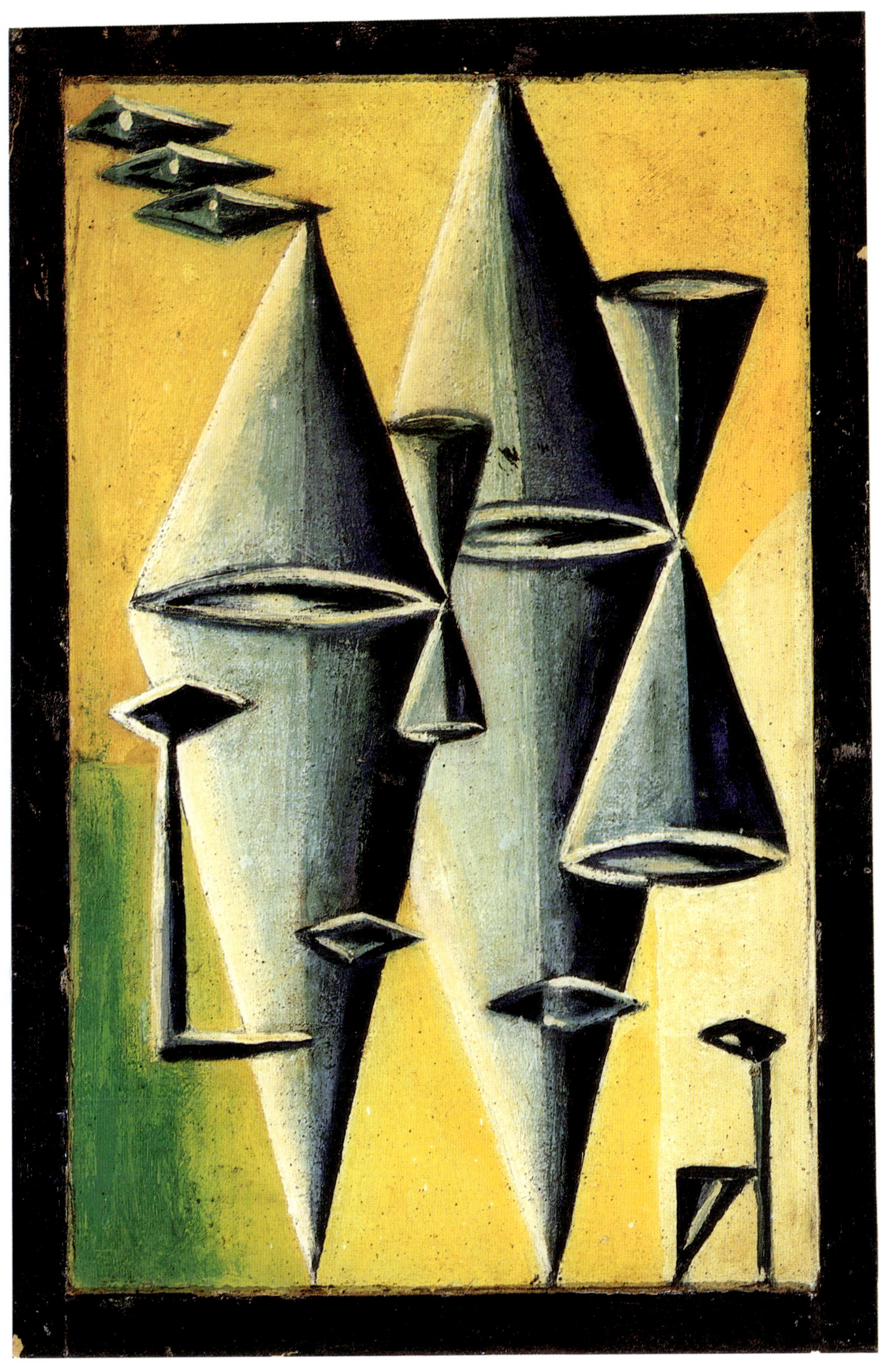

Two Abstract Tiki-like Faces

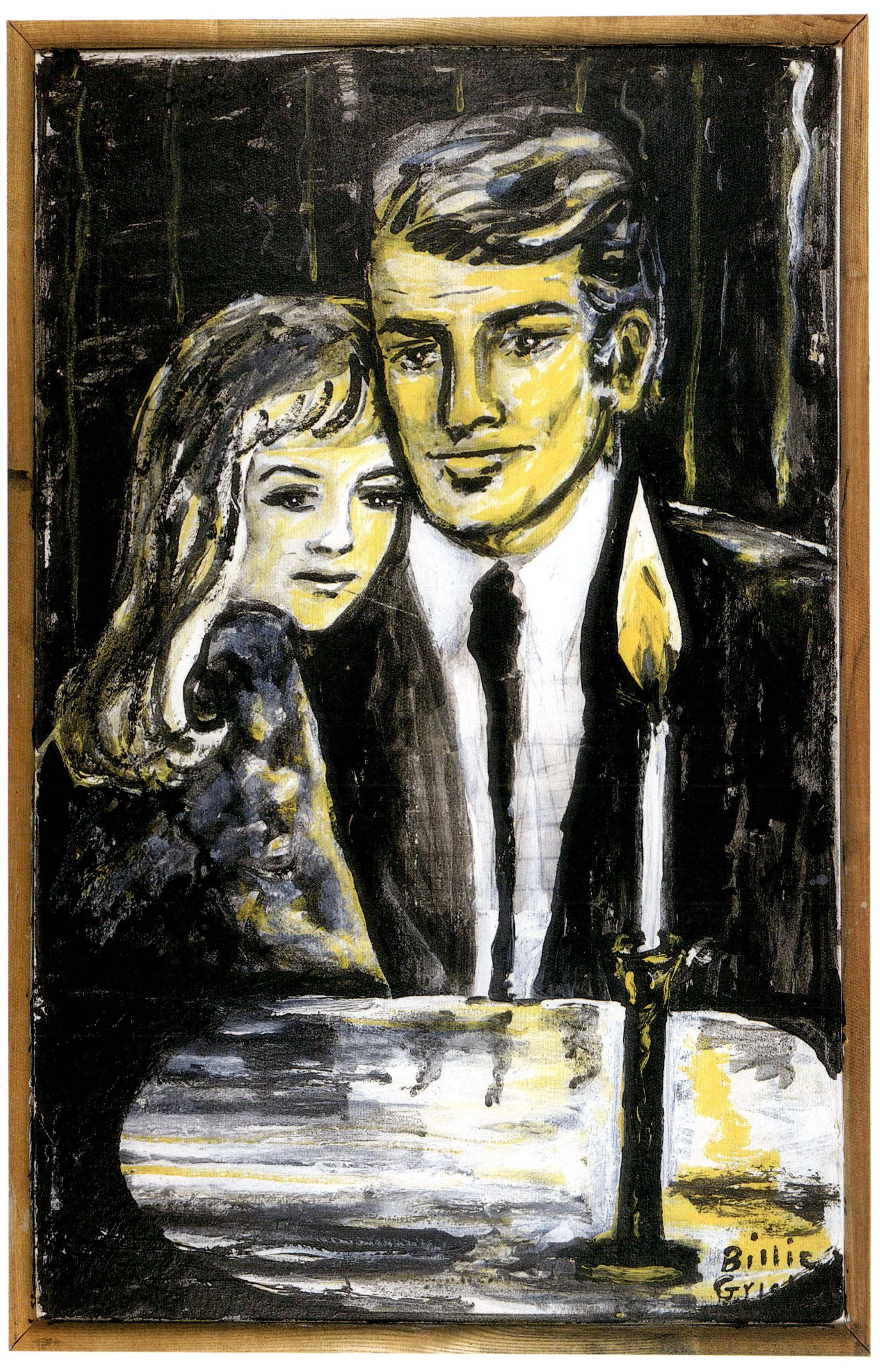

Couple with Candle in Black and Yellow

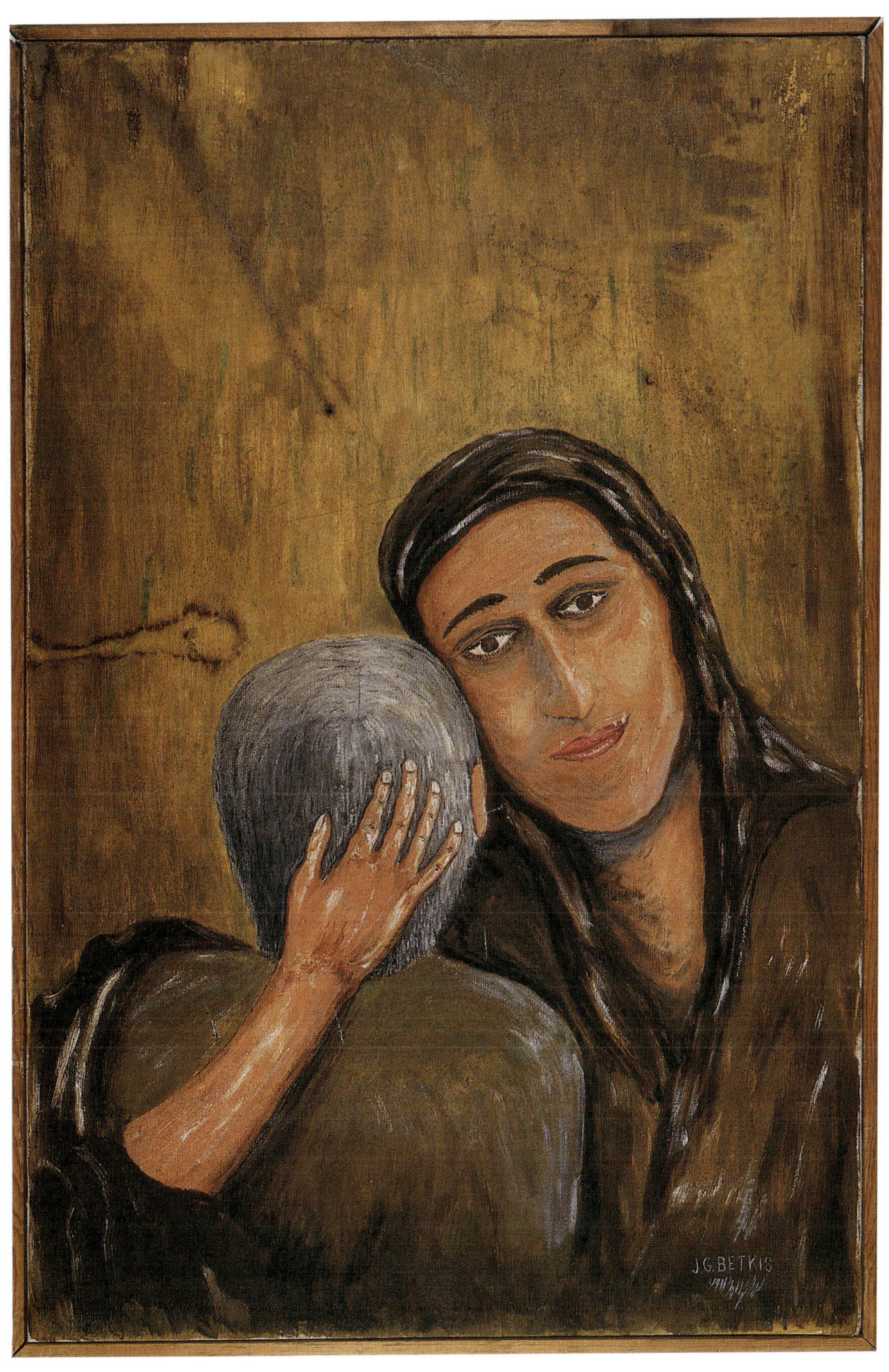

Woman on Ochre Background Comforts Gray-haired Person

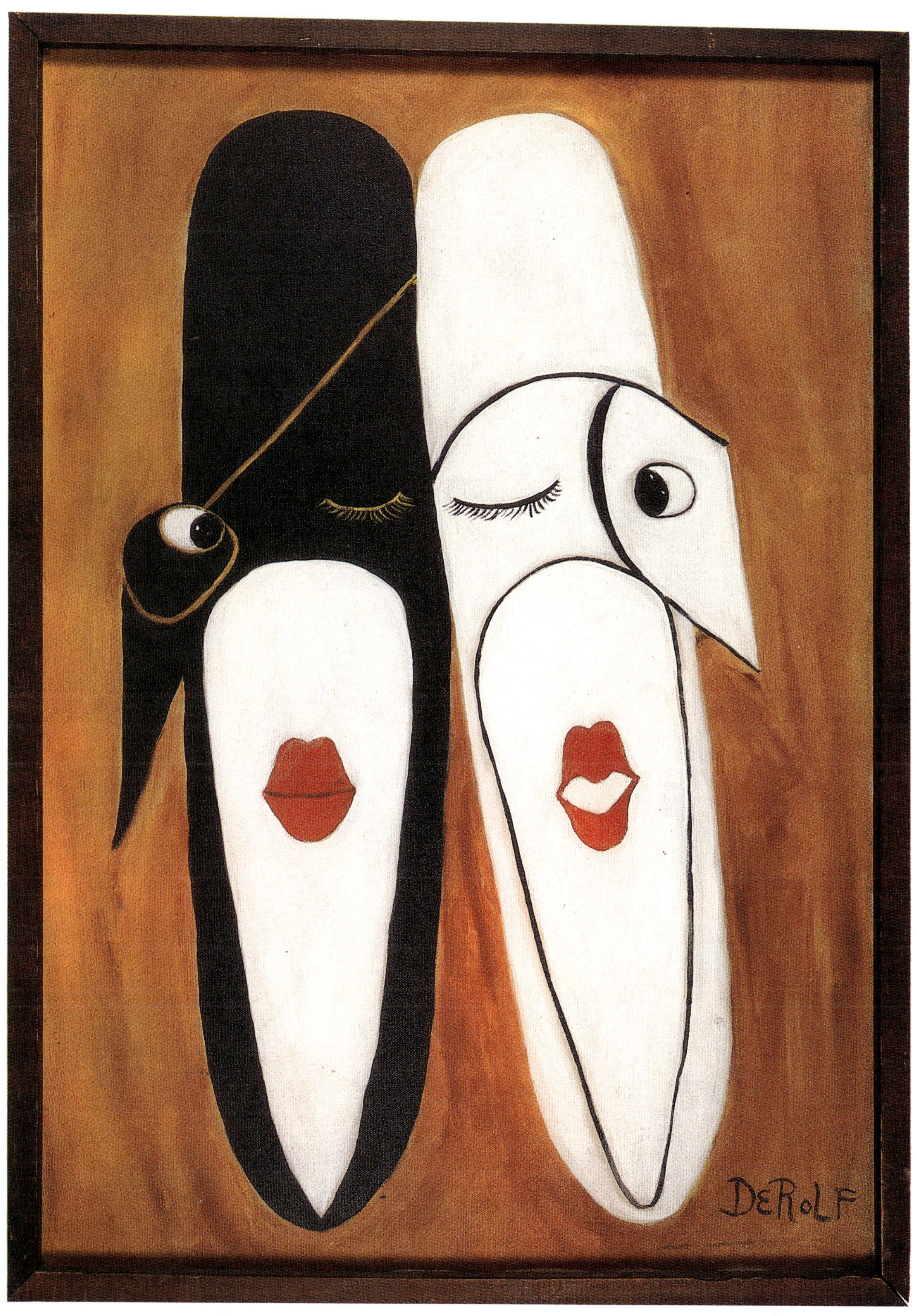

Two Shoes with Faces

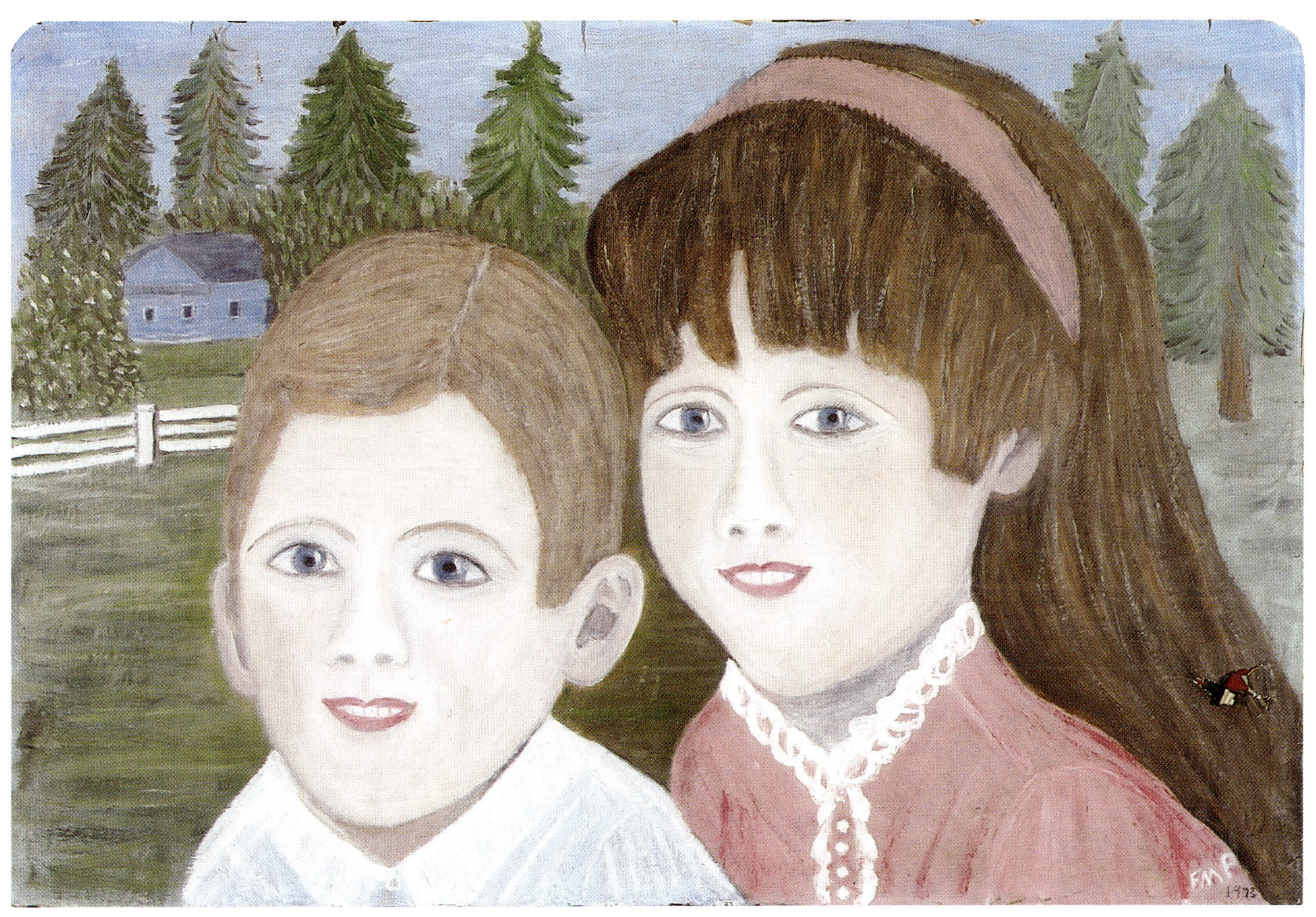

Two Kids with Farm in Background

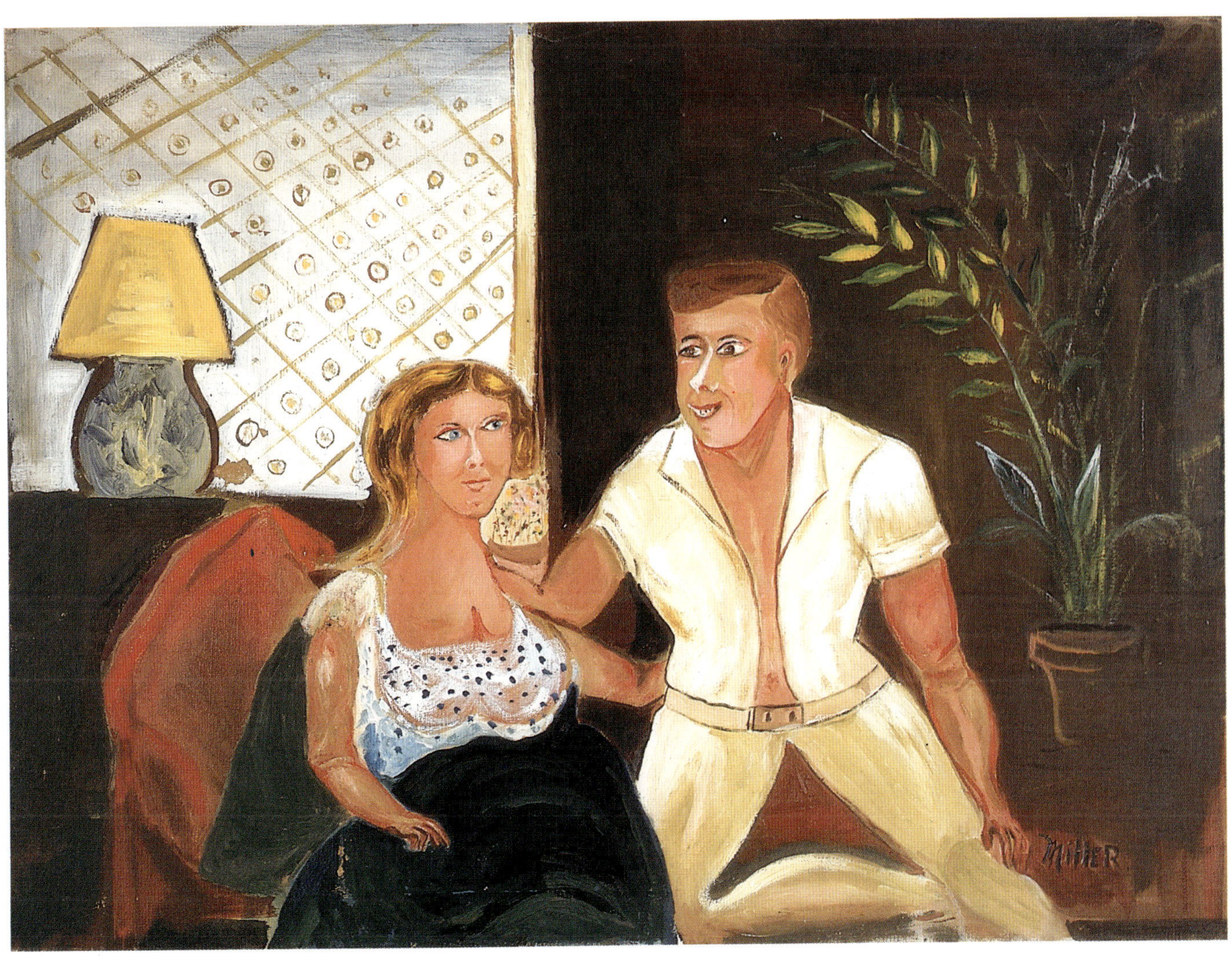

Man with No Crotch Sits Down with Girl

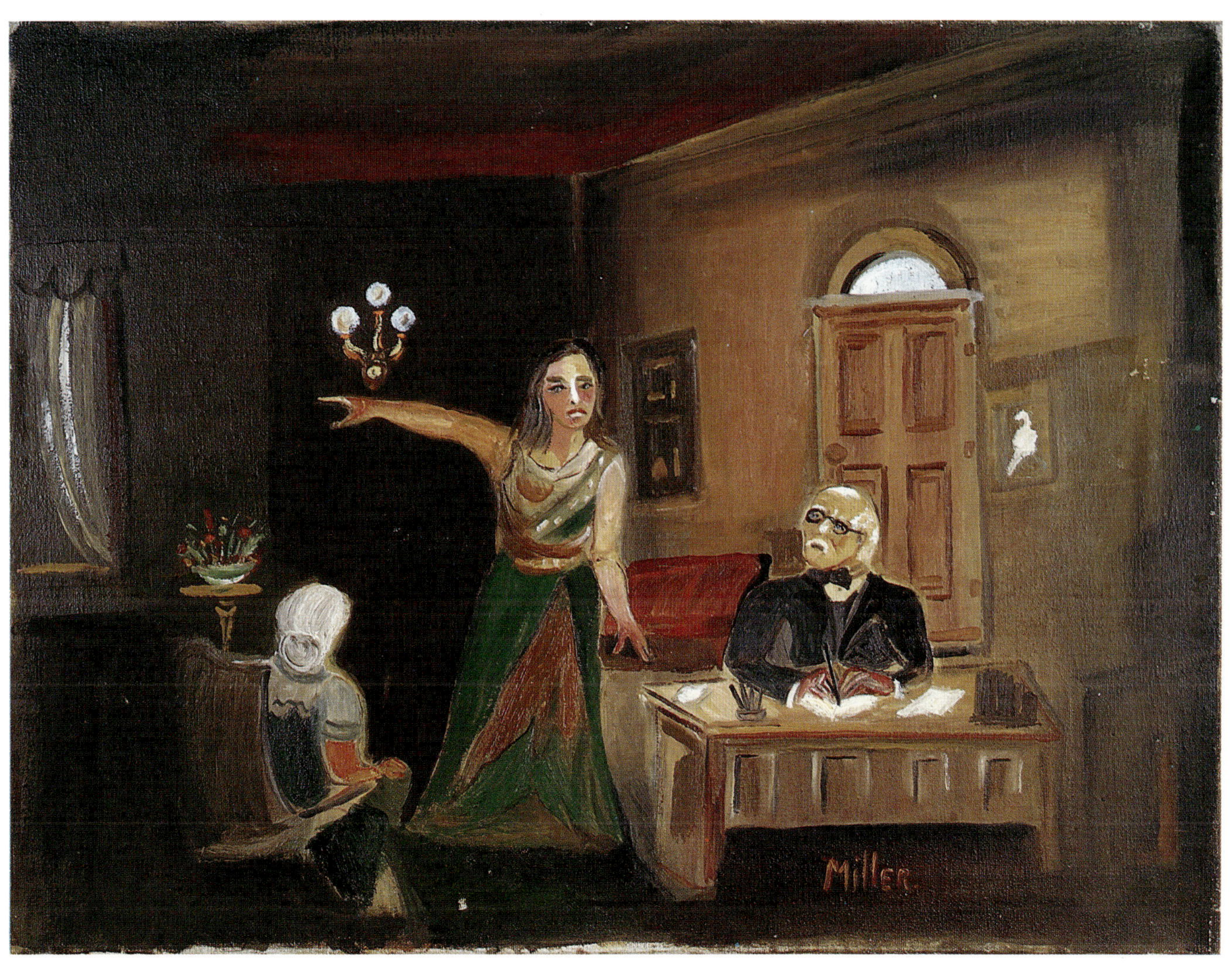

Dramatic Historical Scene

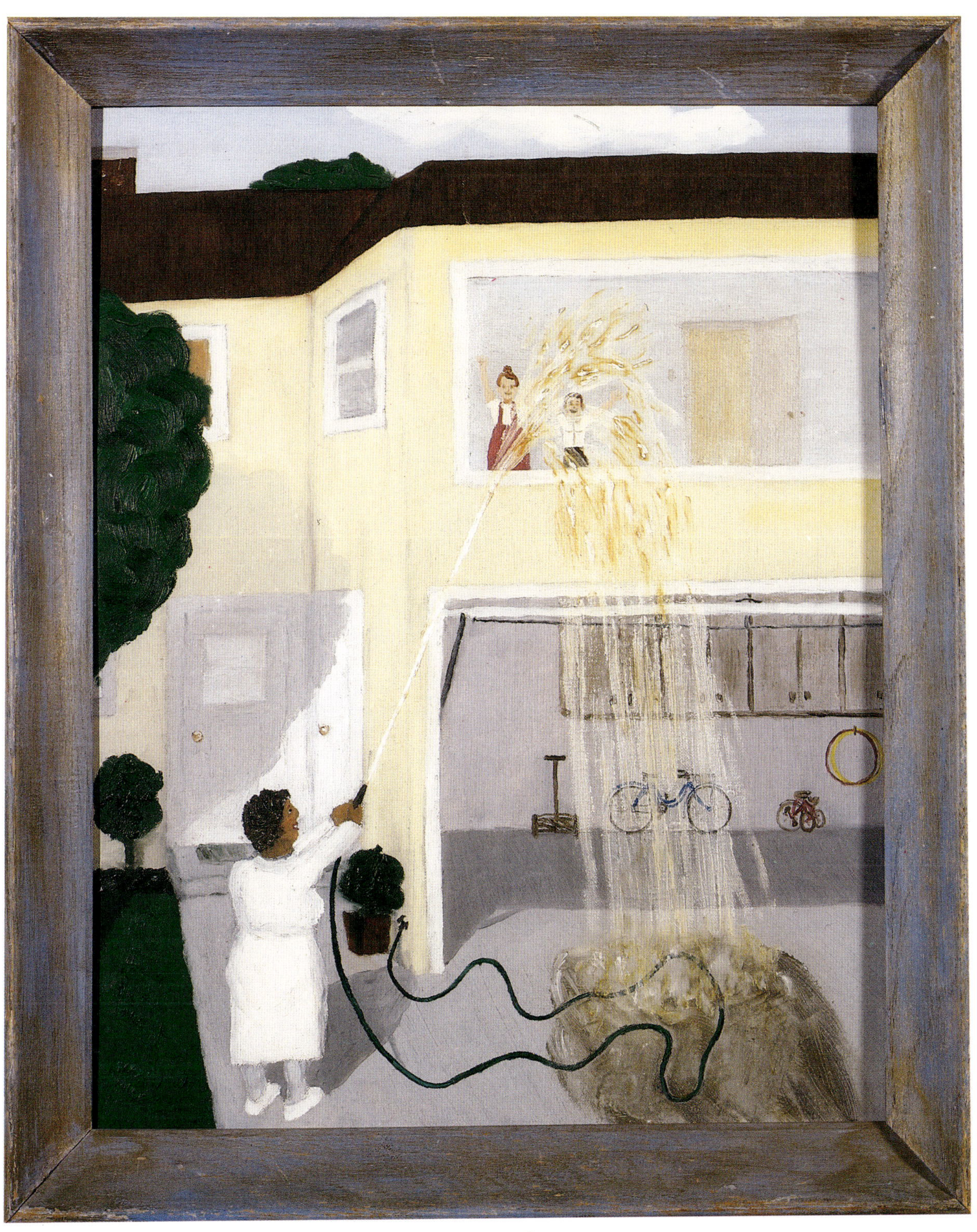

Maid Sprays Kids on Second Floor with Hose

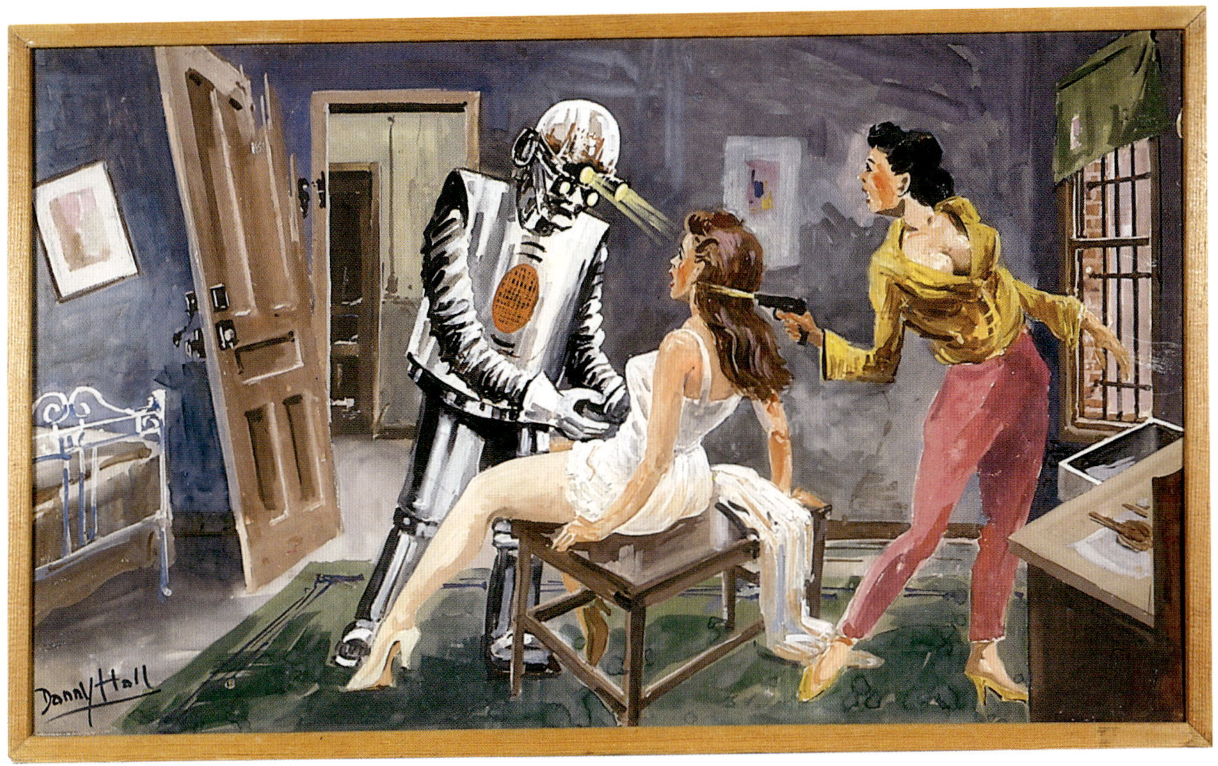

Robot Attacks Two Women

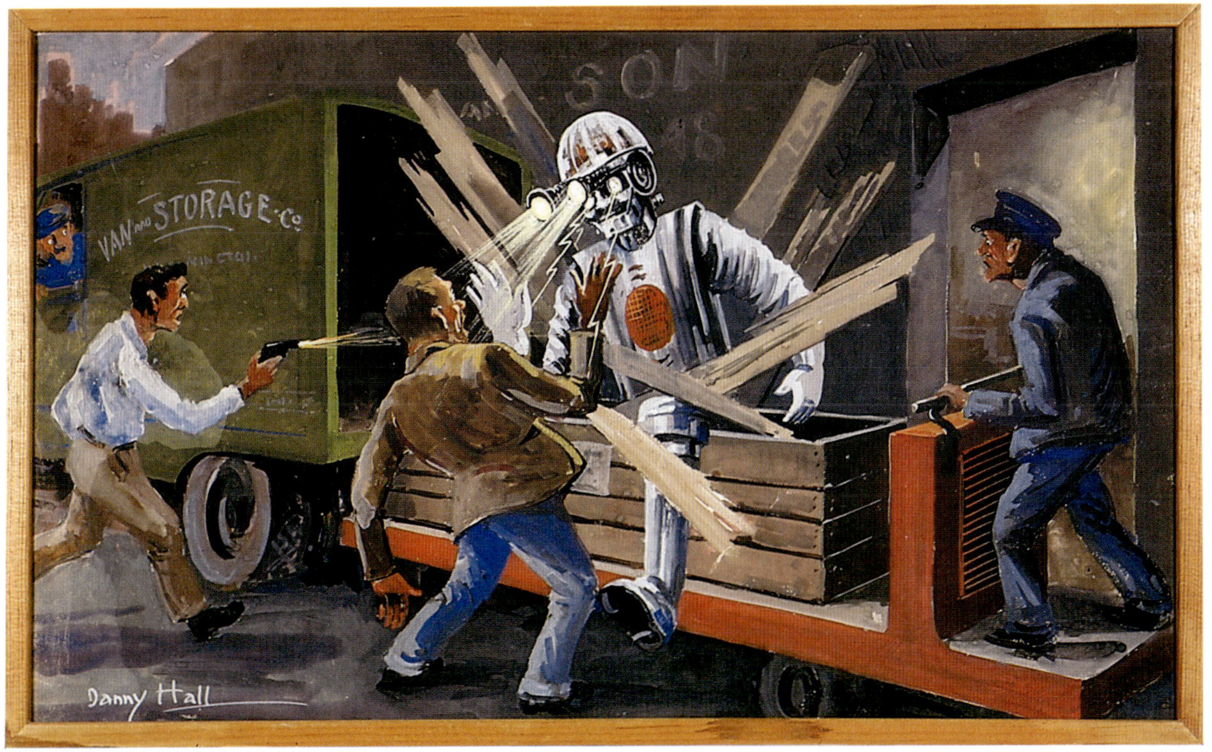

Robot Bursts Out of Crate

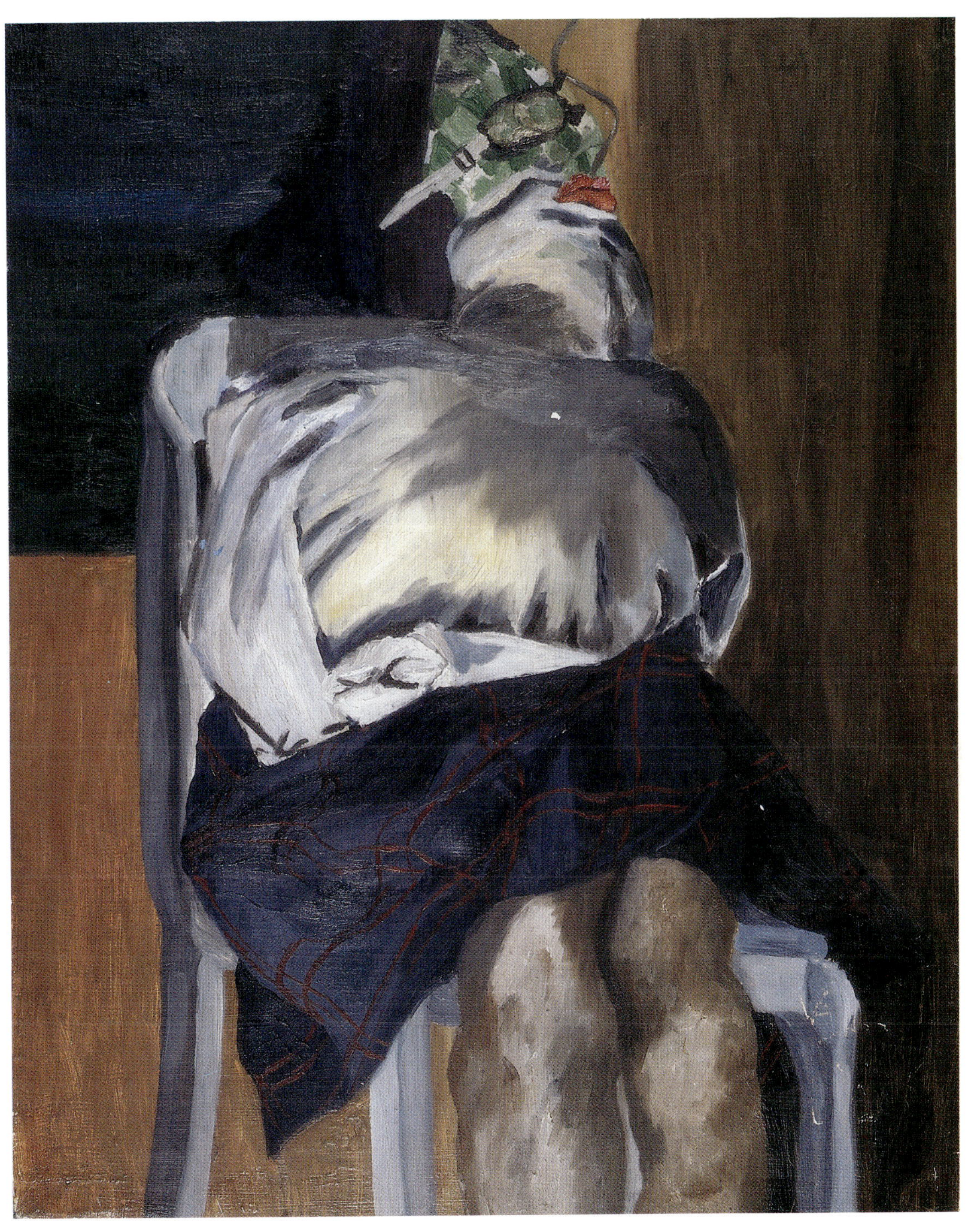

Woman Made of Pillow, Wax Lips, Green Thing

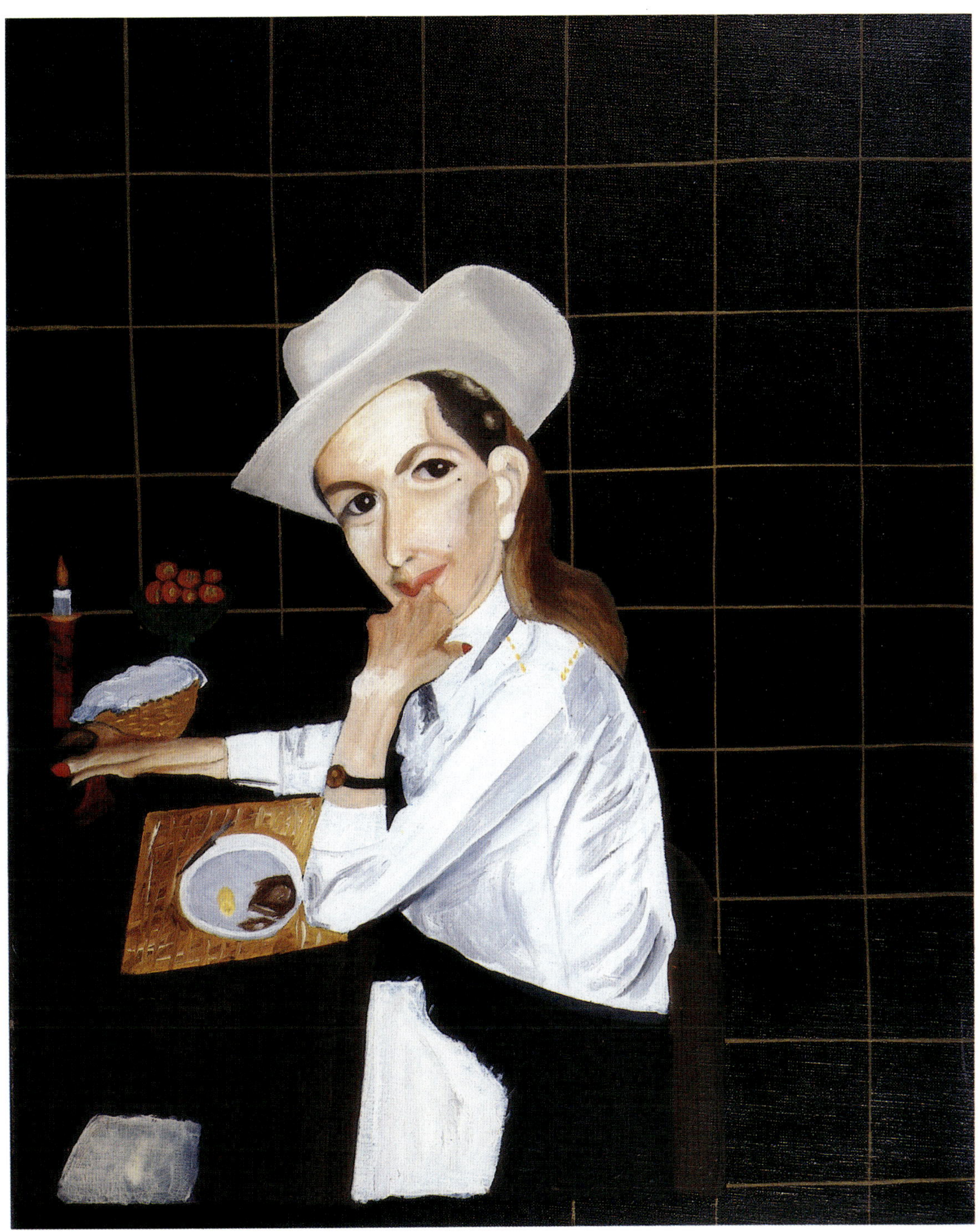

Distorted Woman in Western Clothes with Grid

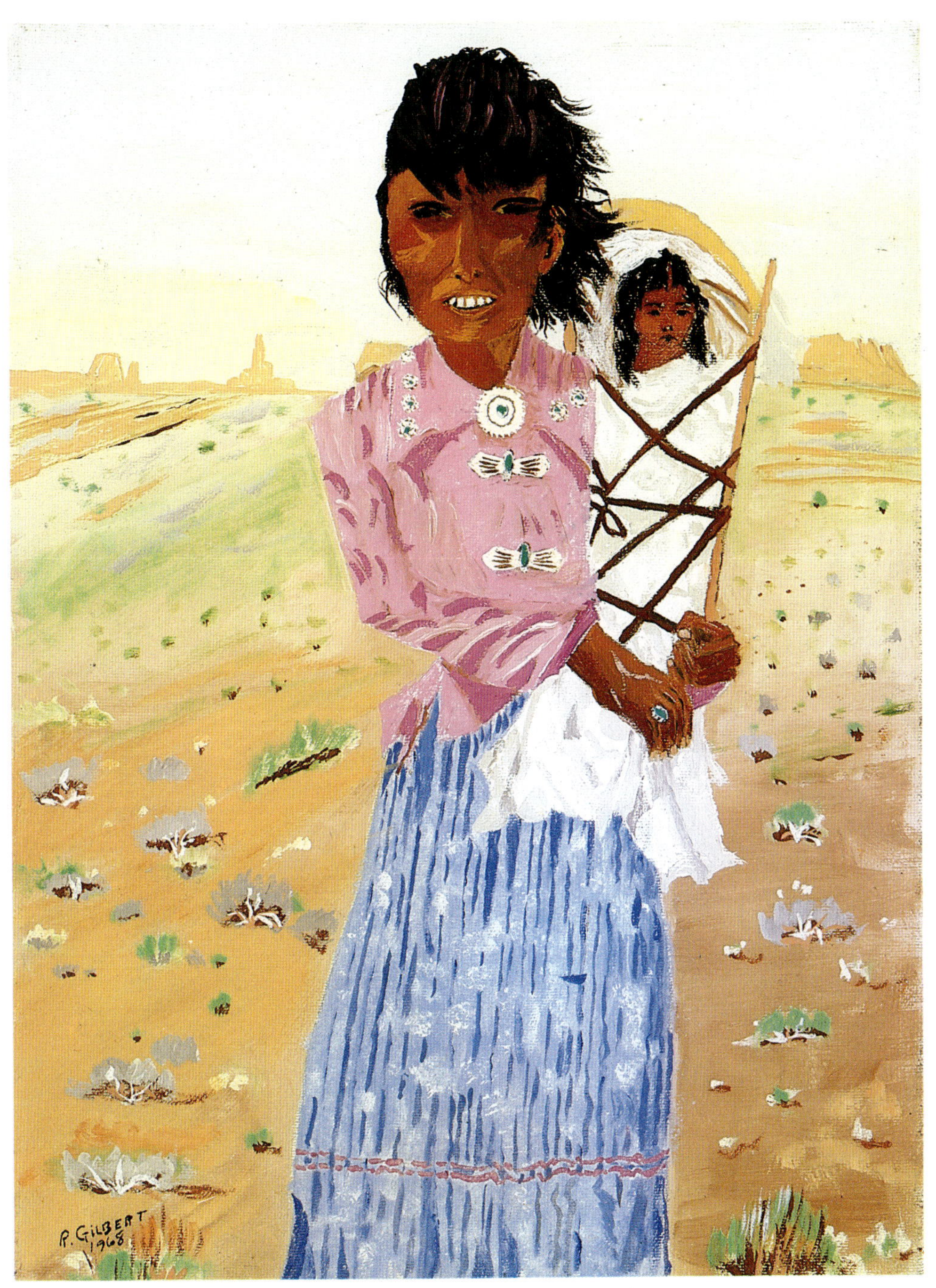

Indian Woman and Papoose

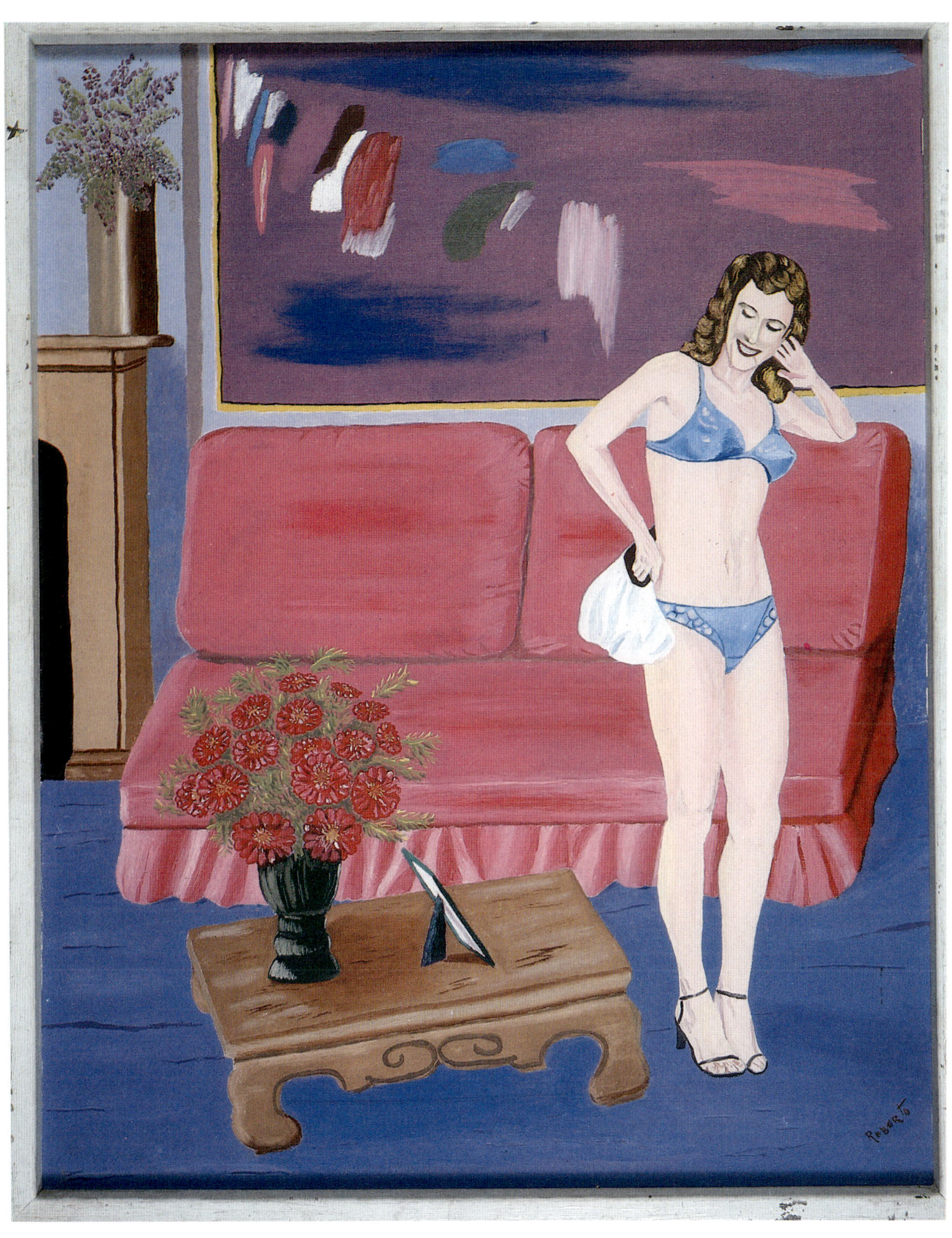

Woman in Underwear Smiles at Photo by Pink Couch and Painting

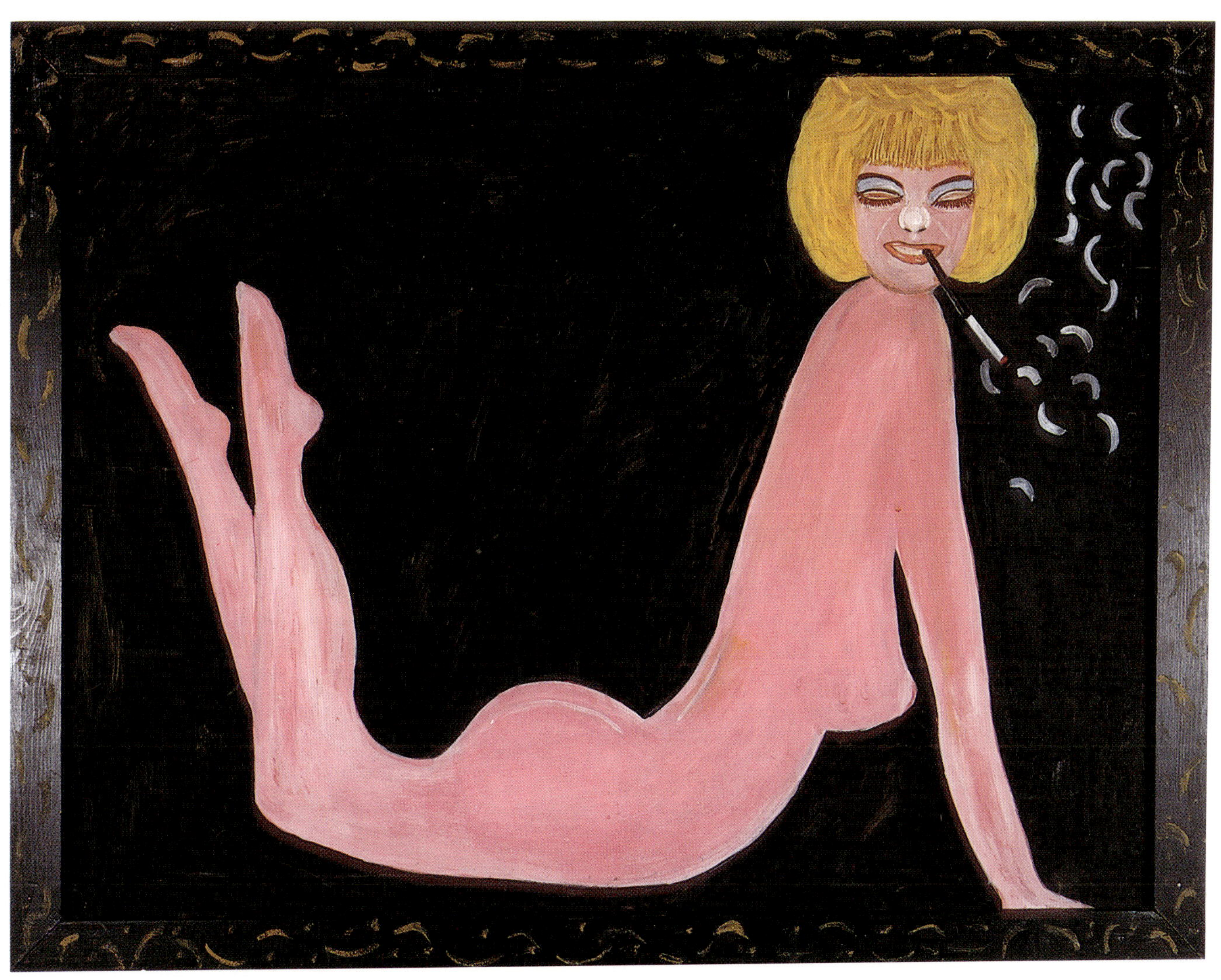

Nude Blonde Woman with Cigarette Holder

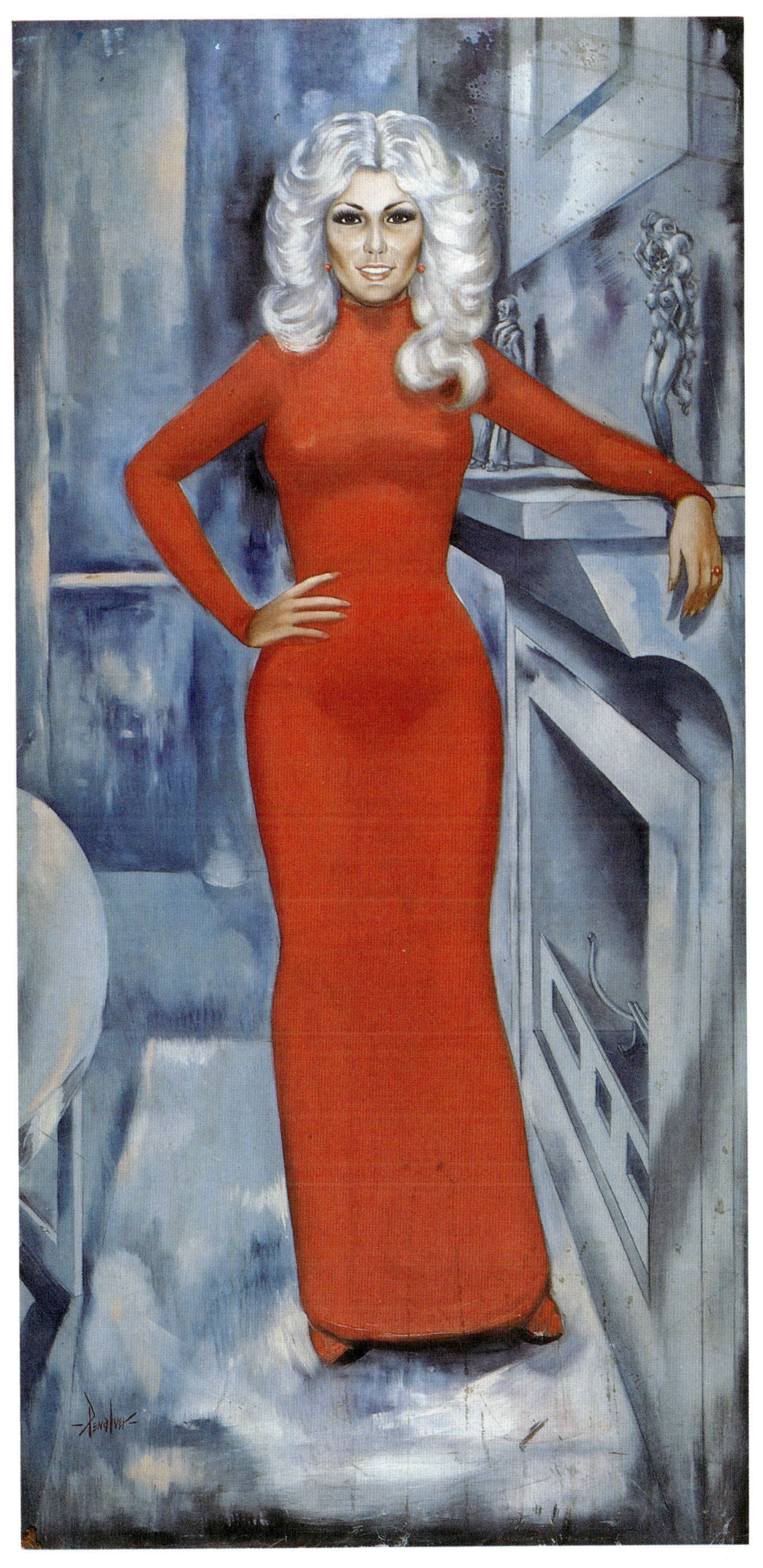

Platinum Blonde Woman in Red Dress in Blue Room

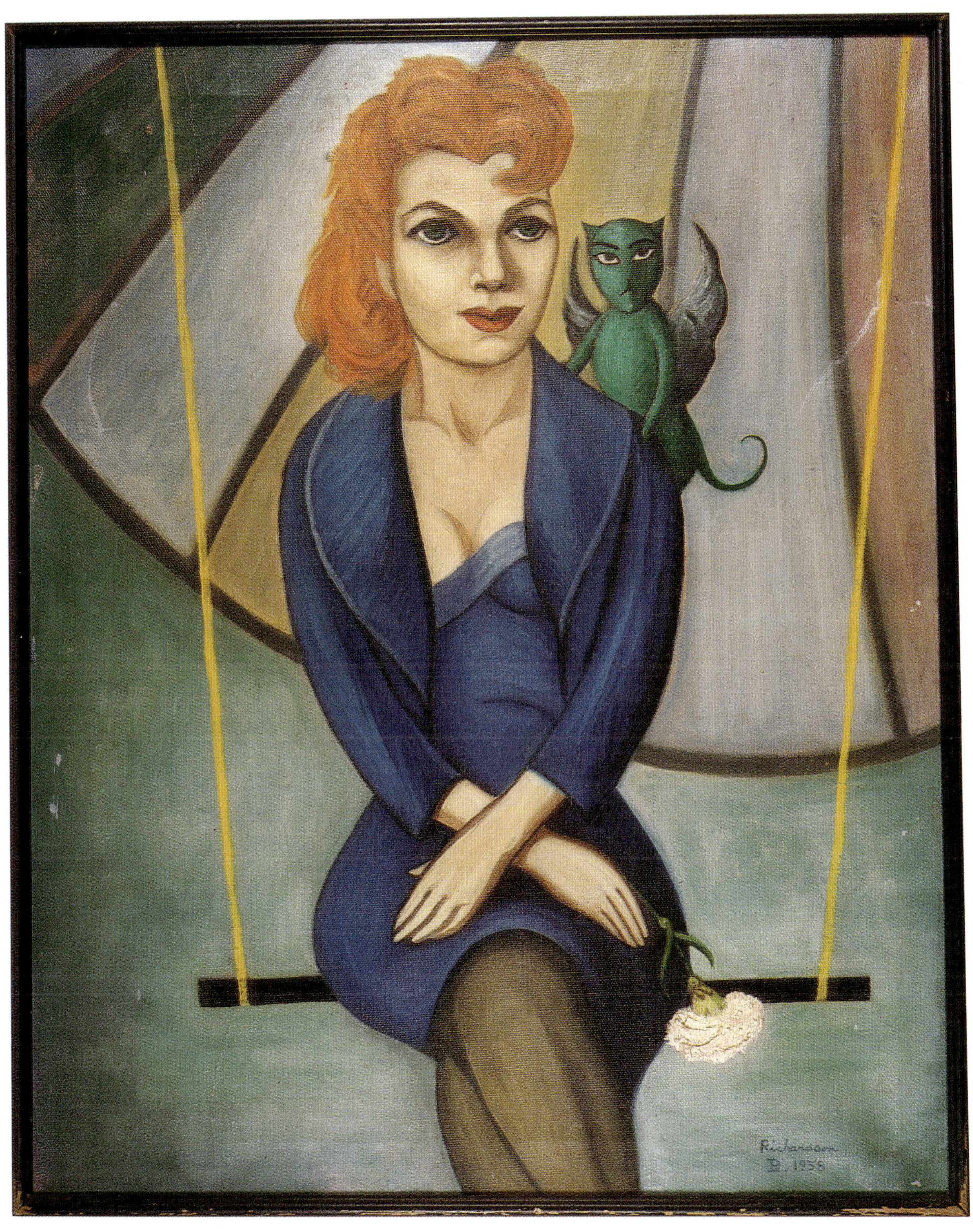

Red-haired Woman in Blue Suit and Demon on Swing

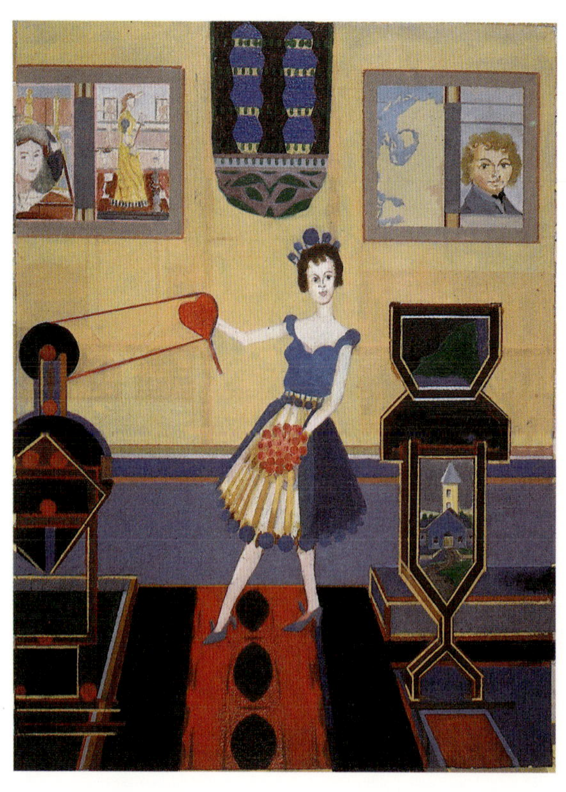

Unknown First Lady

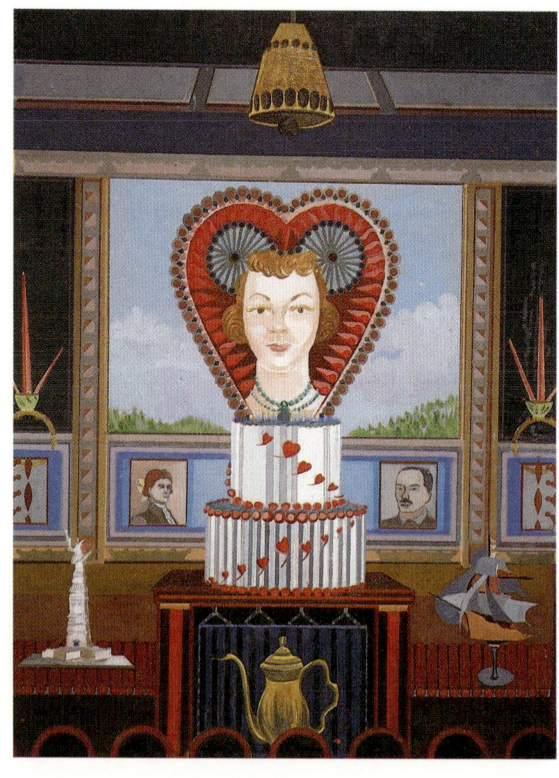

Mrs. Cleveland "1st Wedding in White House"

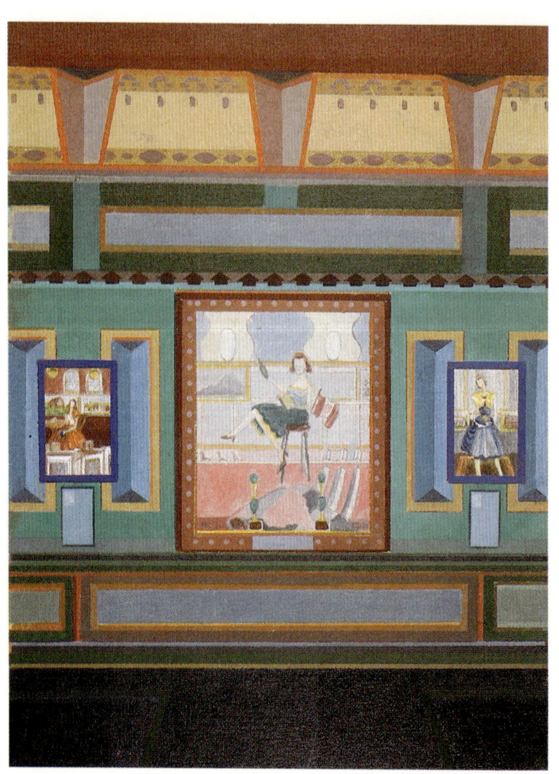

Mrs. Monroe

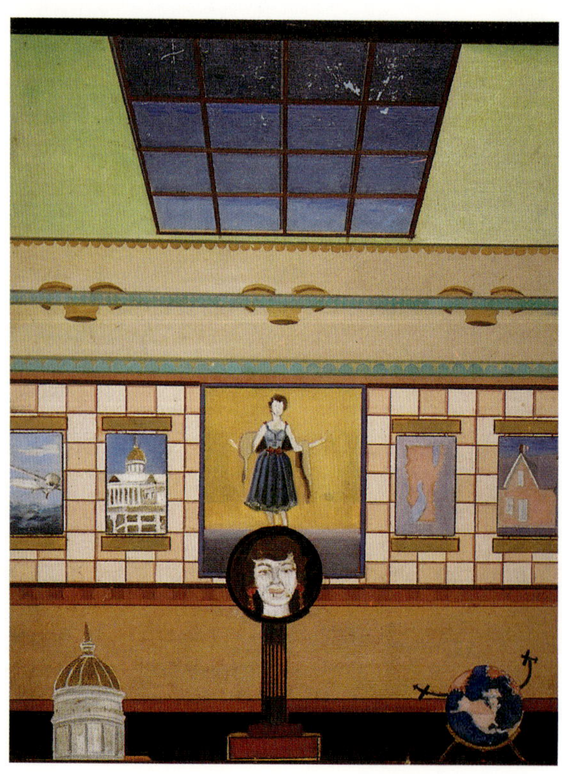

Grace Goodhue Coolidge

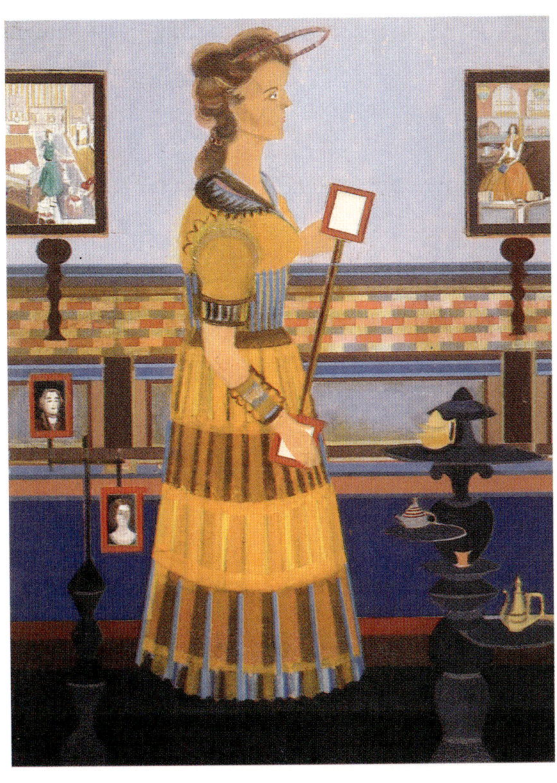

Dolly Payne Todd Madison "Most Popular First Lady"

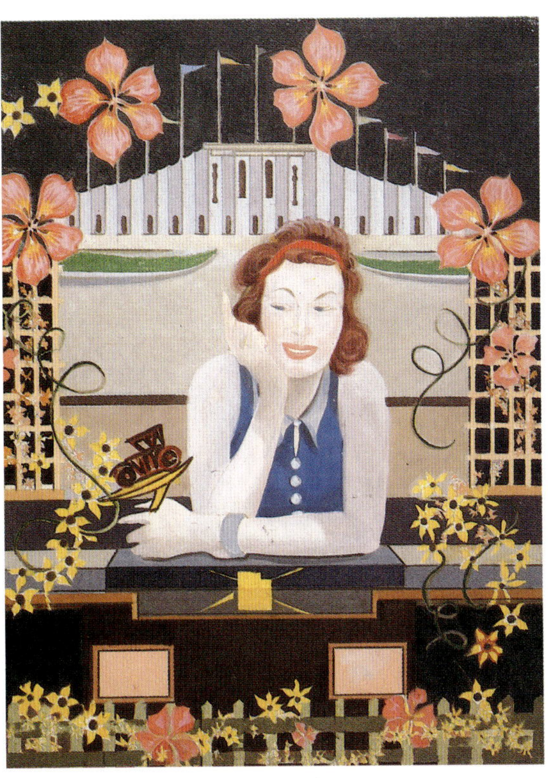

Frances Folsom Cleveland "First Lady to be Married"

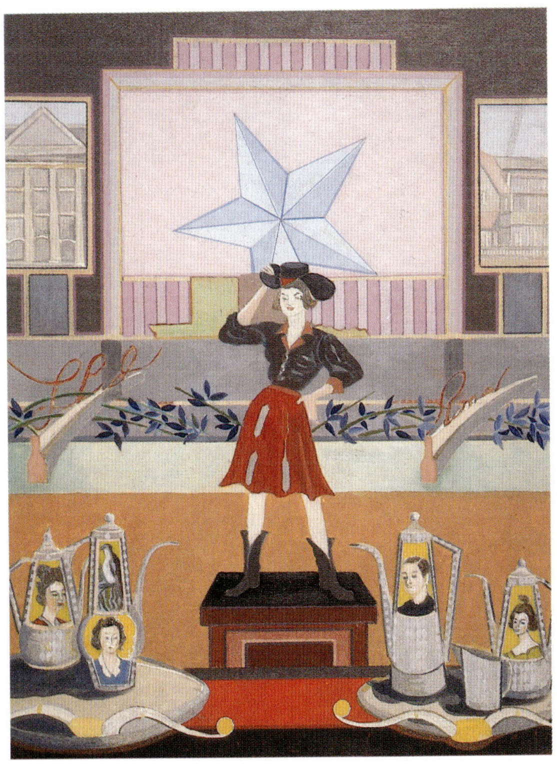

Lady Bird Johnson

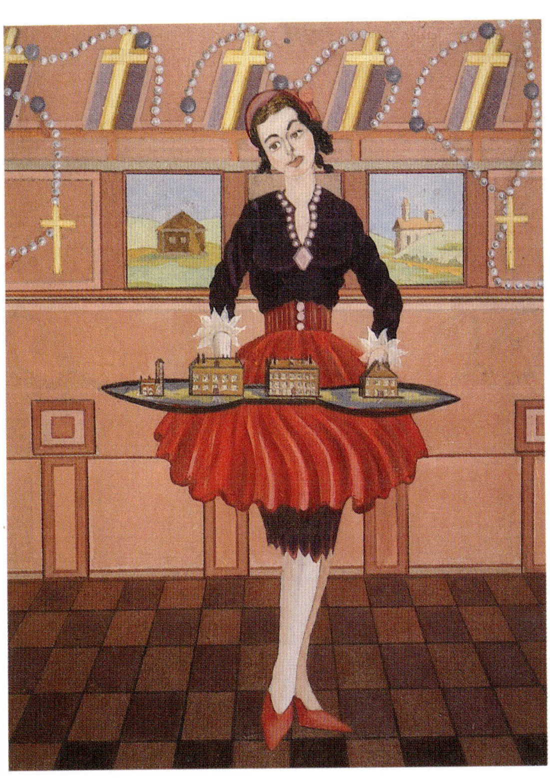

Jane Means Appleton Pierce "Reluctant First Lady"

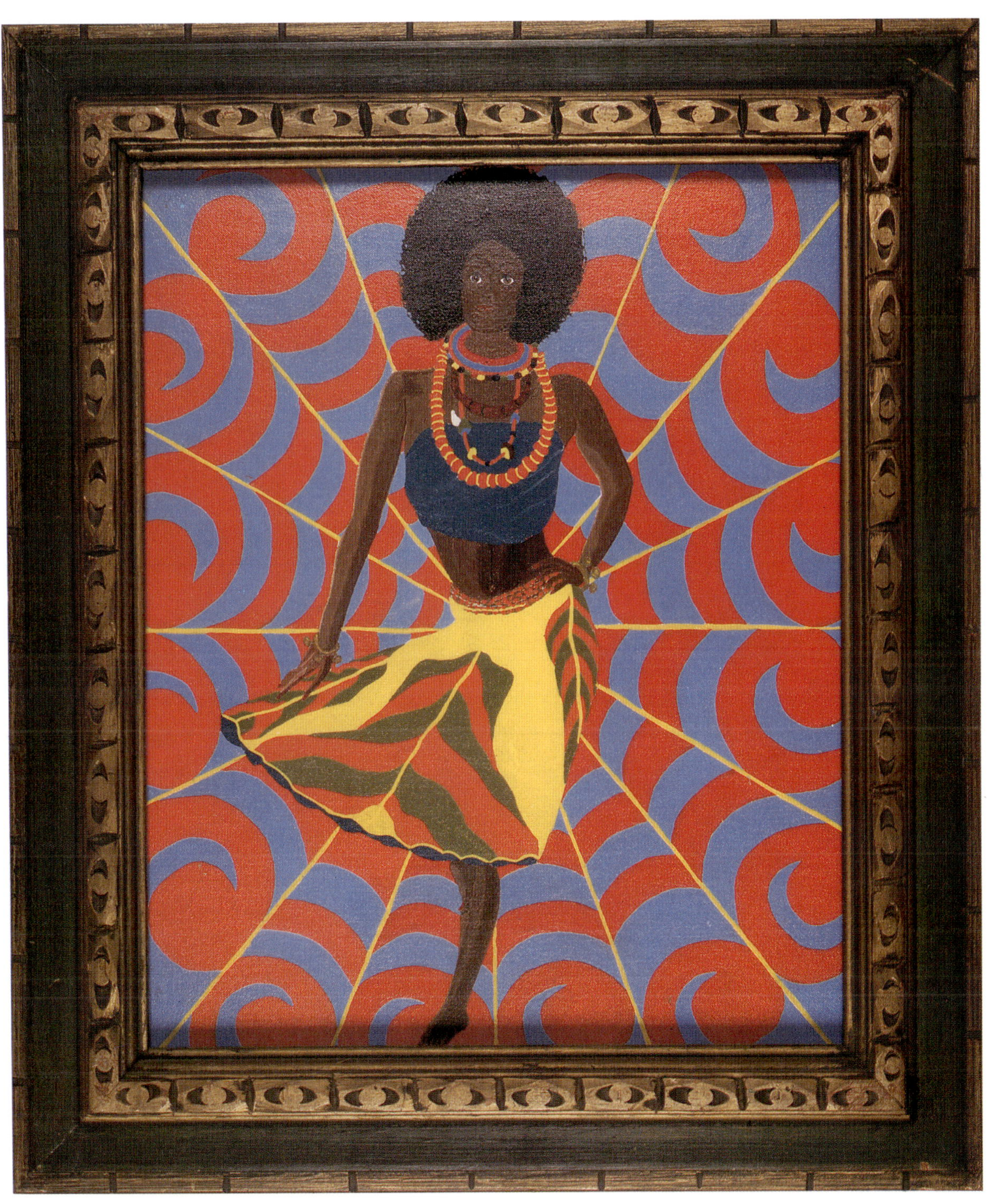

African Woman with Psychedelic Spider Web 2

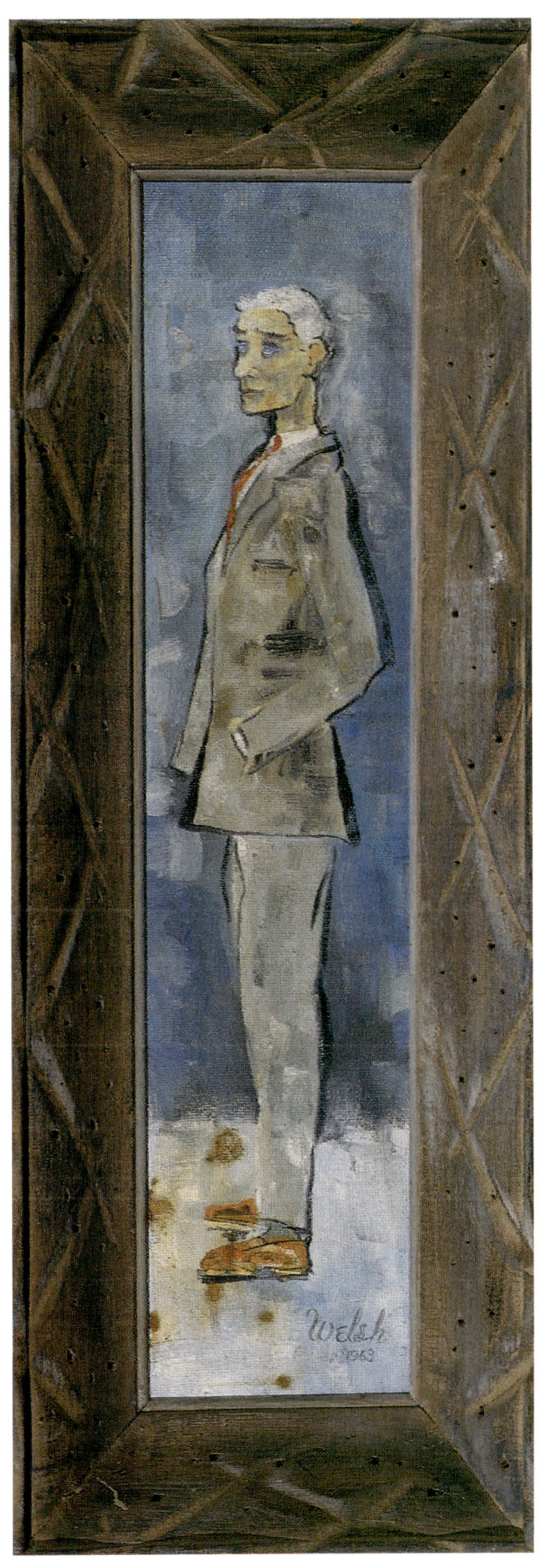

Thin, White-haired Man

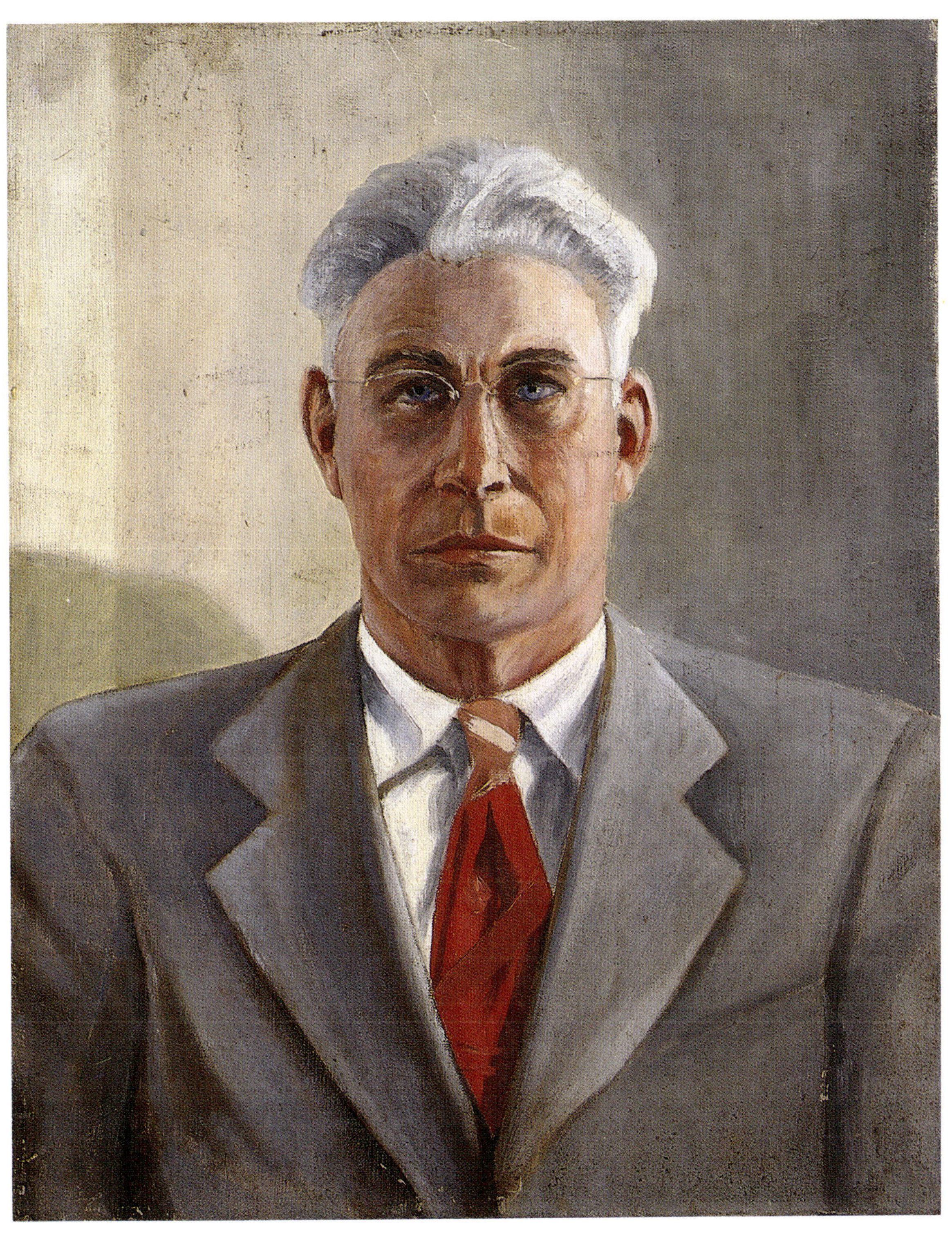

Man with White Hair, Wide Shoulders

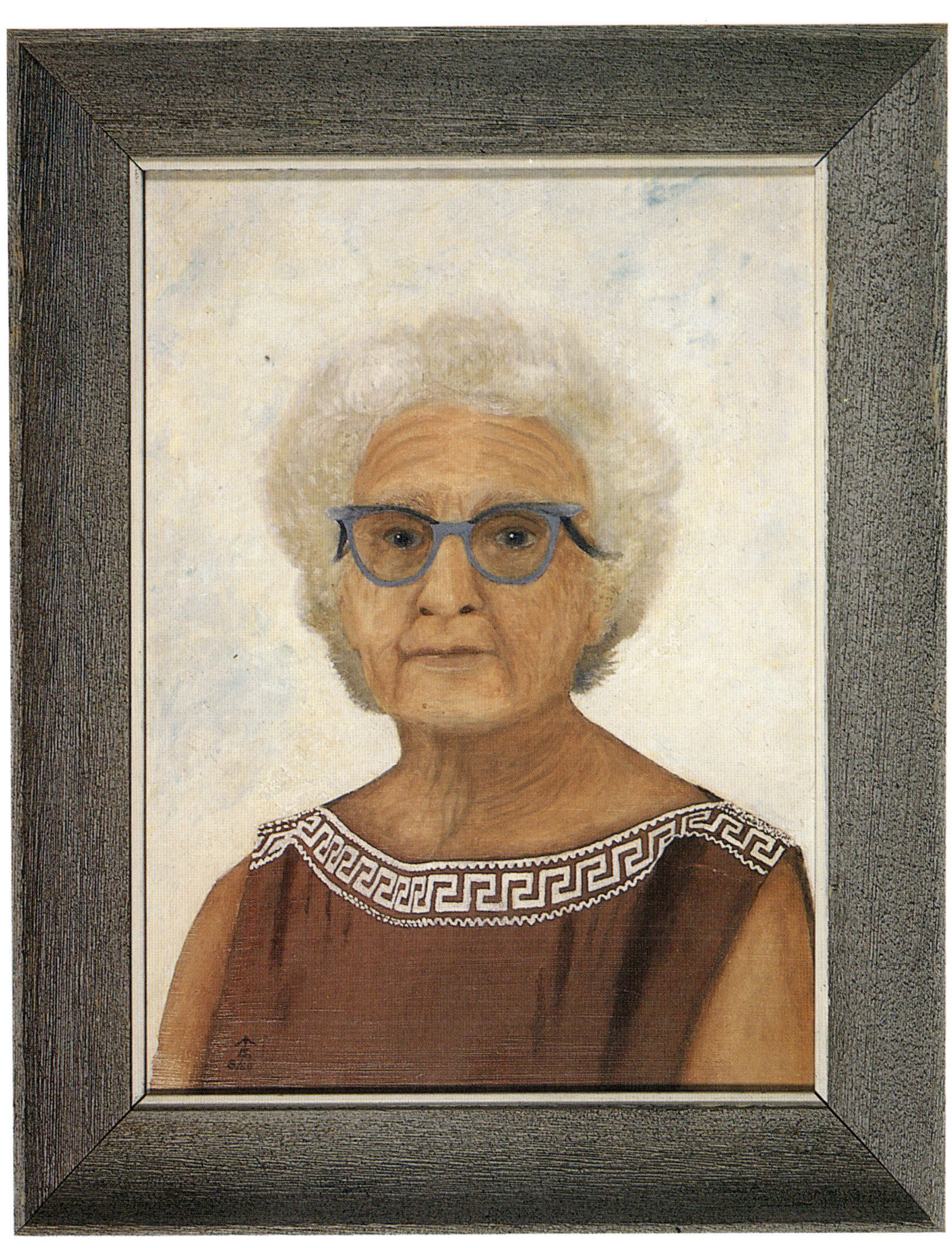

Grandma with Blue Glasses and Brown Dress

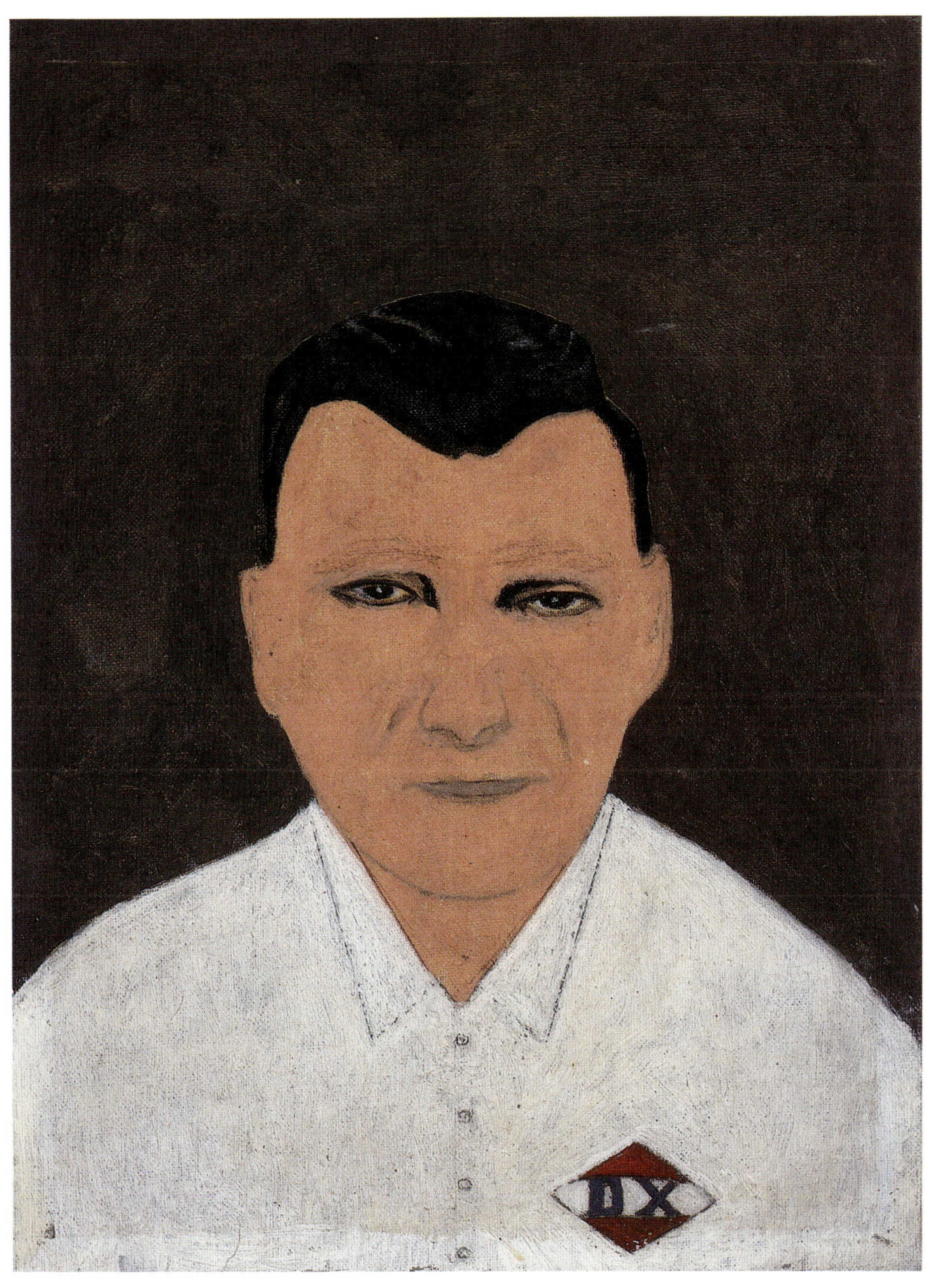

Gas Station Owner

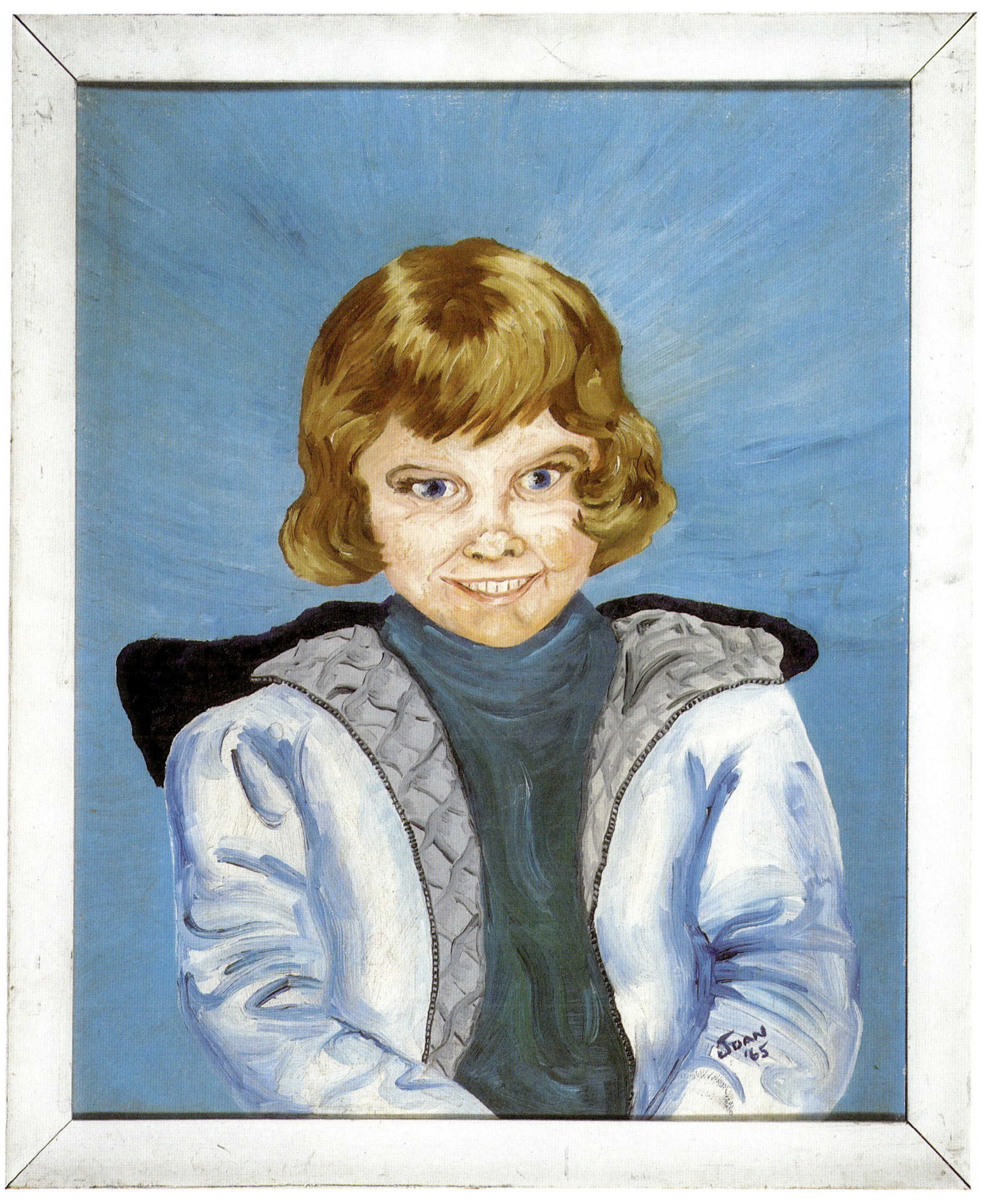

Little Girl with Teeth

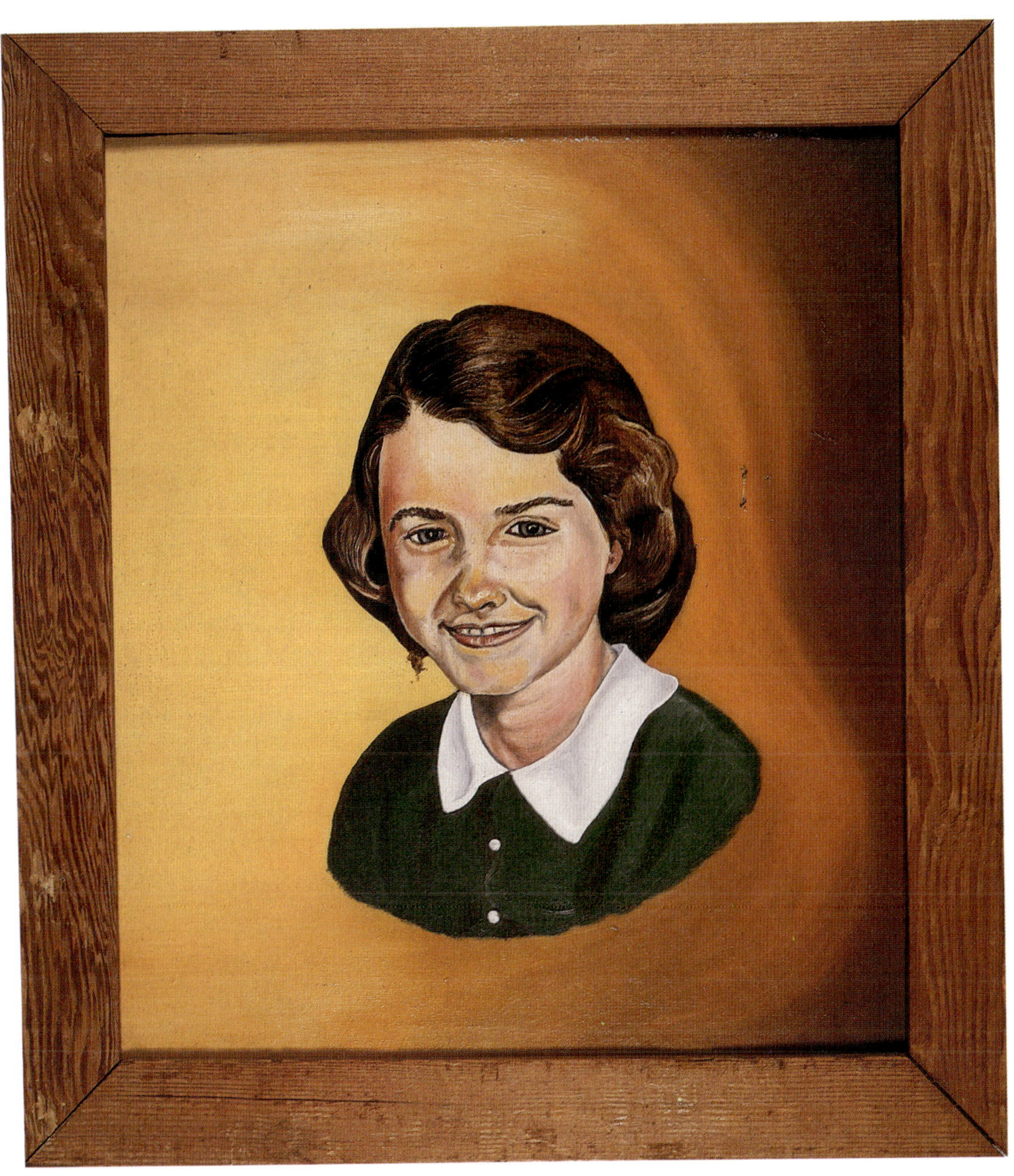

Girl Floating on Yellow Field

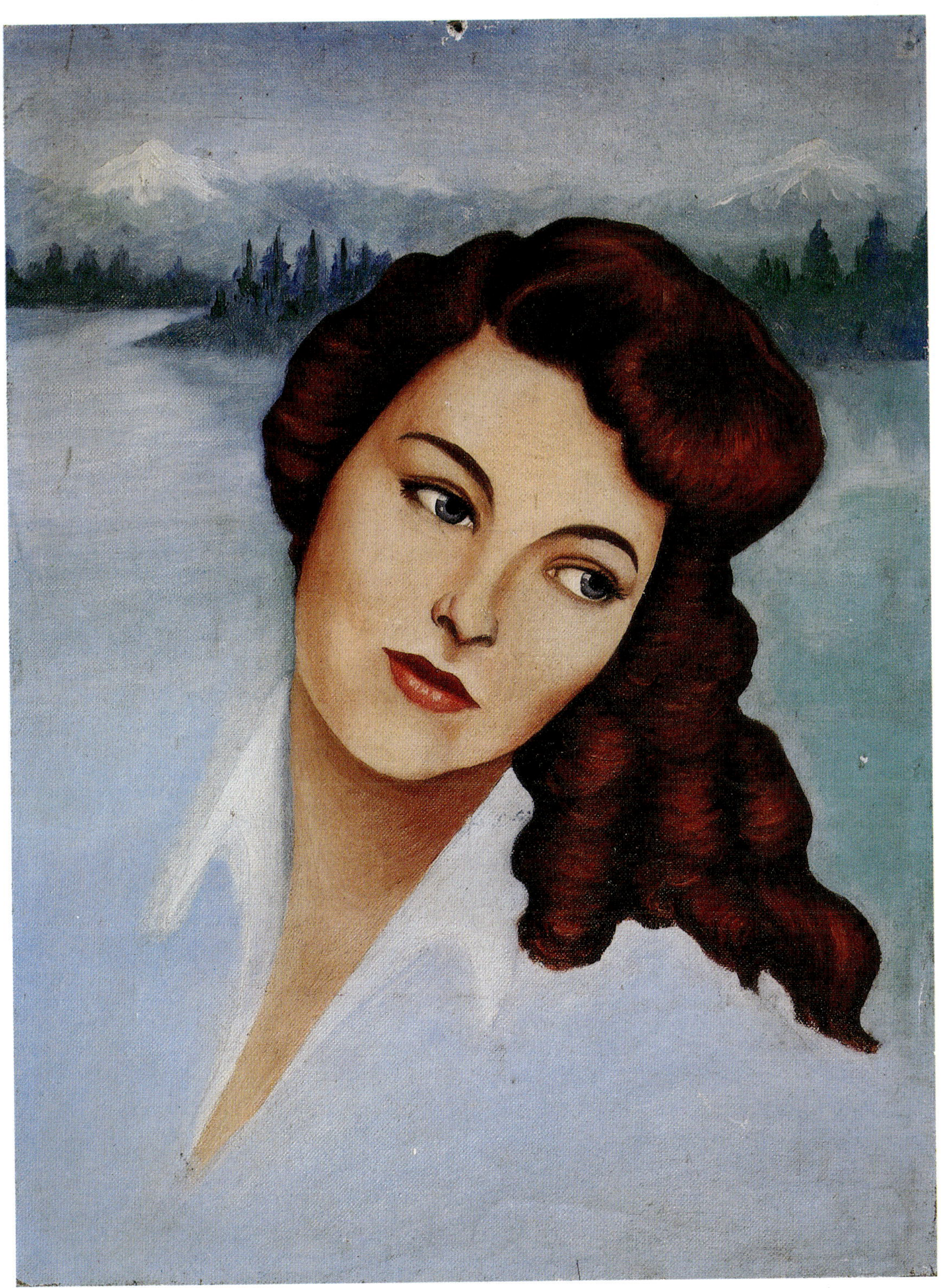

Woman's Head in Blue Landscape

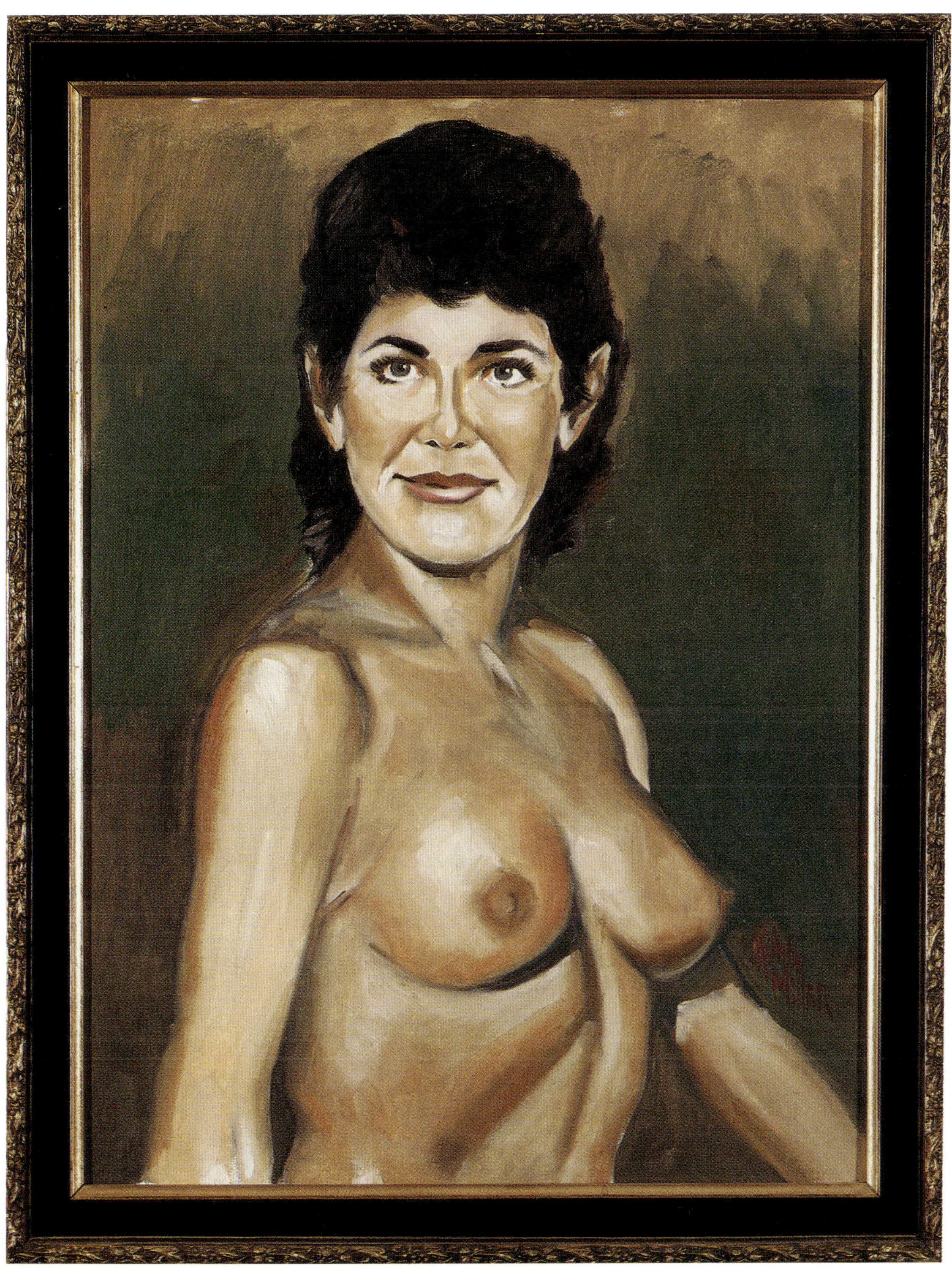

Topless Woman's Portrait

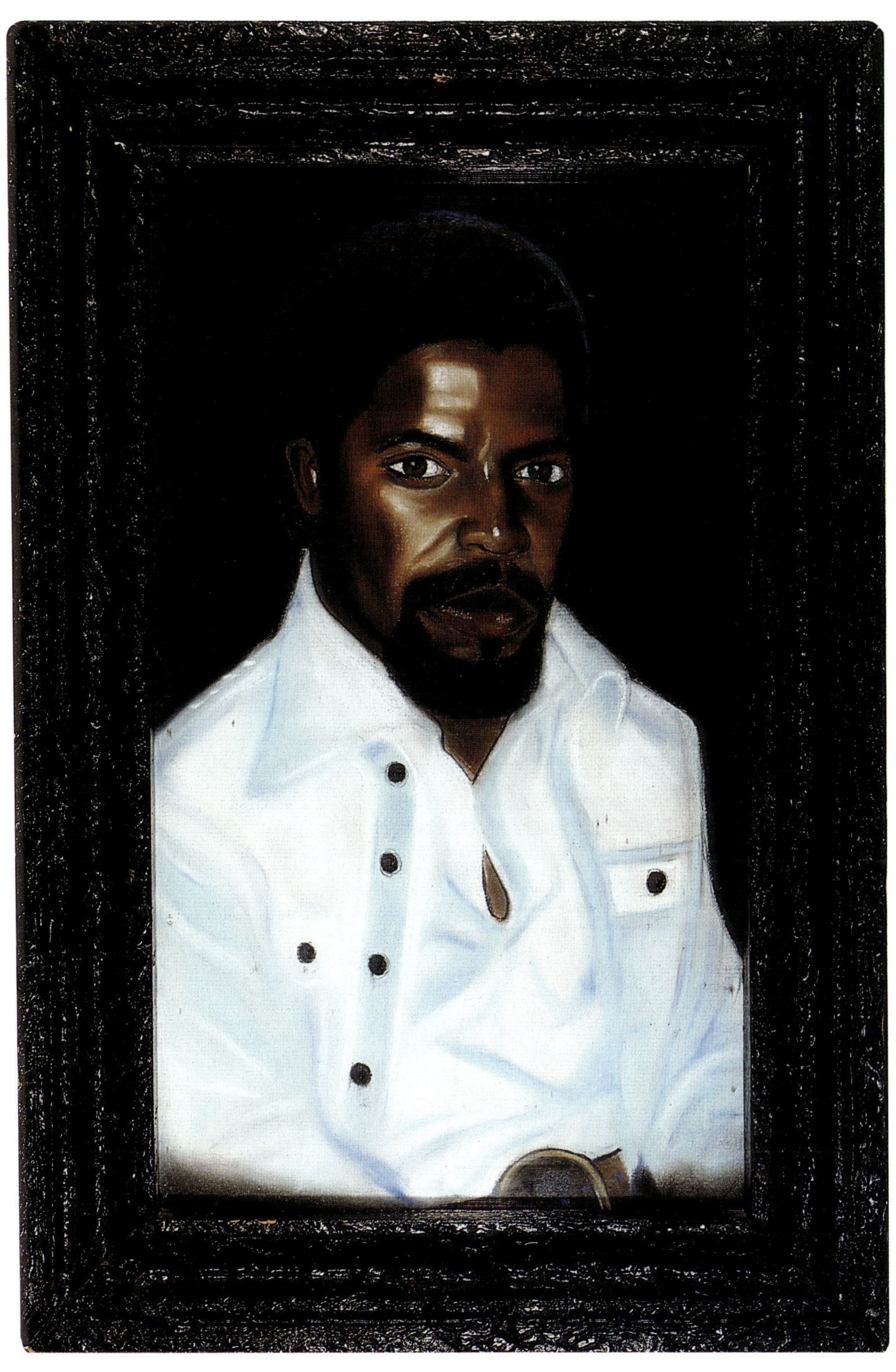

Bearded Black Man in White Shirt

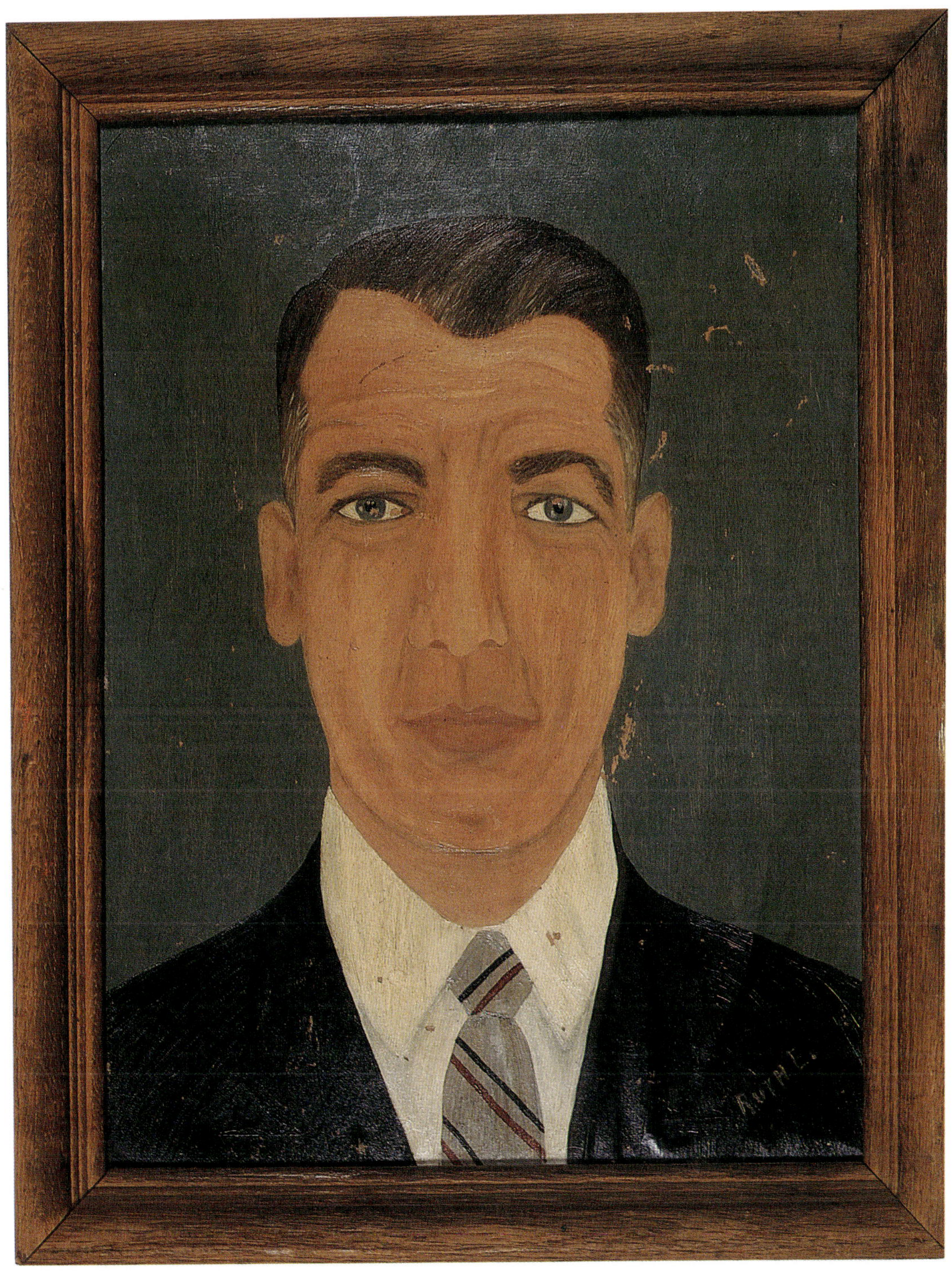

Long-faced Man with Tie

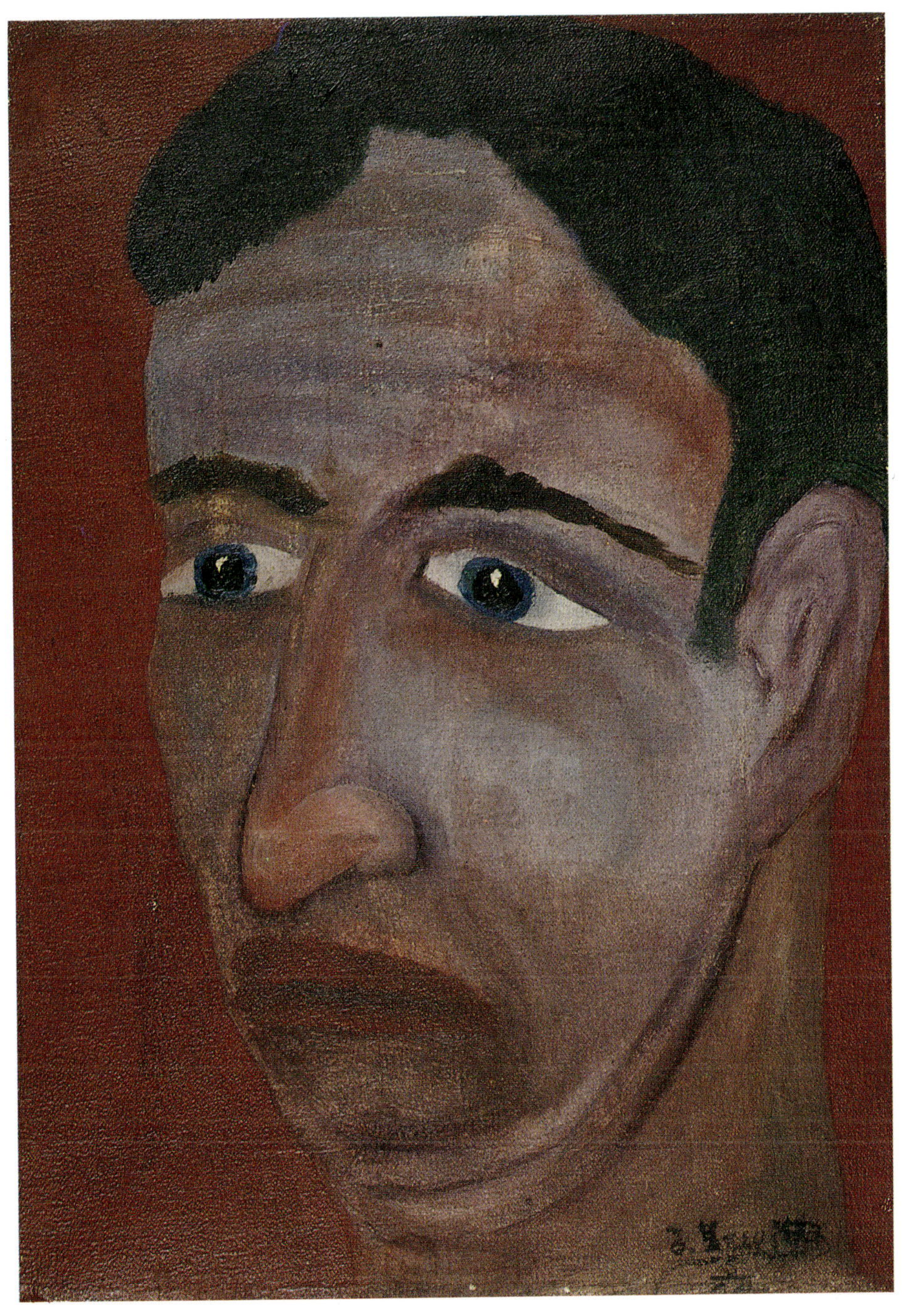

Purple Man

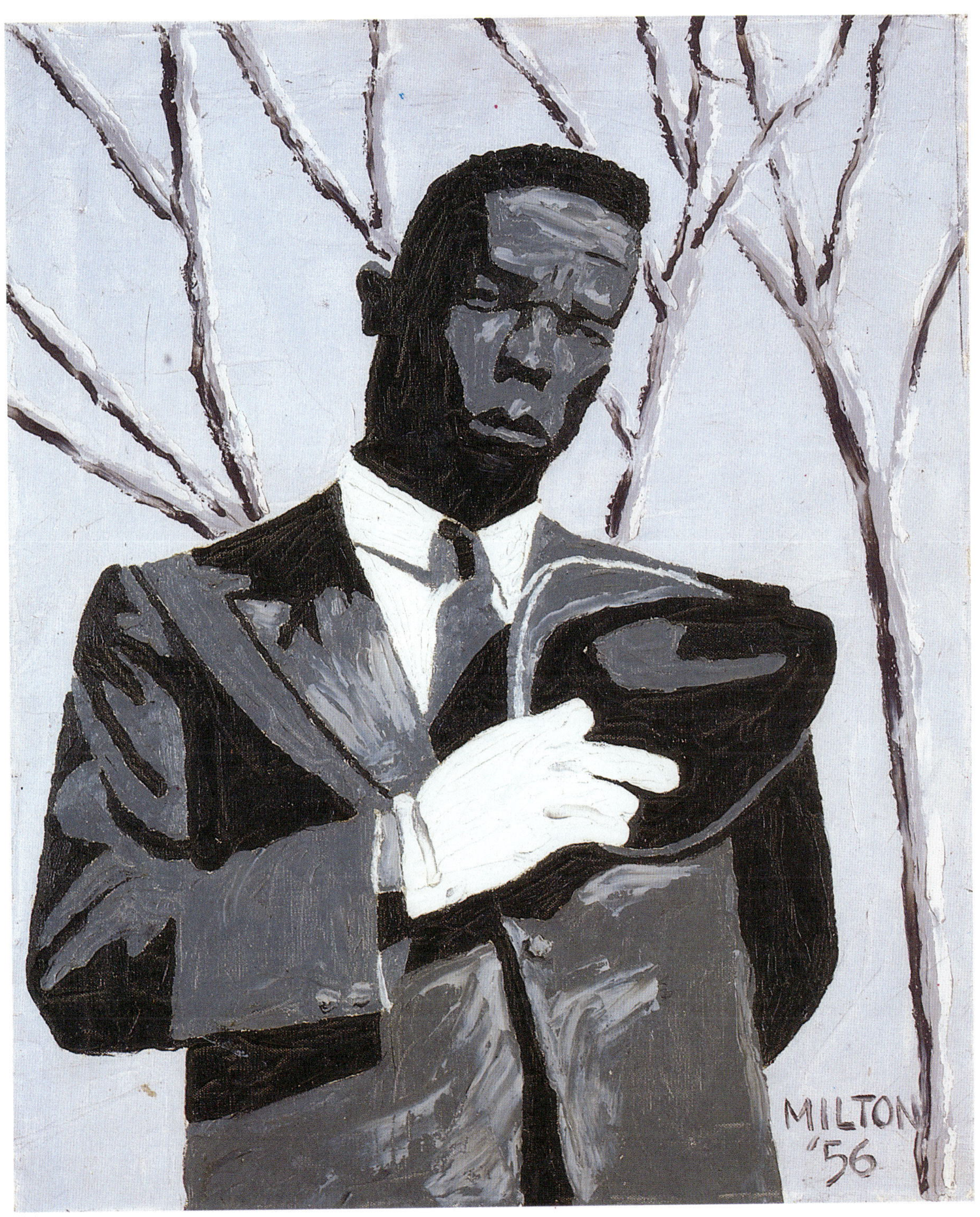

Black Man Mourning in Tones of Grey

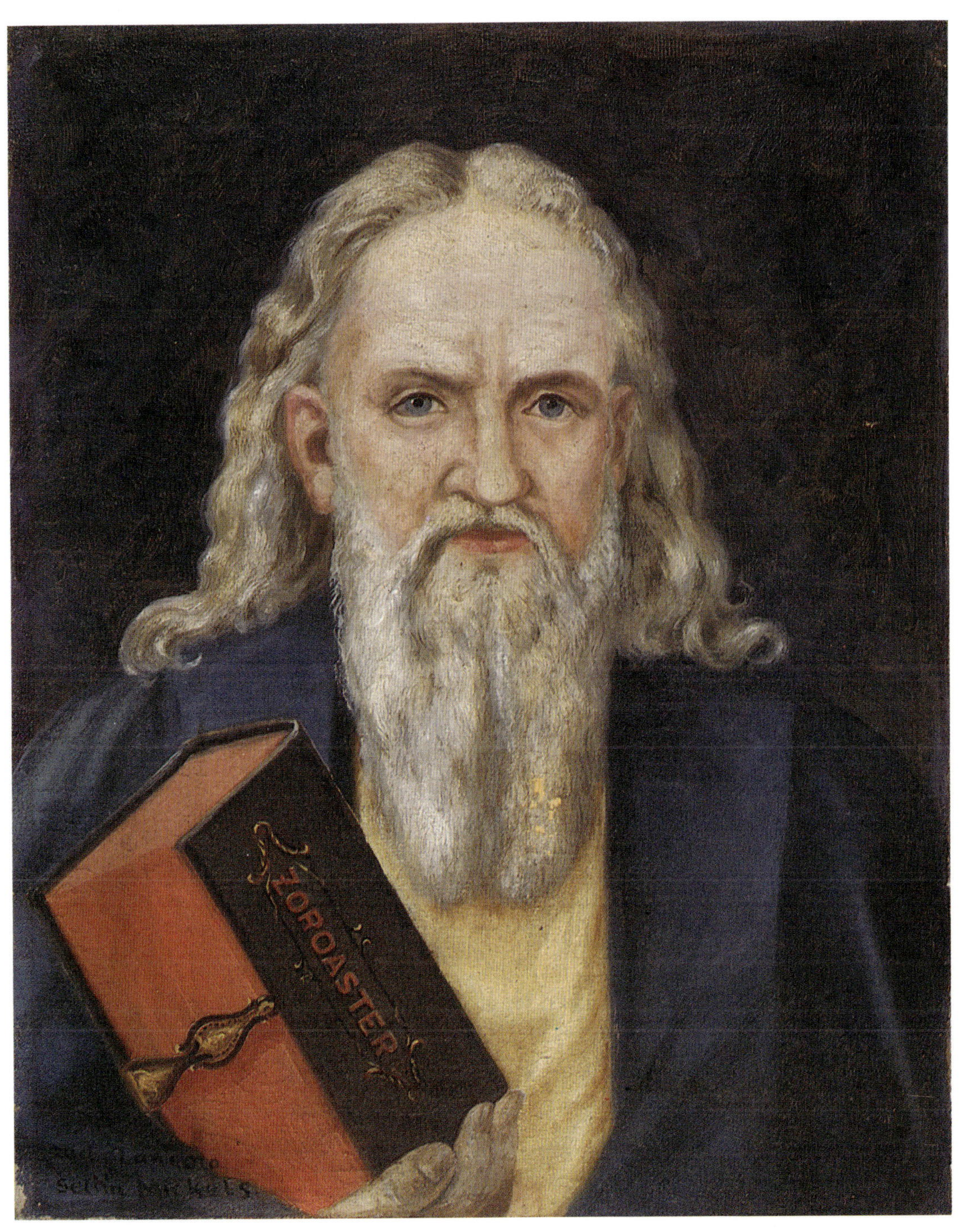

Old Man with Zoroaster Book

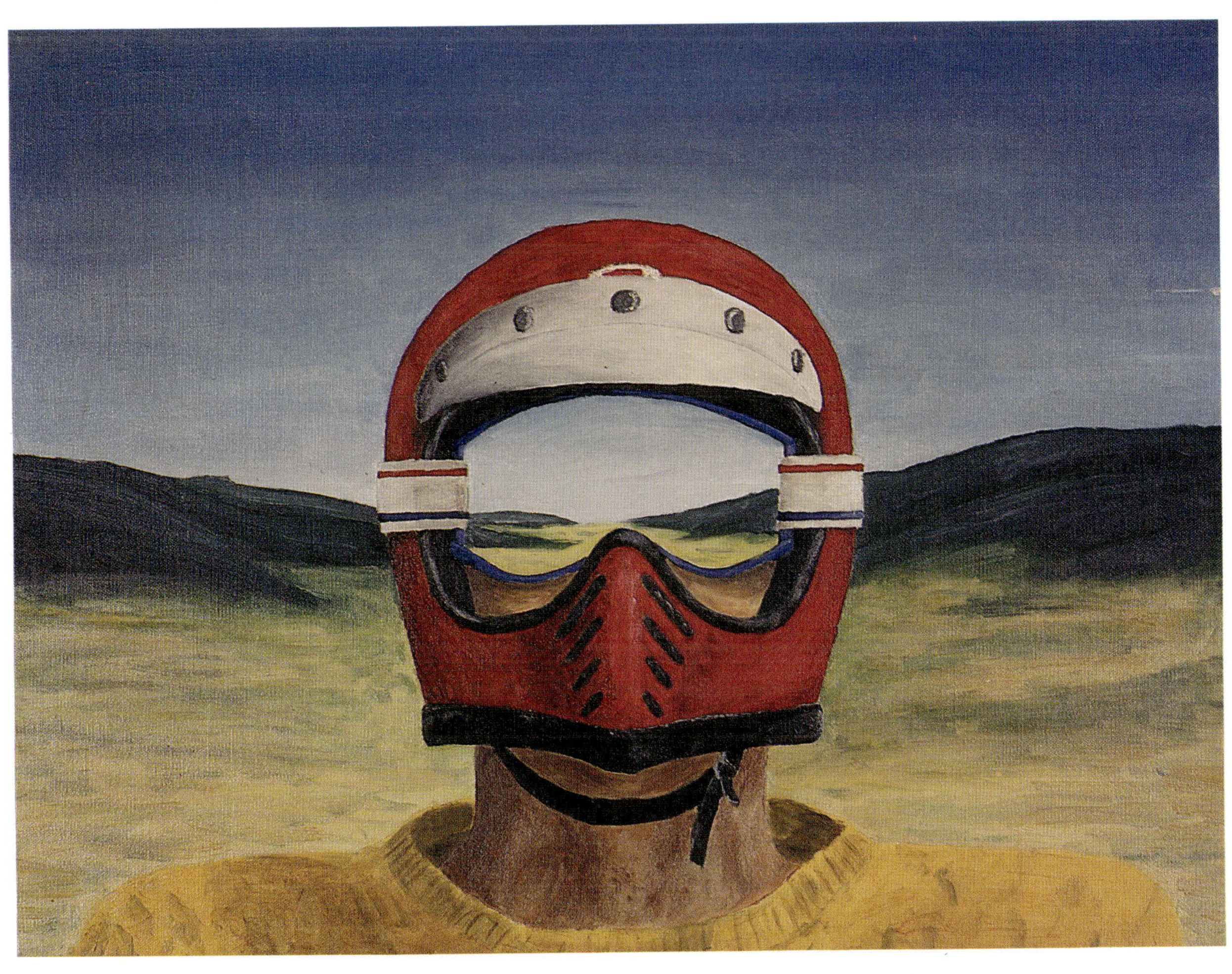

Off-road Helmet Merges with Landscape

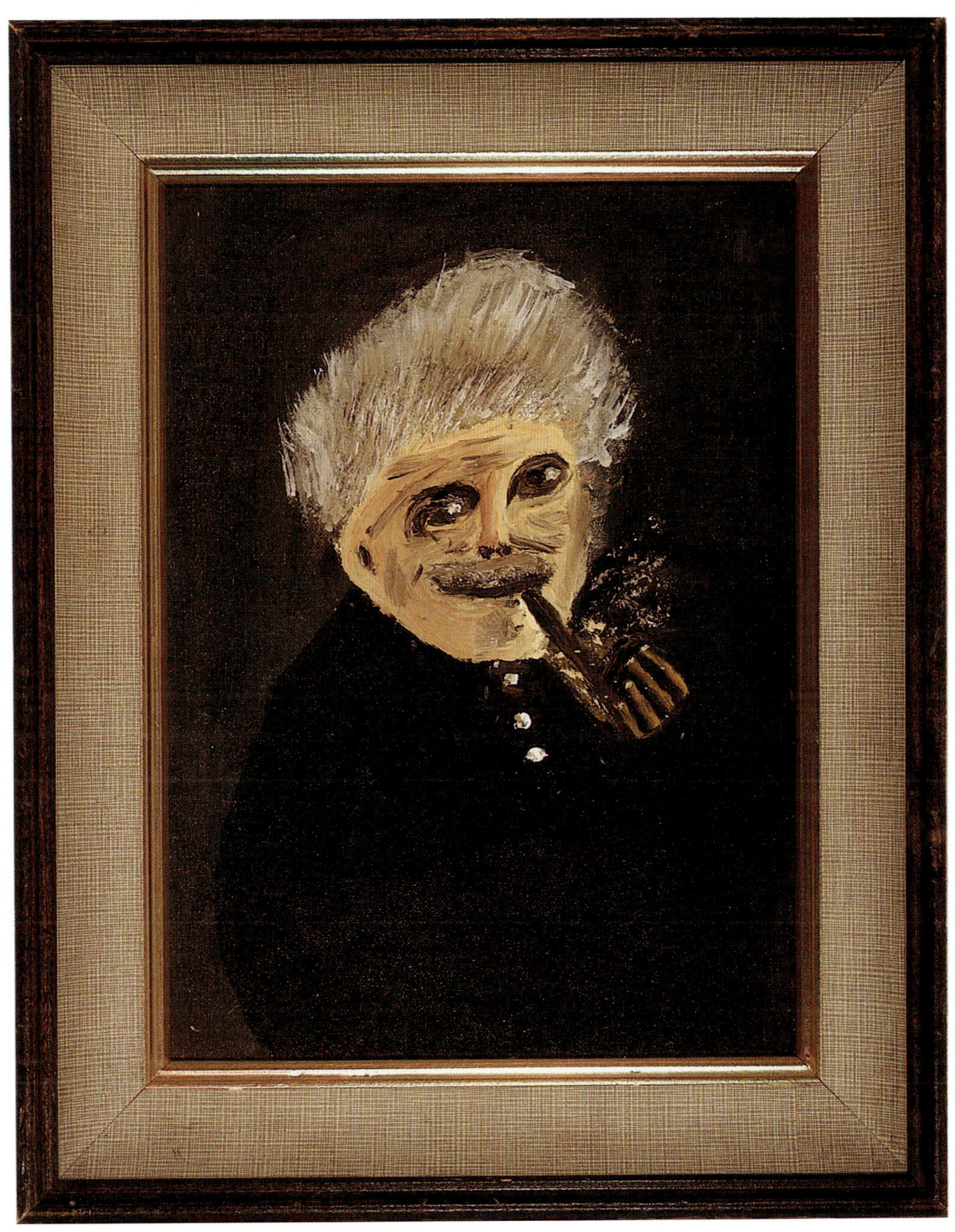

Old Man with Pipe

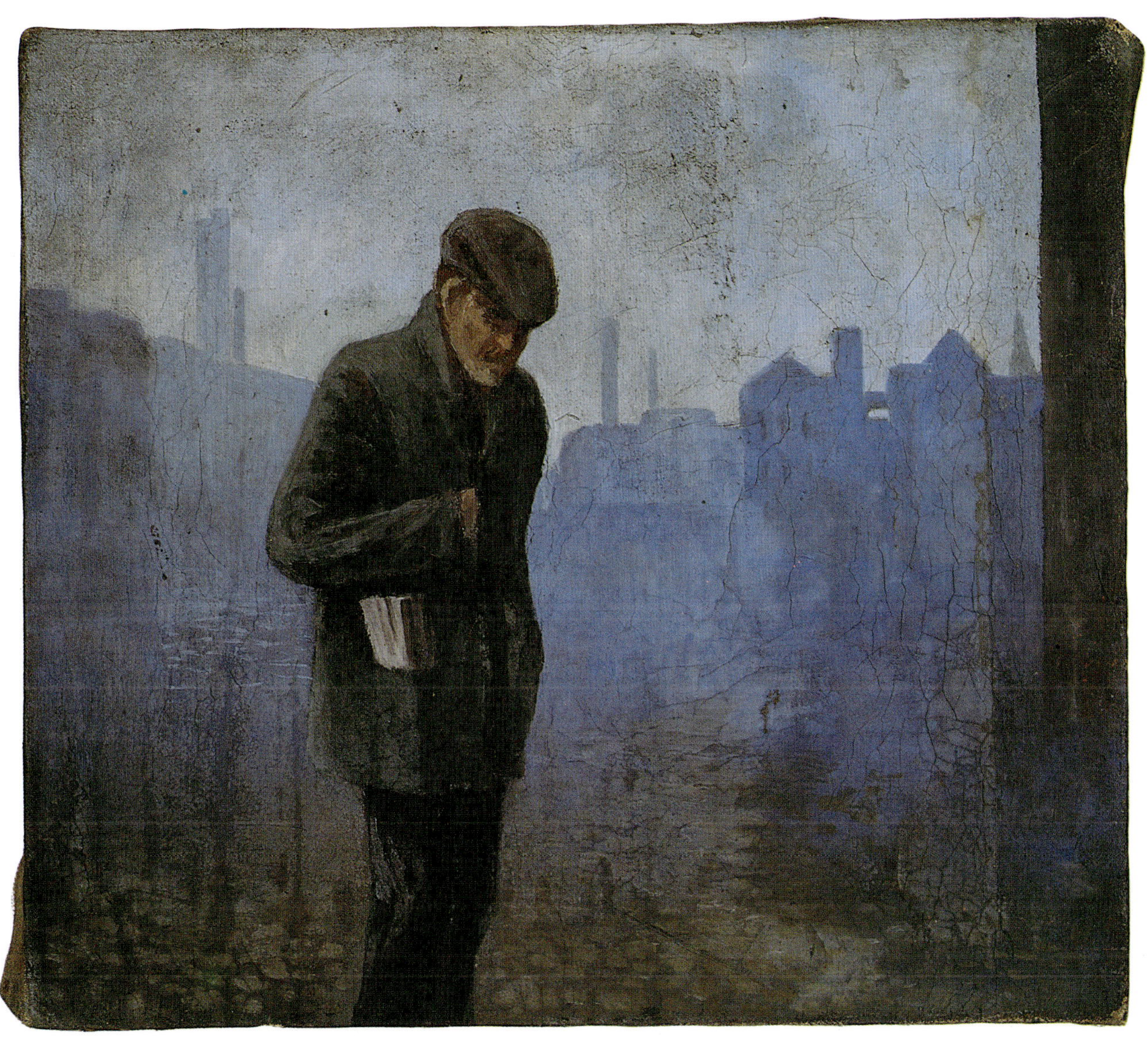

Blue Collar Worker

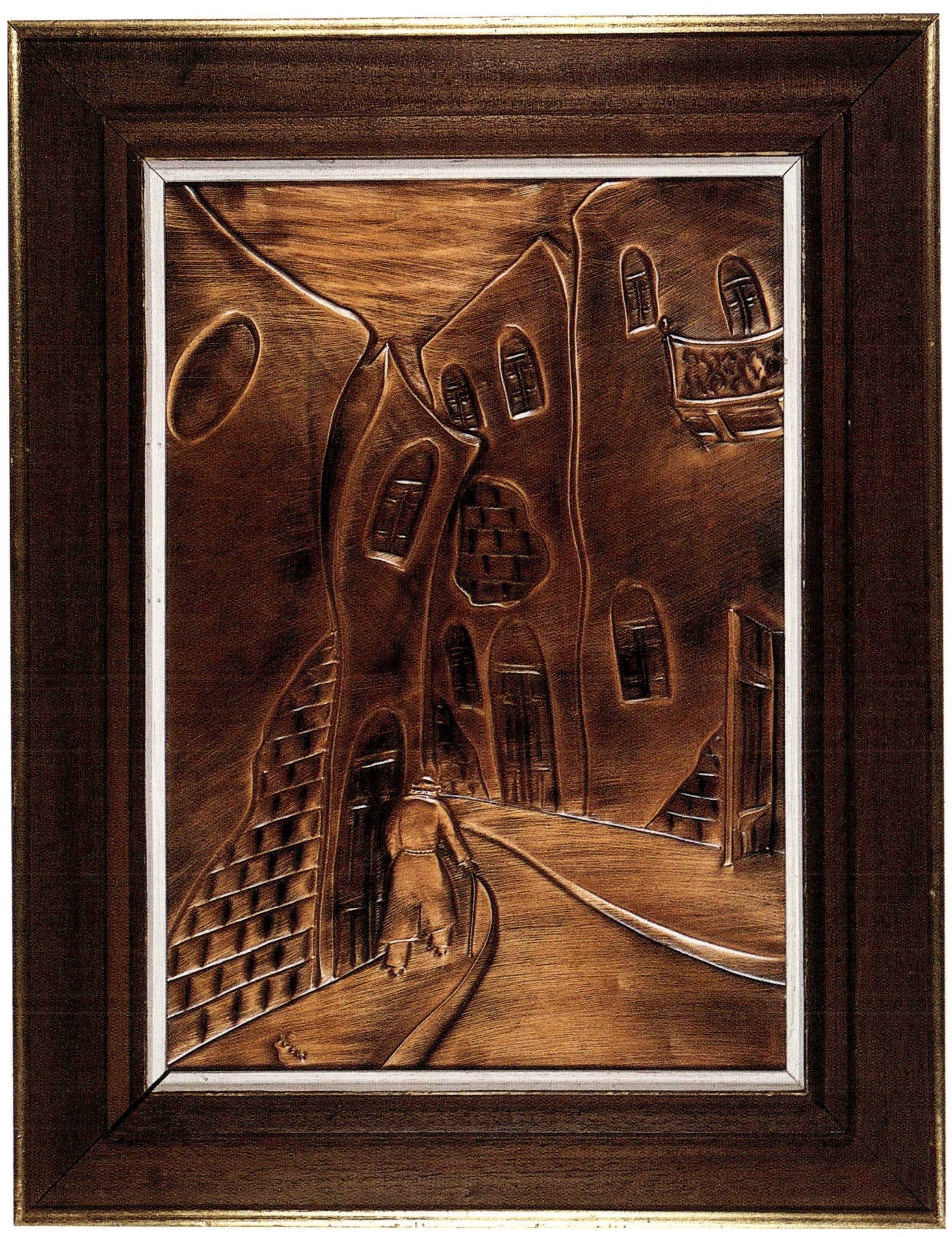

Embossed Surrealist/Expressionist Cityscape

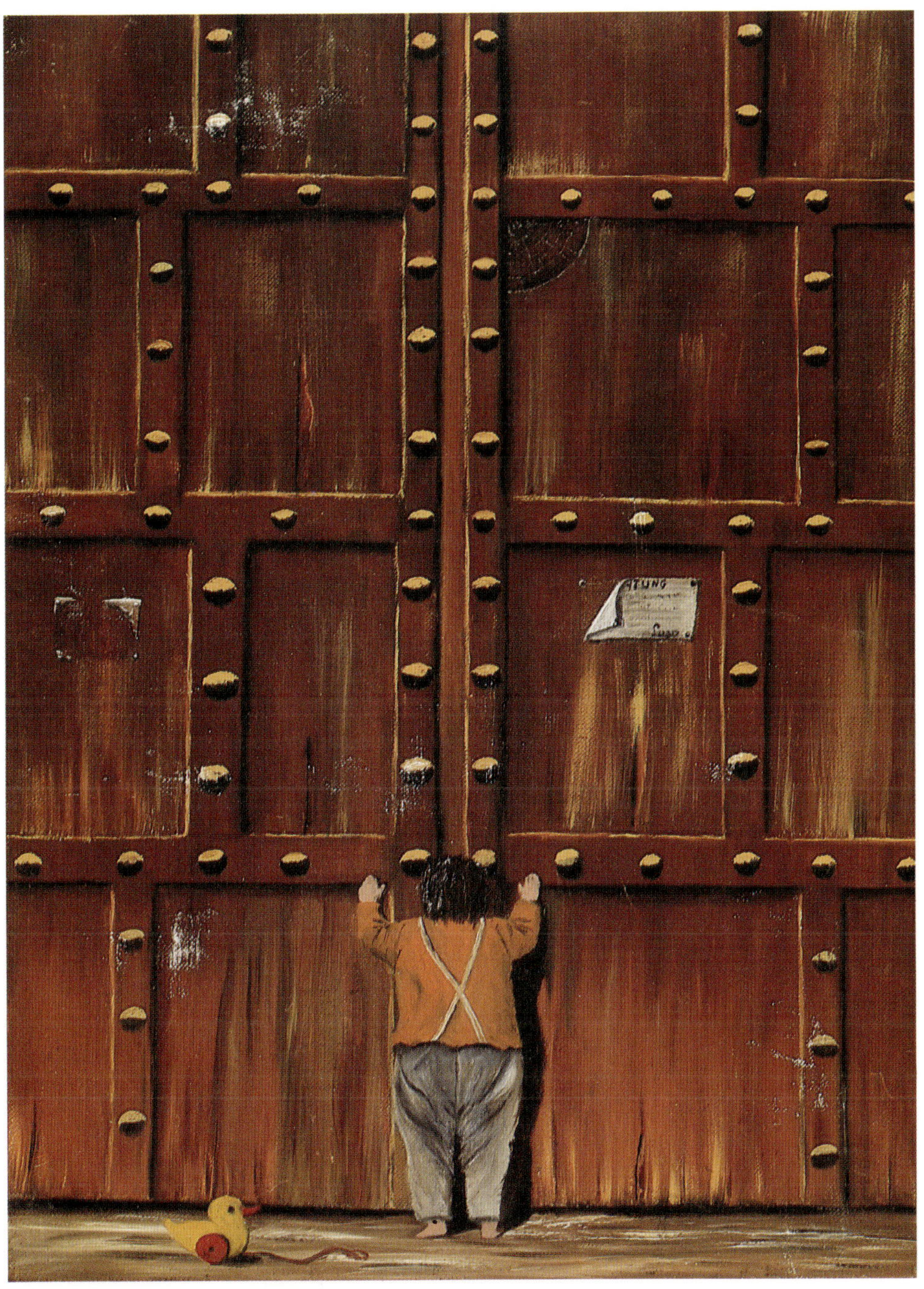

Boy with Duck Toy Peers through Rusty Gates

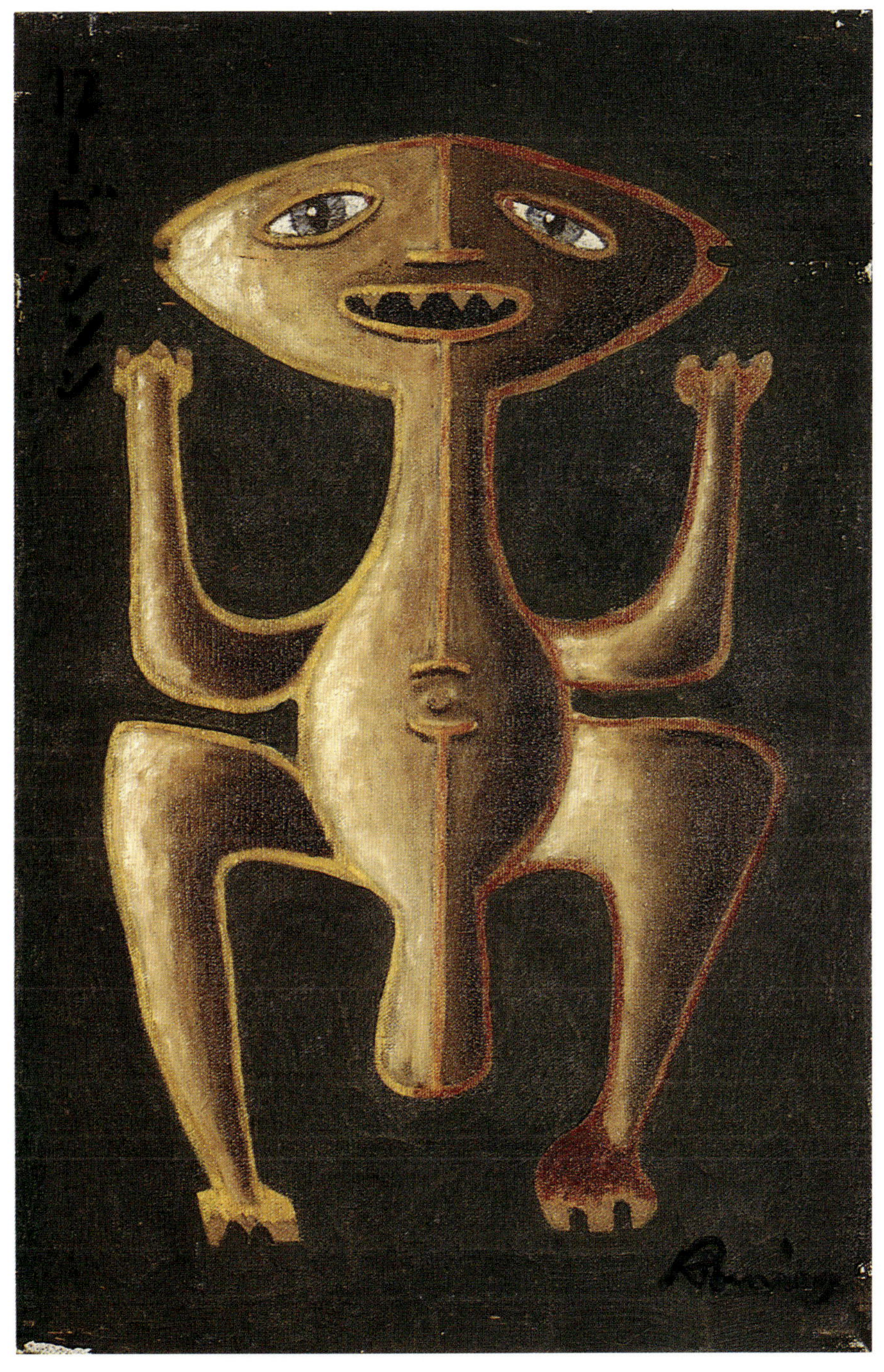

Tiki God

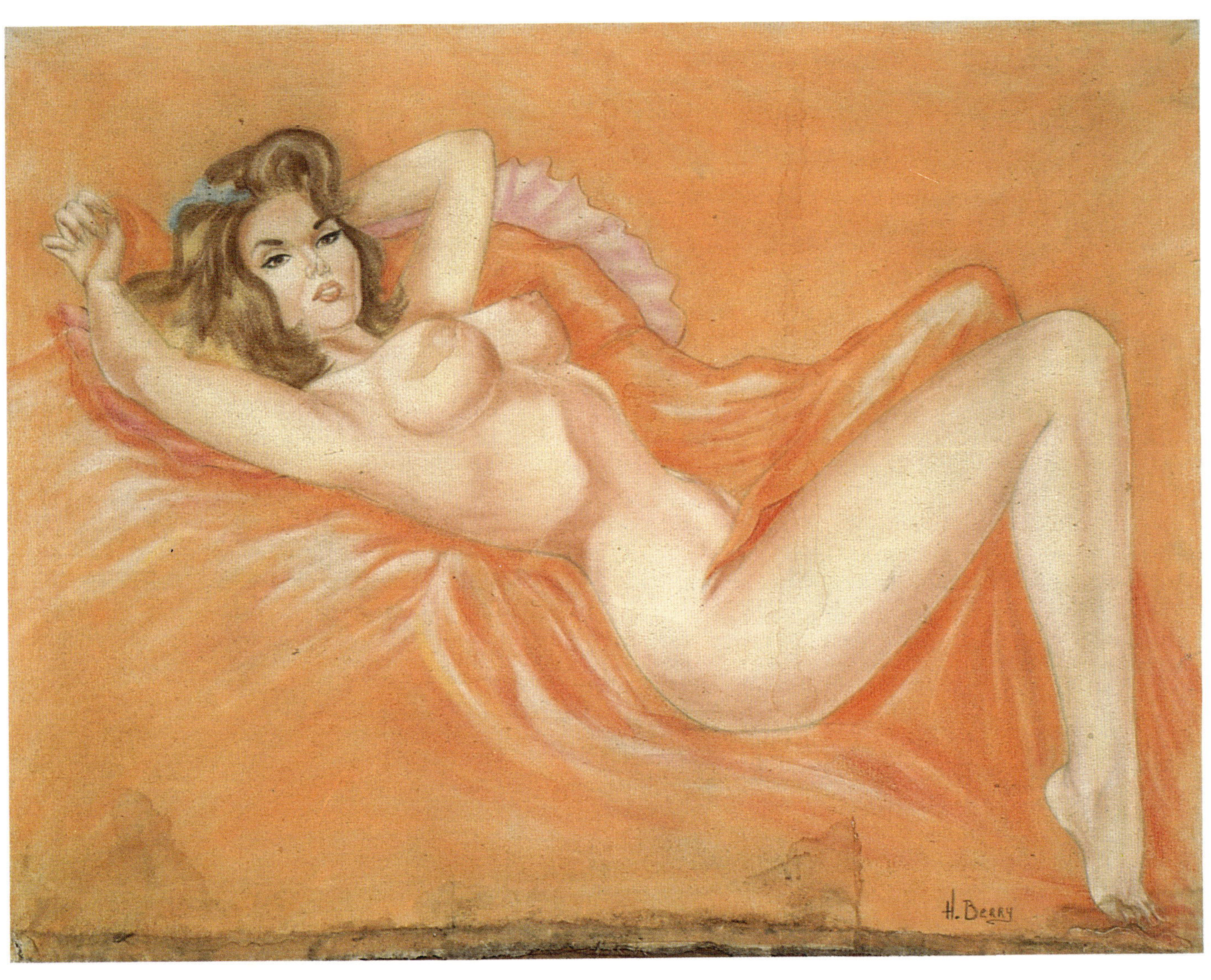

Nude Woman Reclining on Orange Bed

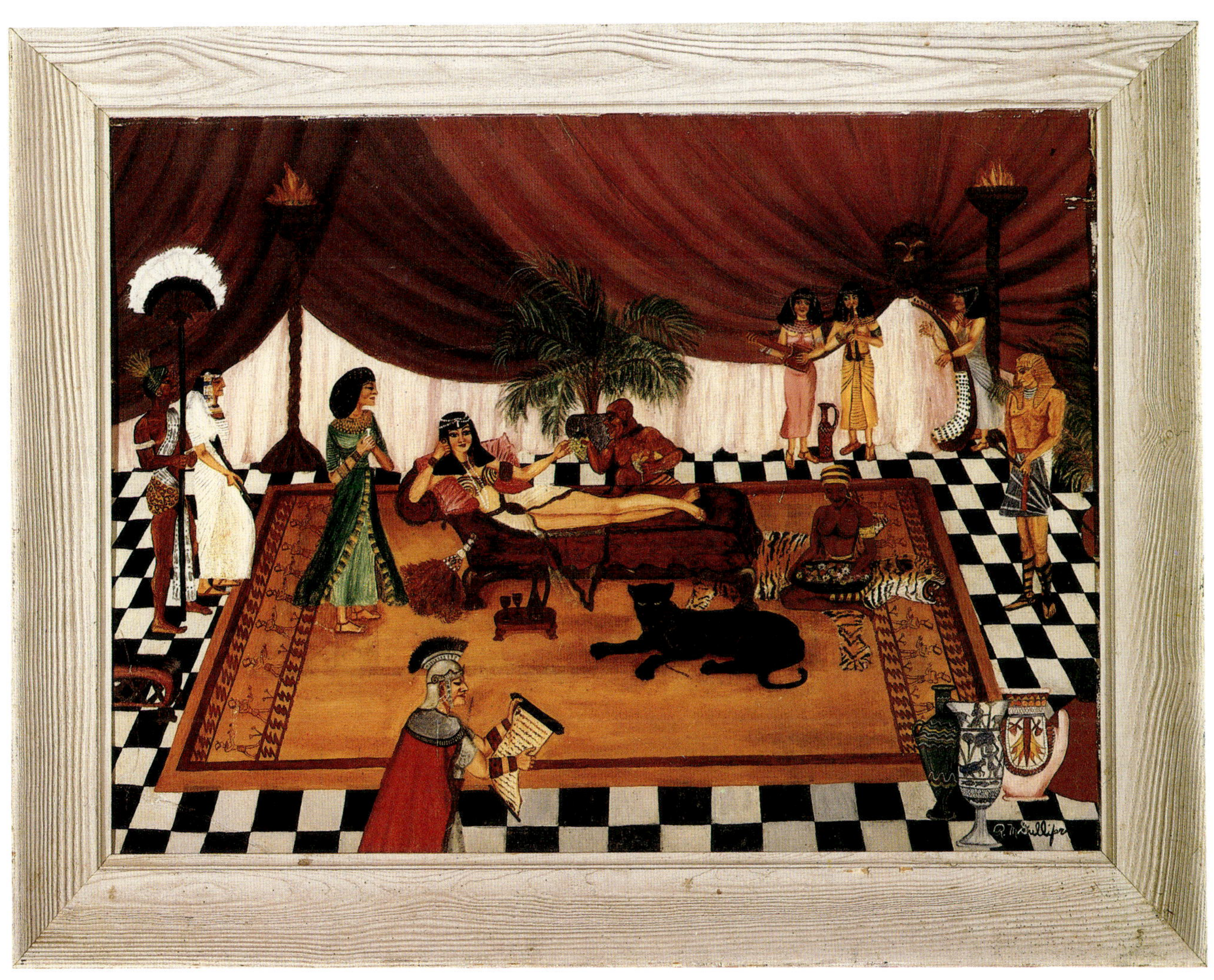

Cleopatra with Cats and Tiled Floor

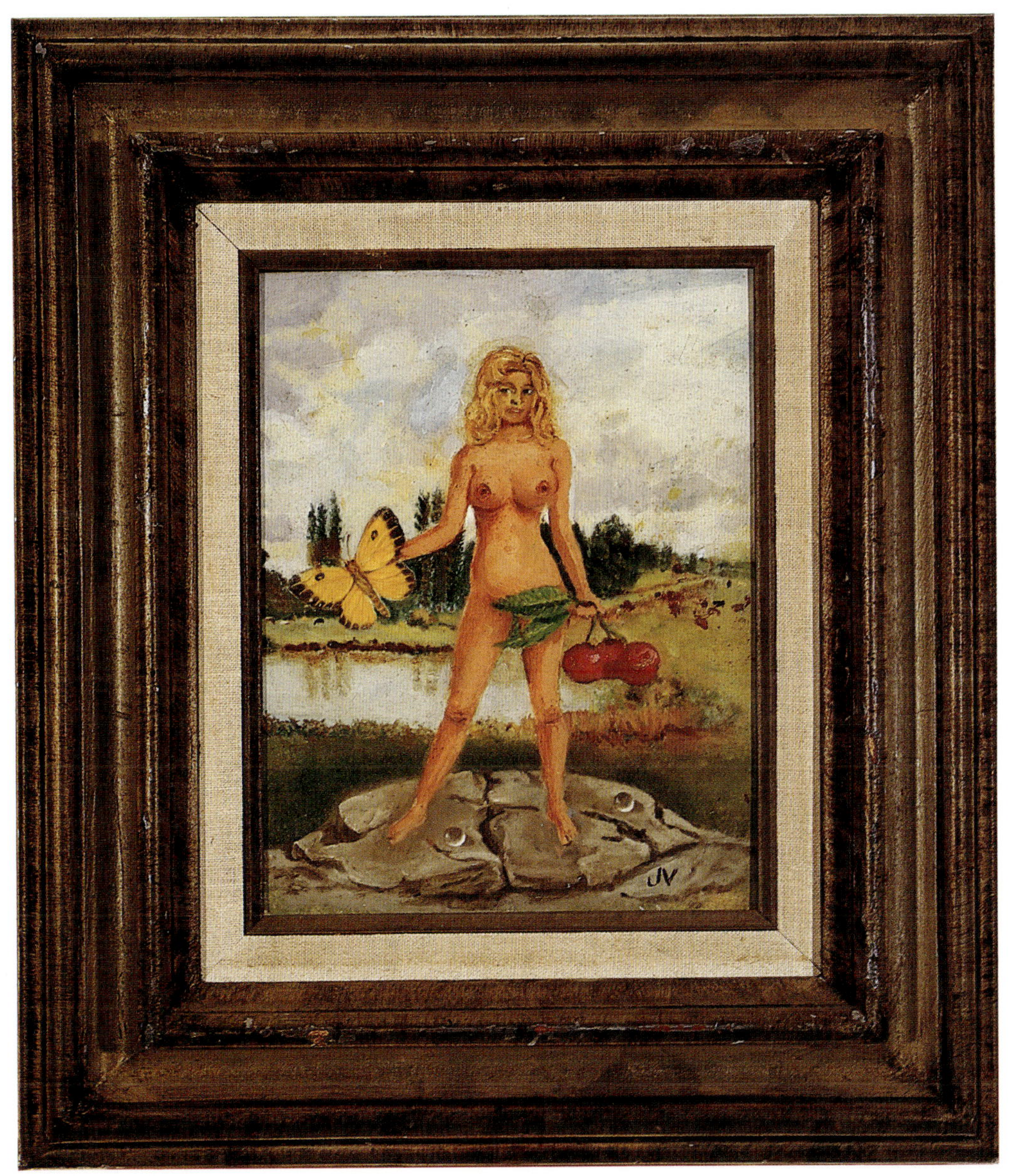

Nude Blonde Woman with Butterfly and Cherries

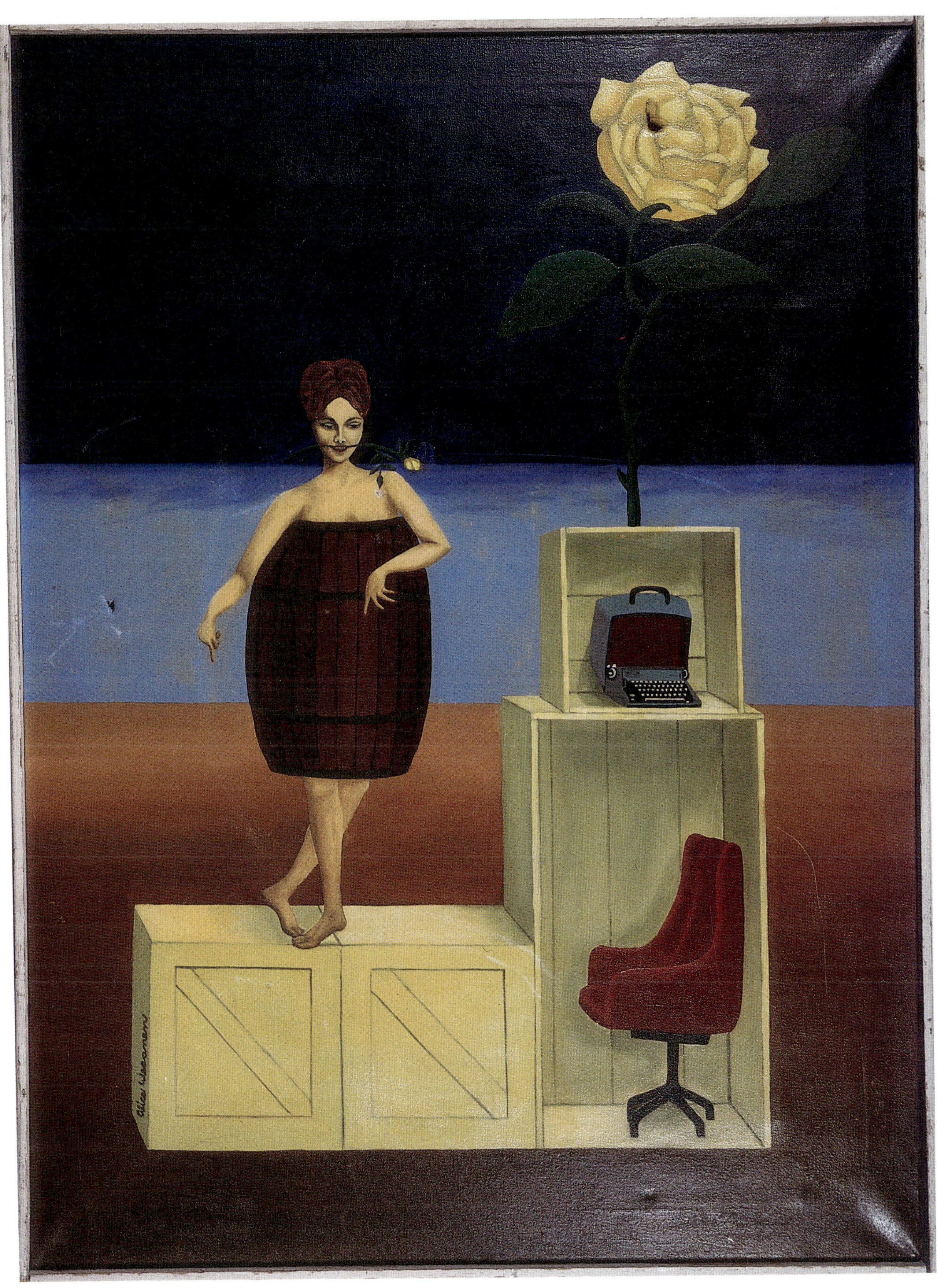

Woman in Barrel with Yellow Roses, Typewriter and Chair on Boxes

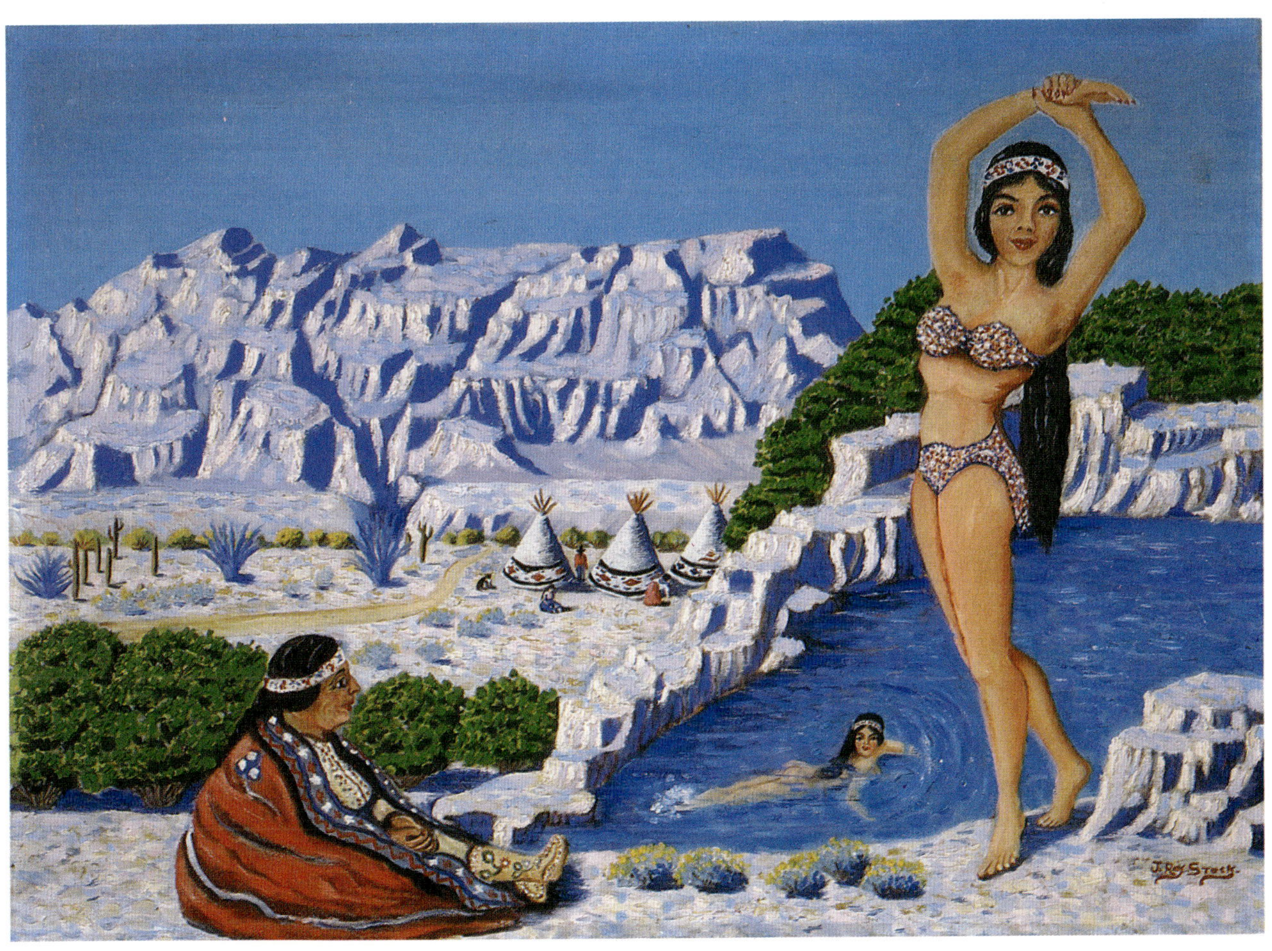

Indian Maidens Frolic in Bikinis

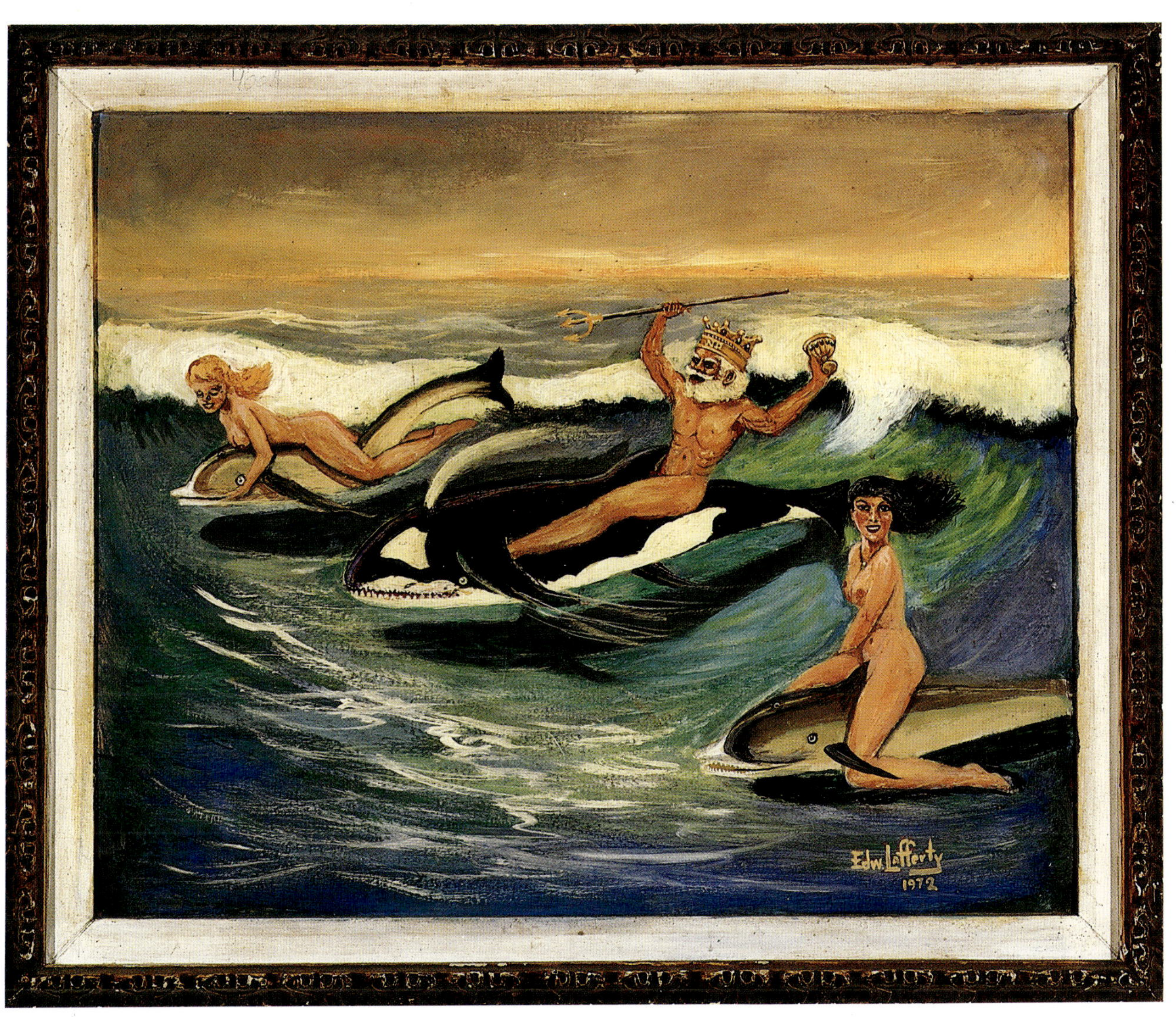

Neptune and Nymphs Astride Sea Mammals

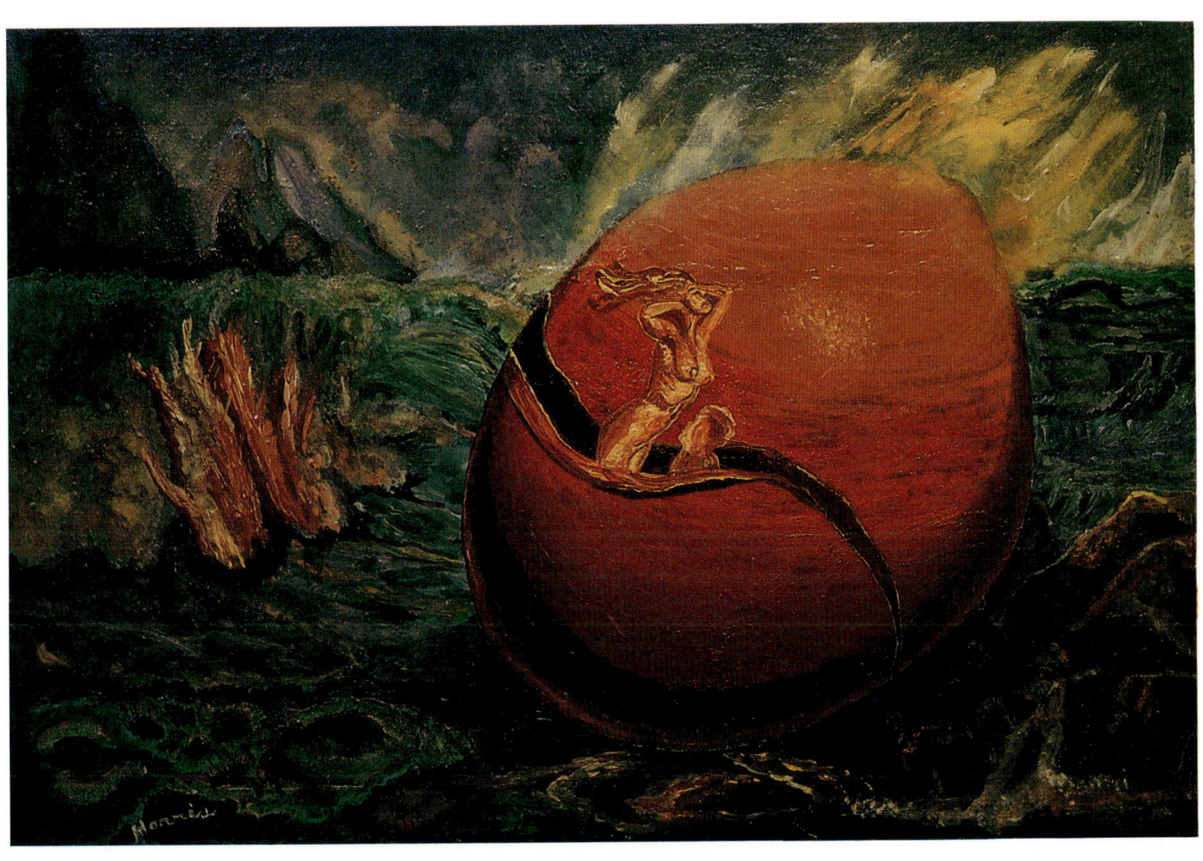

Man and Woman Emerge from Egg in Seascape

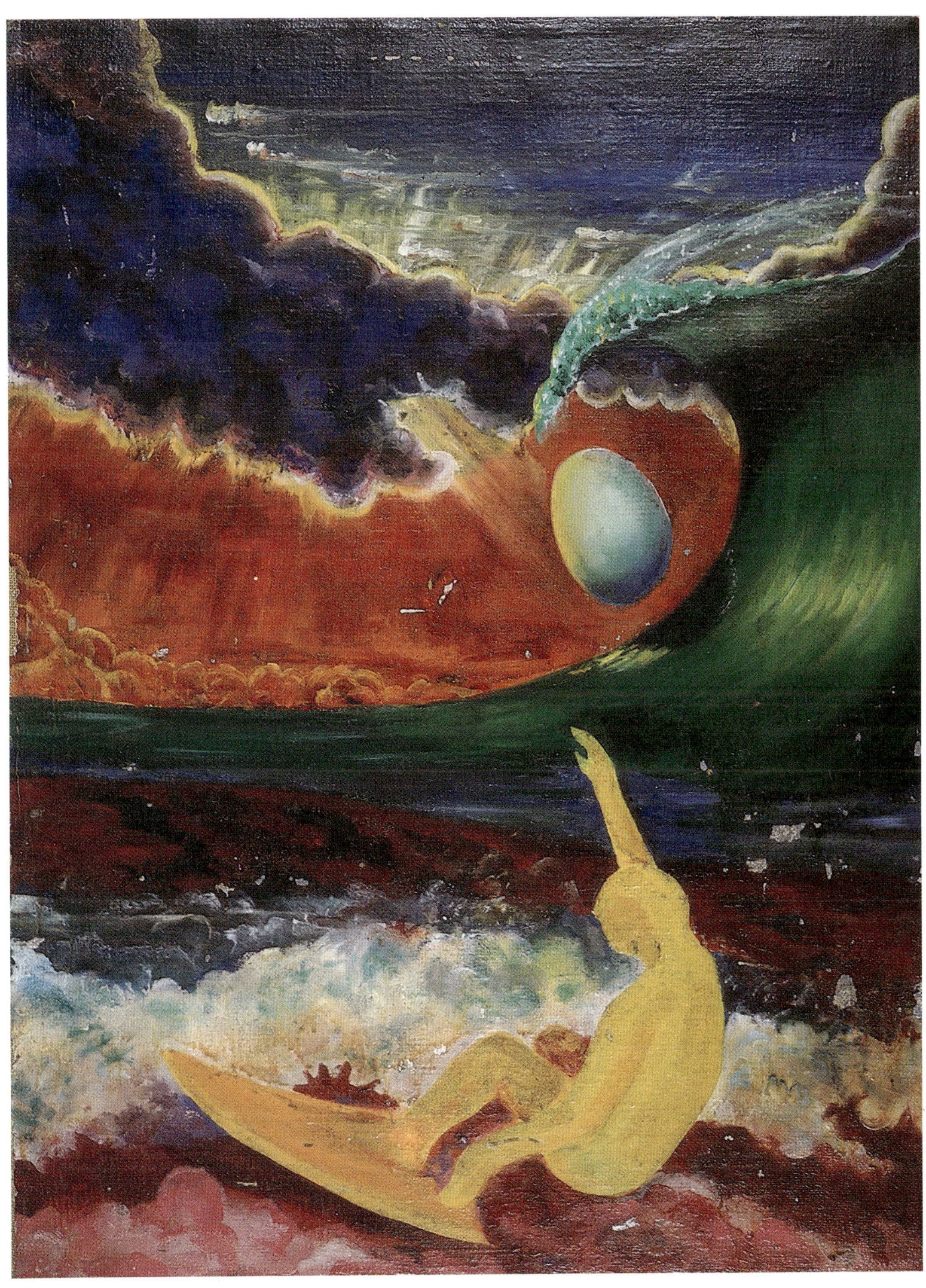

Yellow Surfer and Egg in Curl

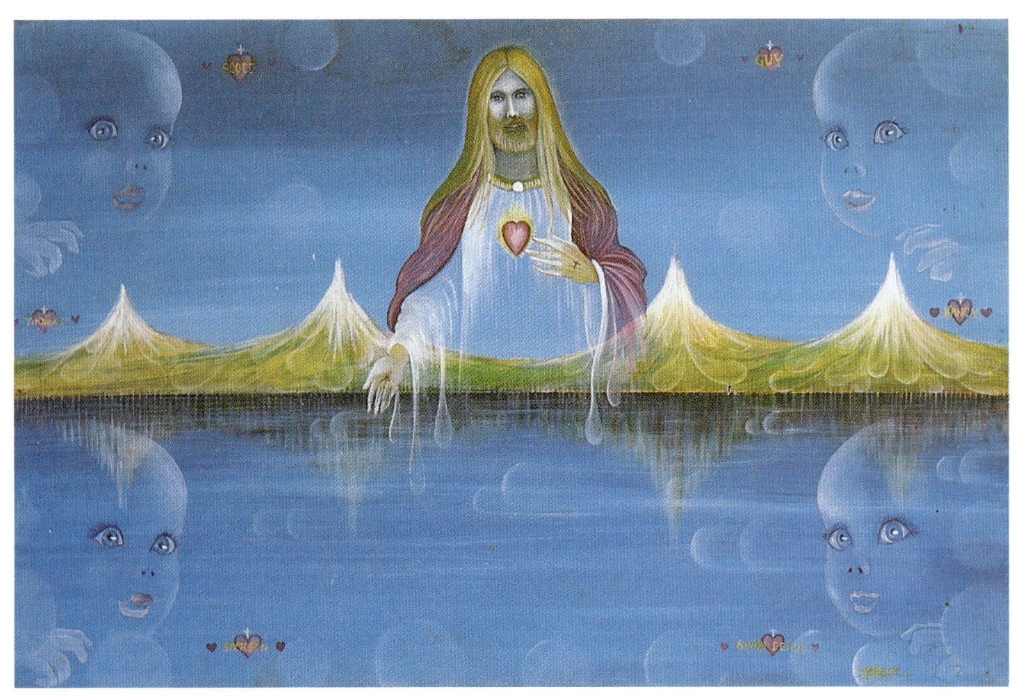

Jesus and Babies Over Mountain Pool Landscape

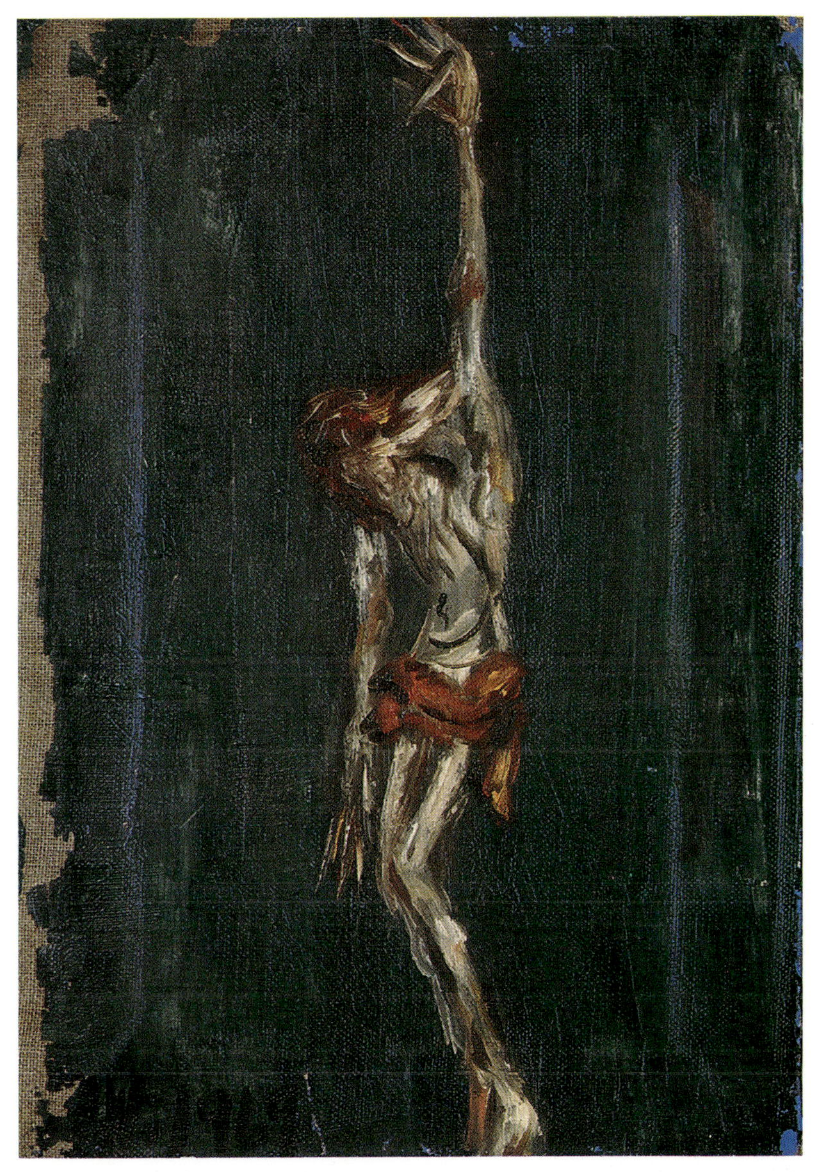

Loin-clothed Man Hanging by One Wrist

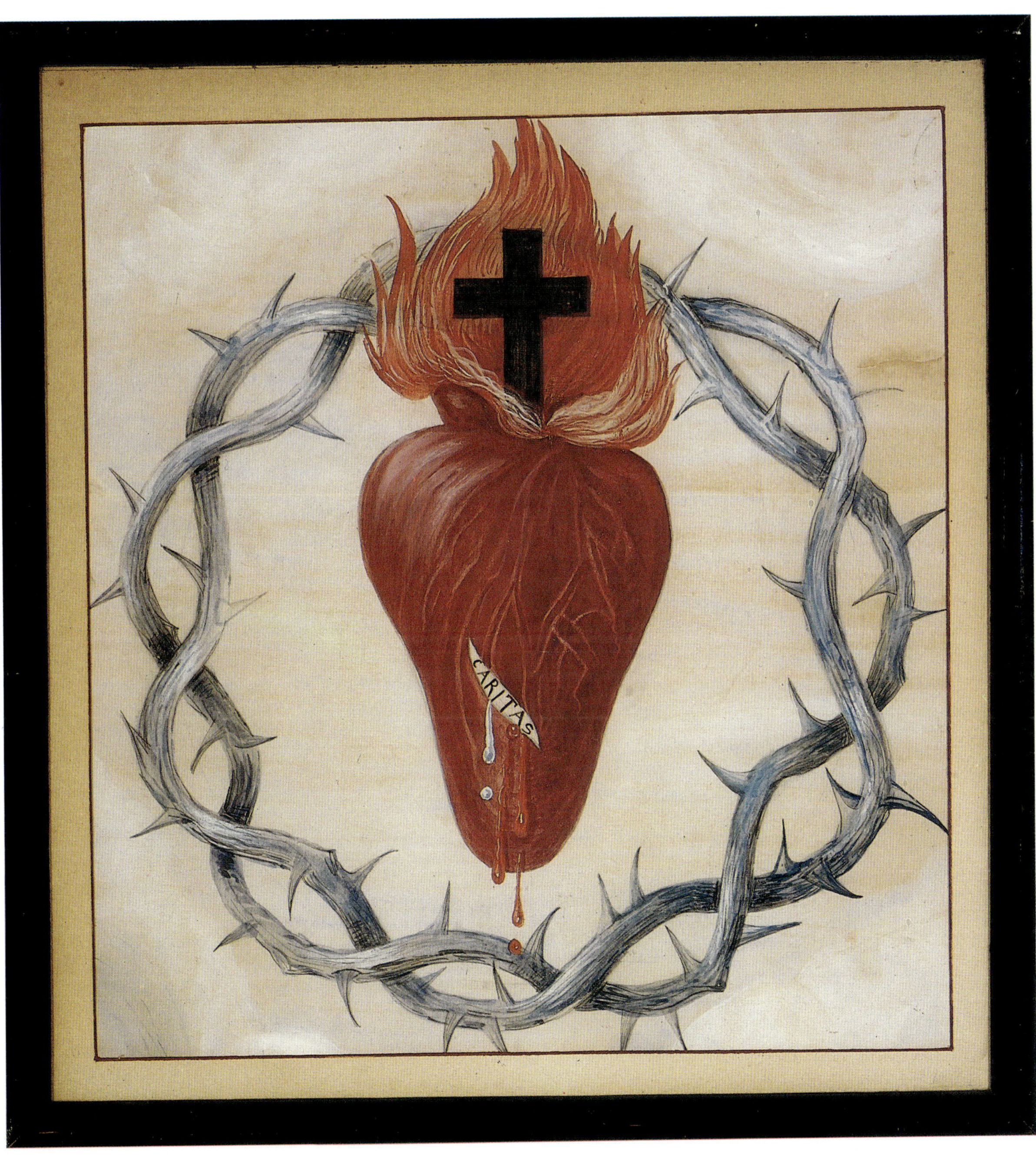

Bleeding Flaming Heart, Thorns and Caritas

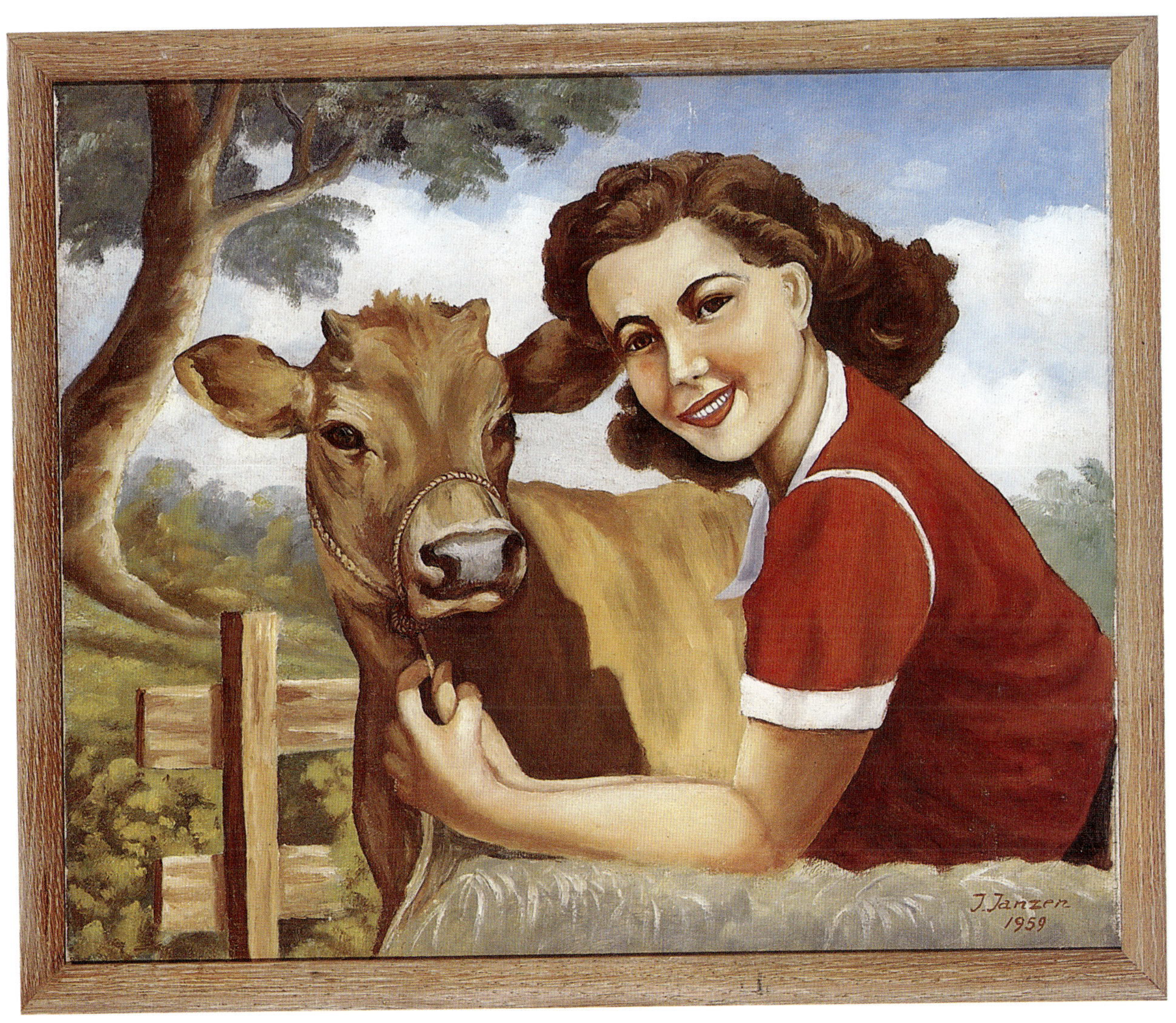

Girl with Calf

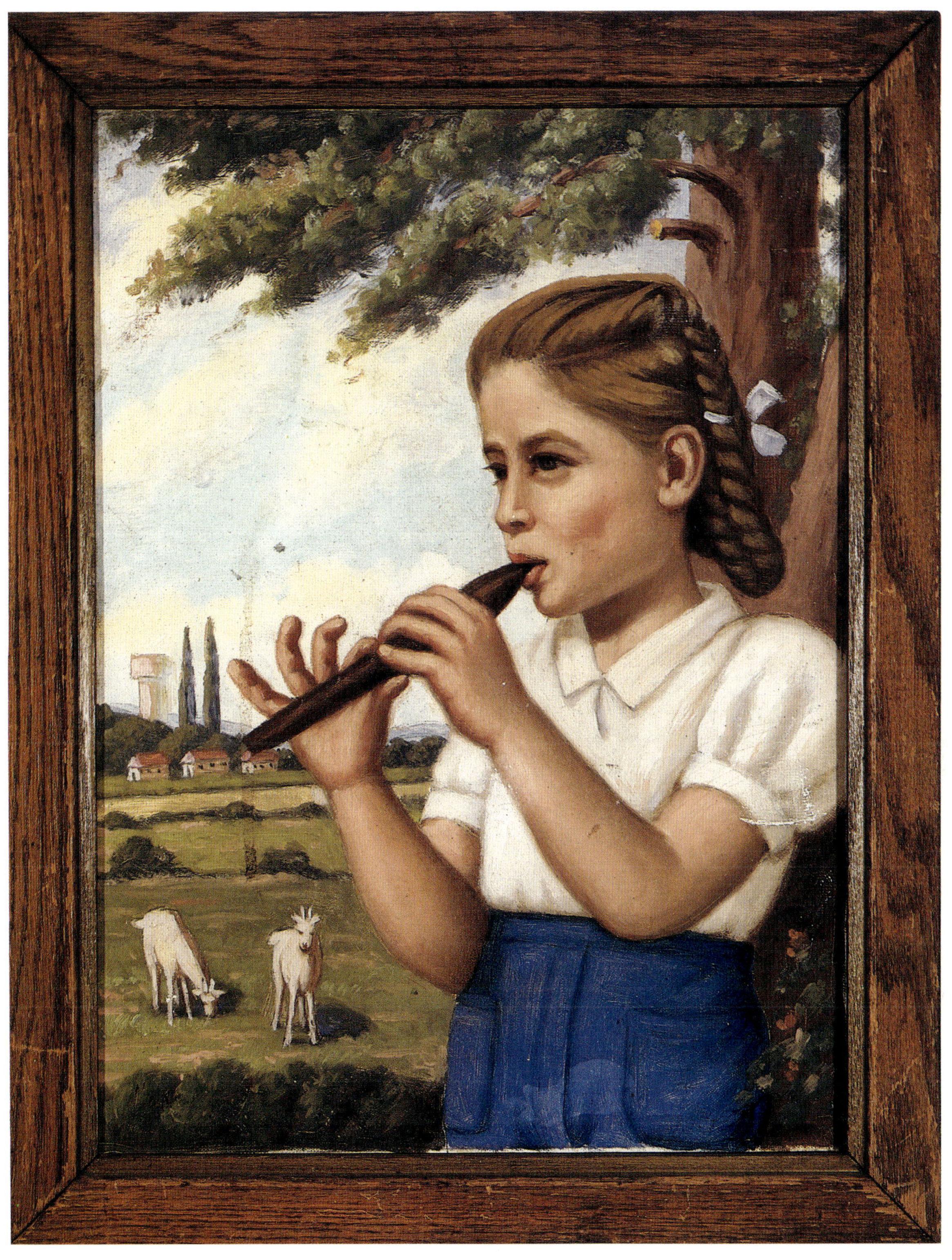

Girl with Cigar-like Flute and Goats

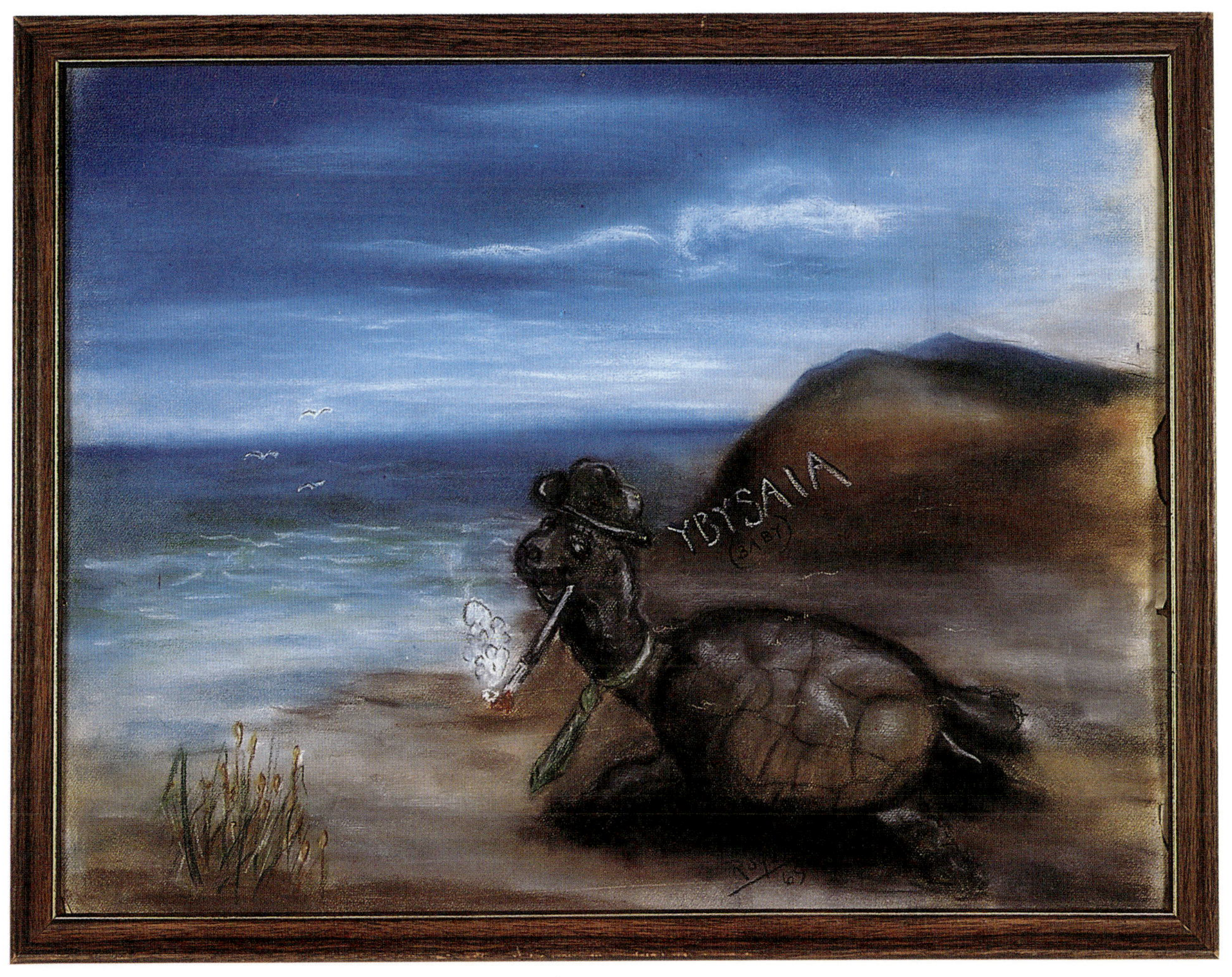

Turtle in Hat with Cigar, Saying "Ybysaia (Baby)"

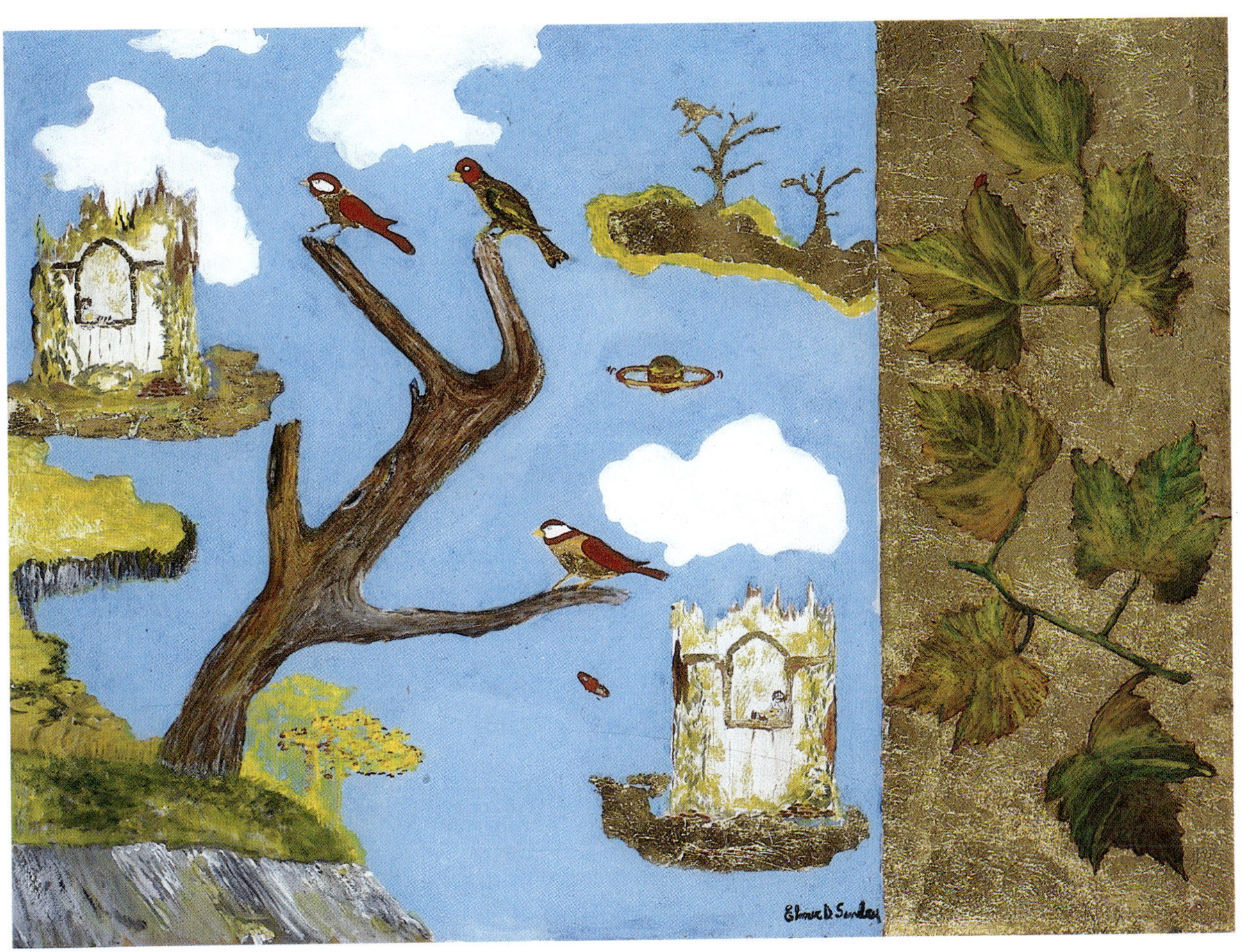

Leaves, Birds, Sky, Gold Leaf, Jupiter, etc.

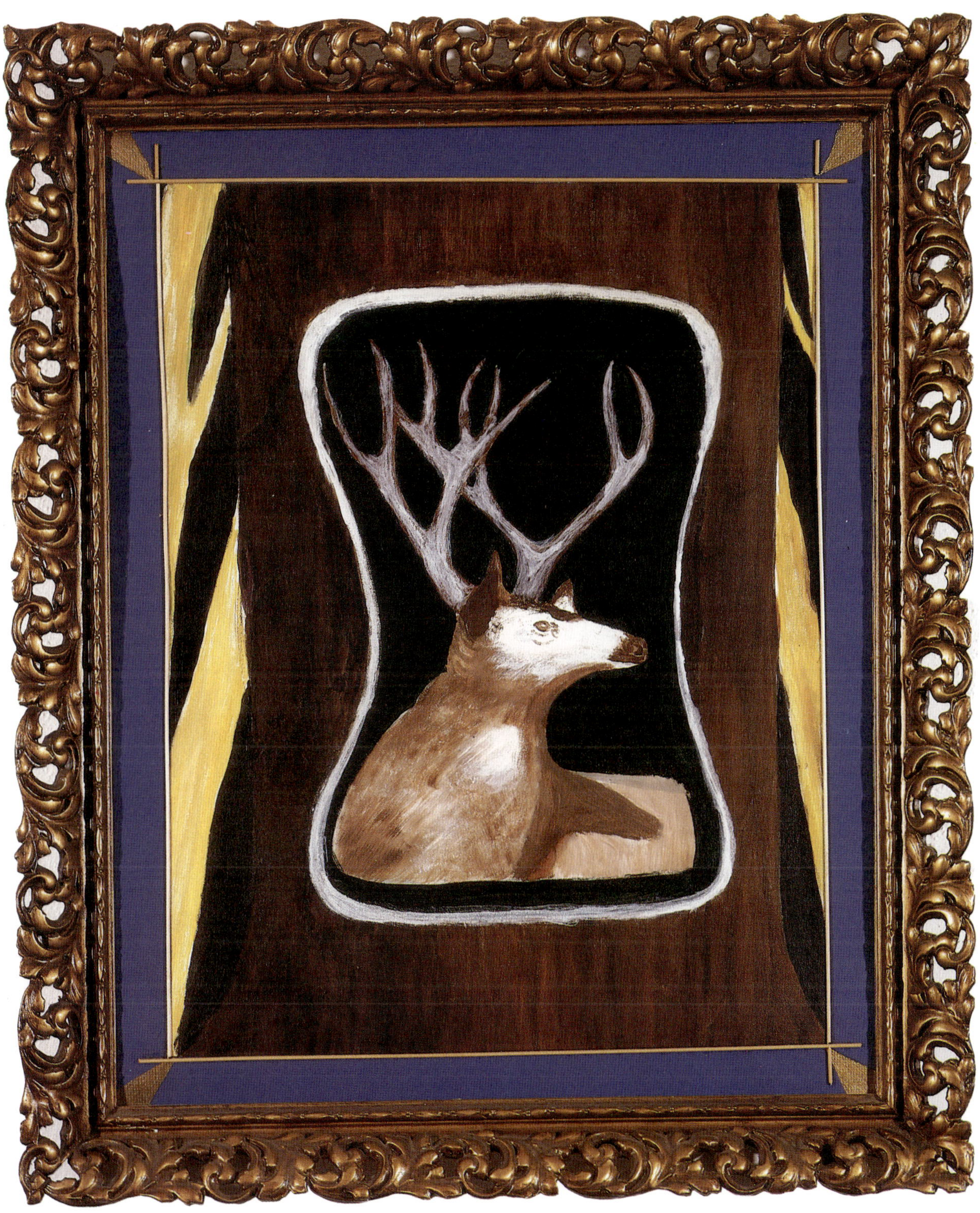

Elk's Head in Multiple Frames

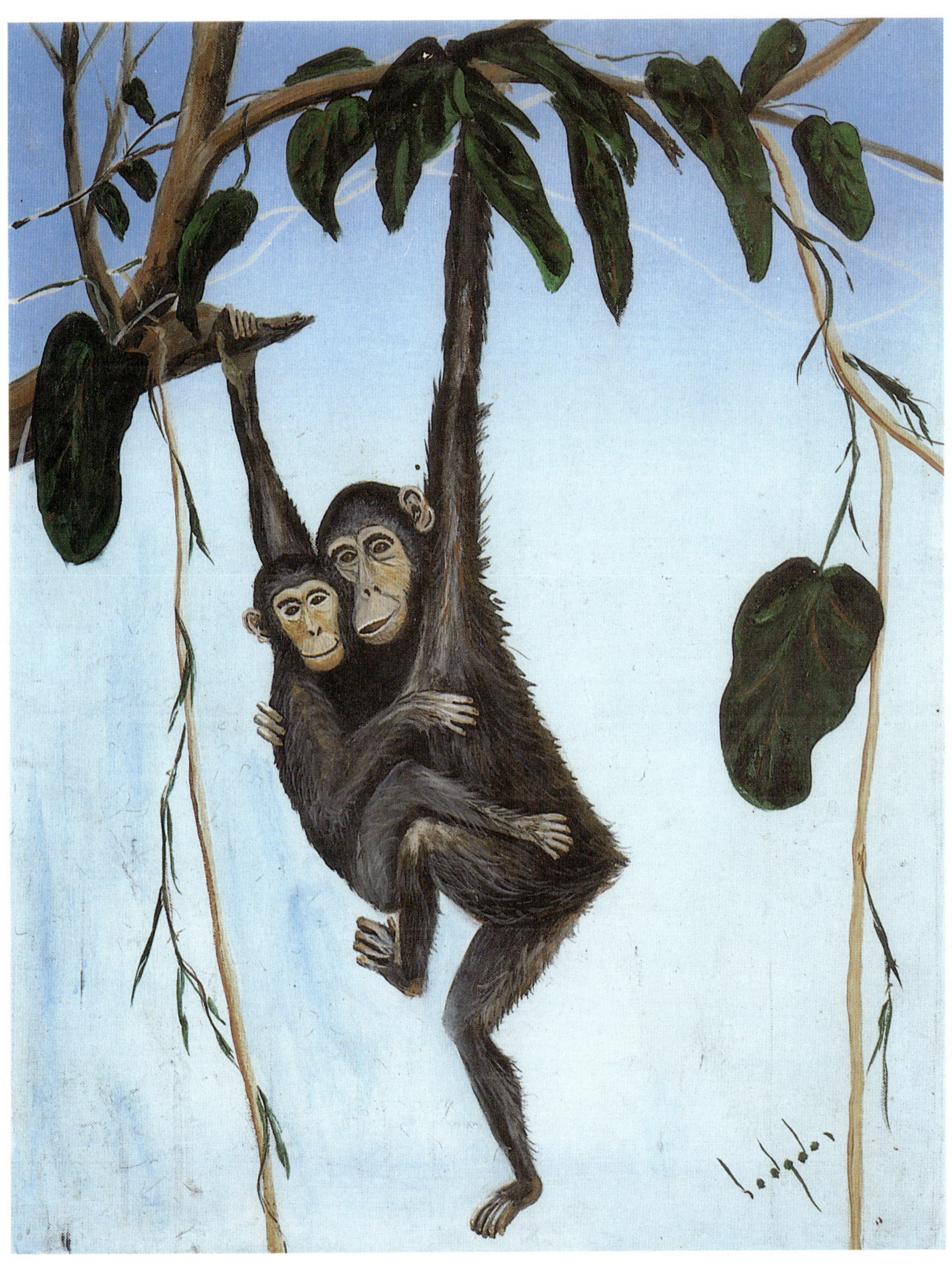

Two Monkeys Hang from Tree

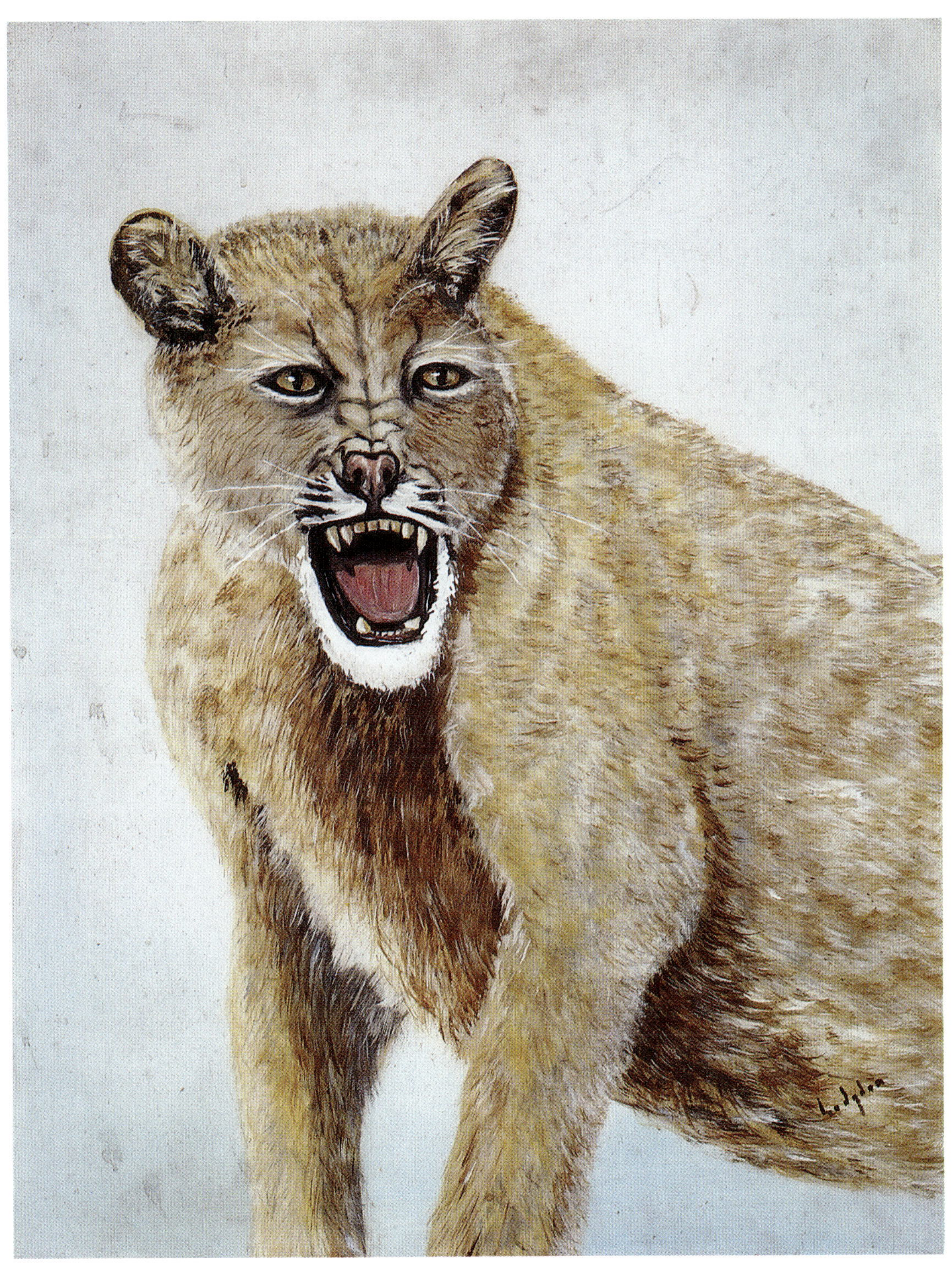

Snarling Mountain Lion

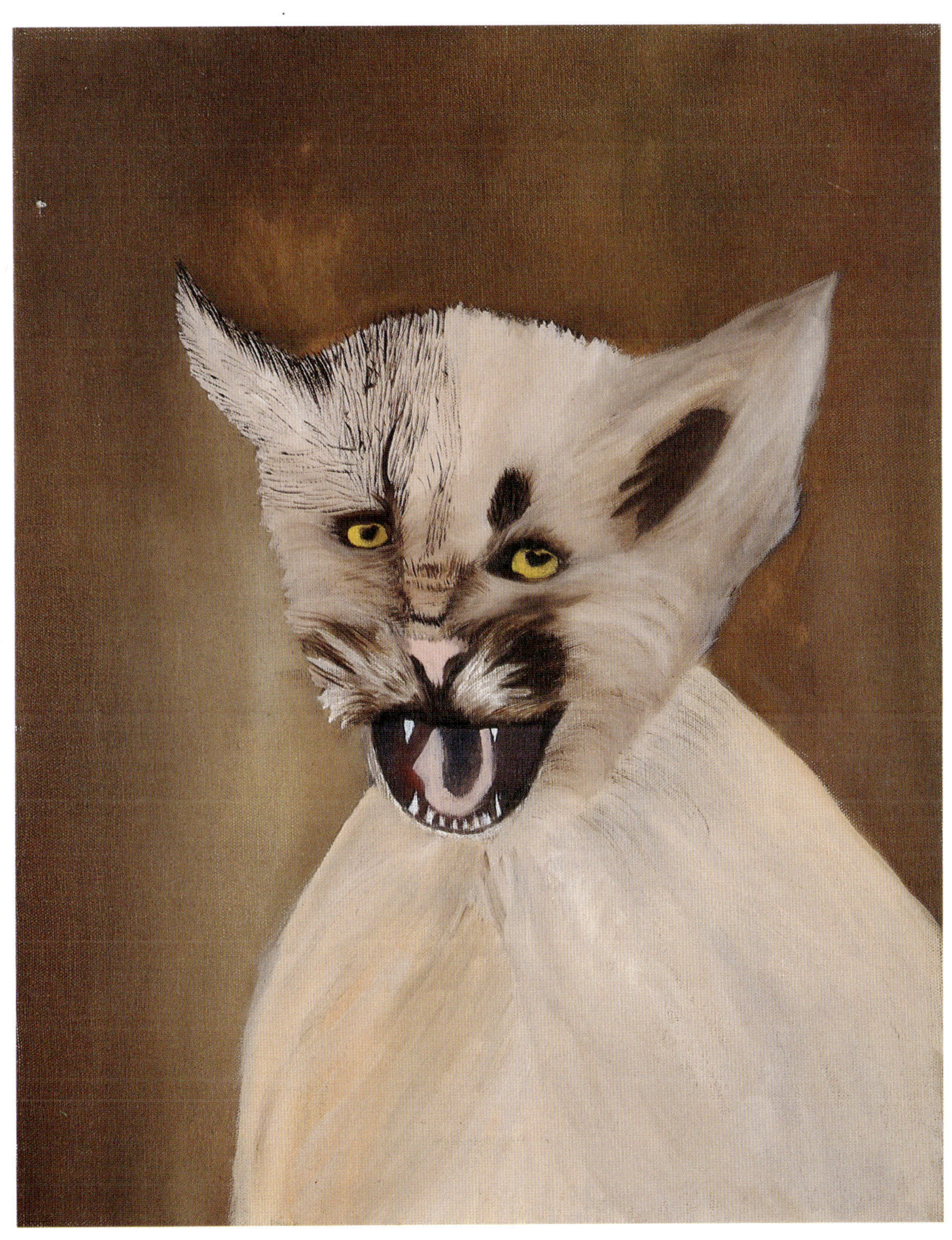

Pink Mountain Lion on Brown Background

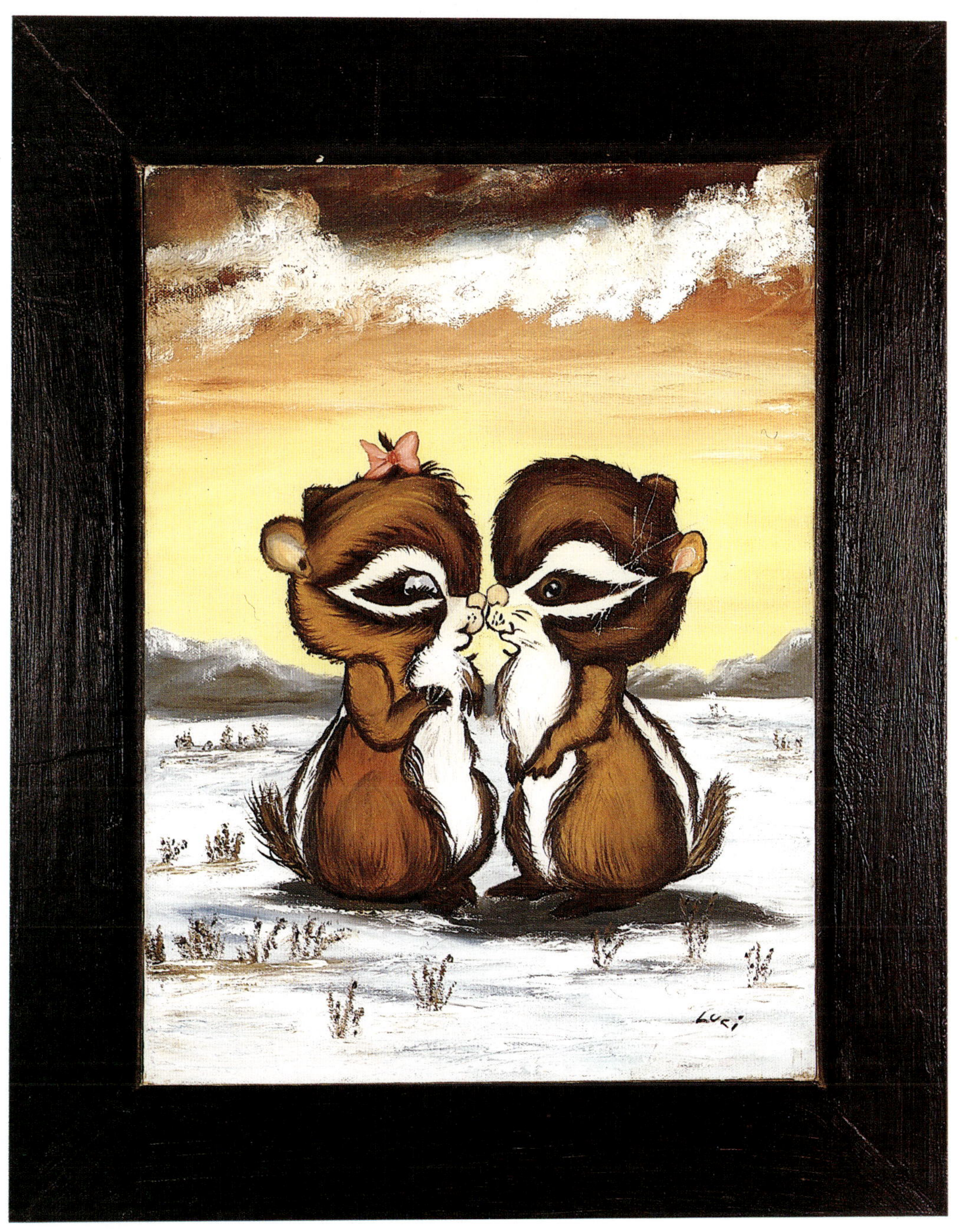

Two Chipmunks

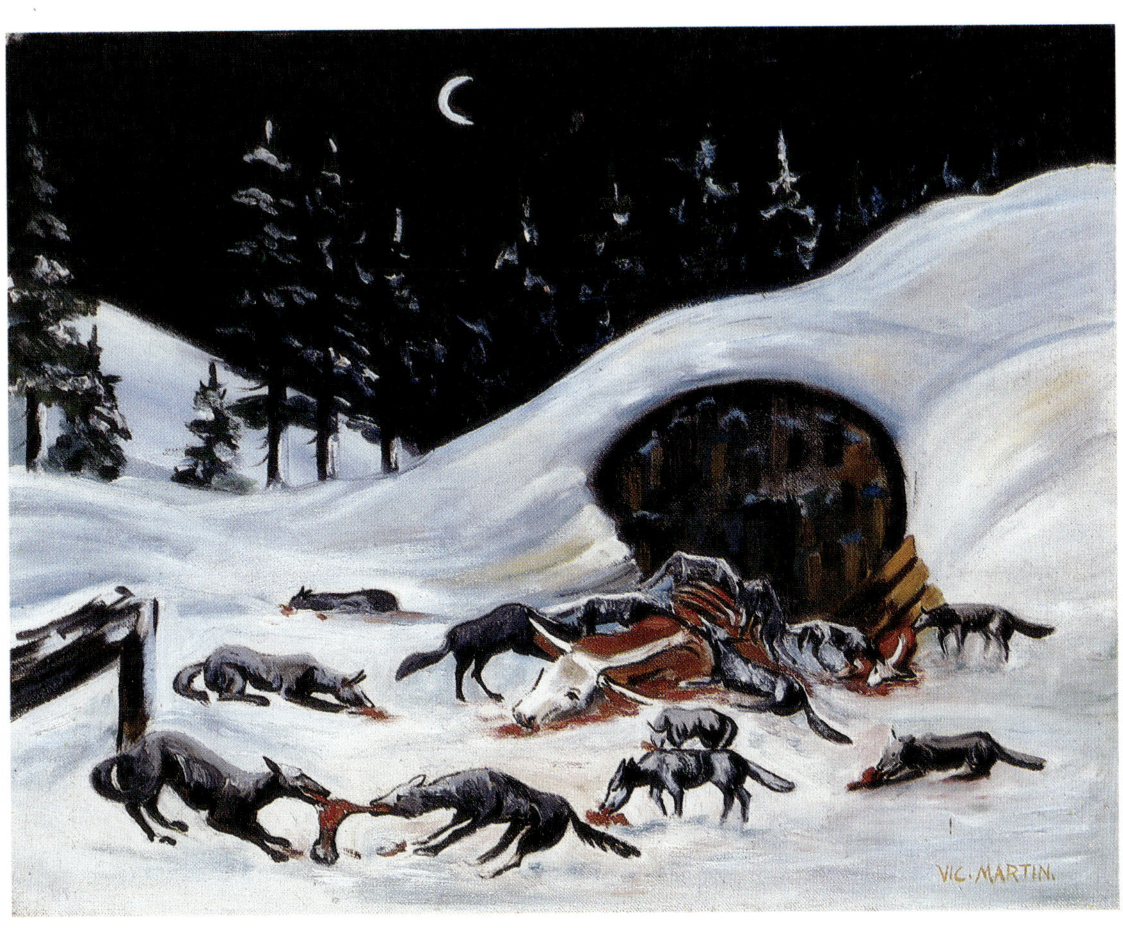

Wolves Attacking Steer Carcass on Snowy Night

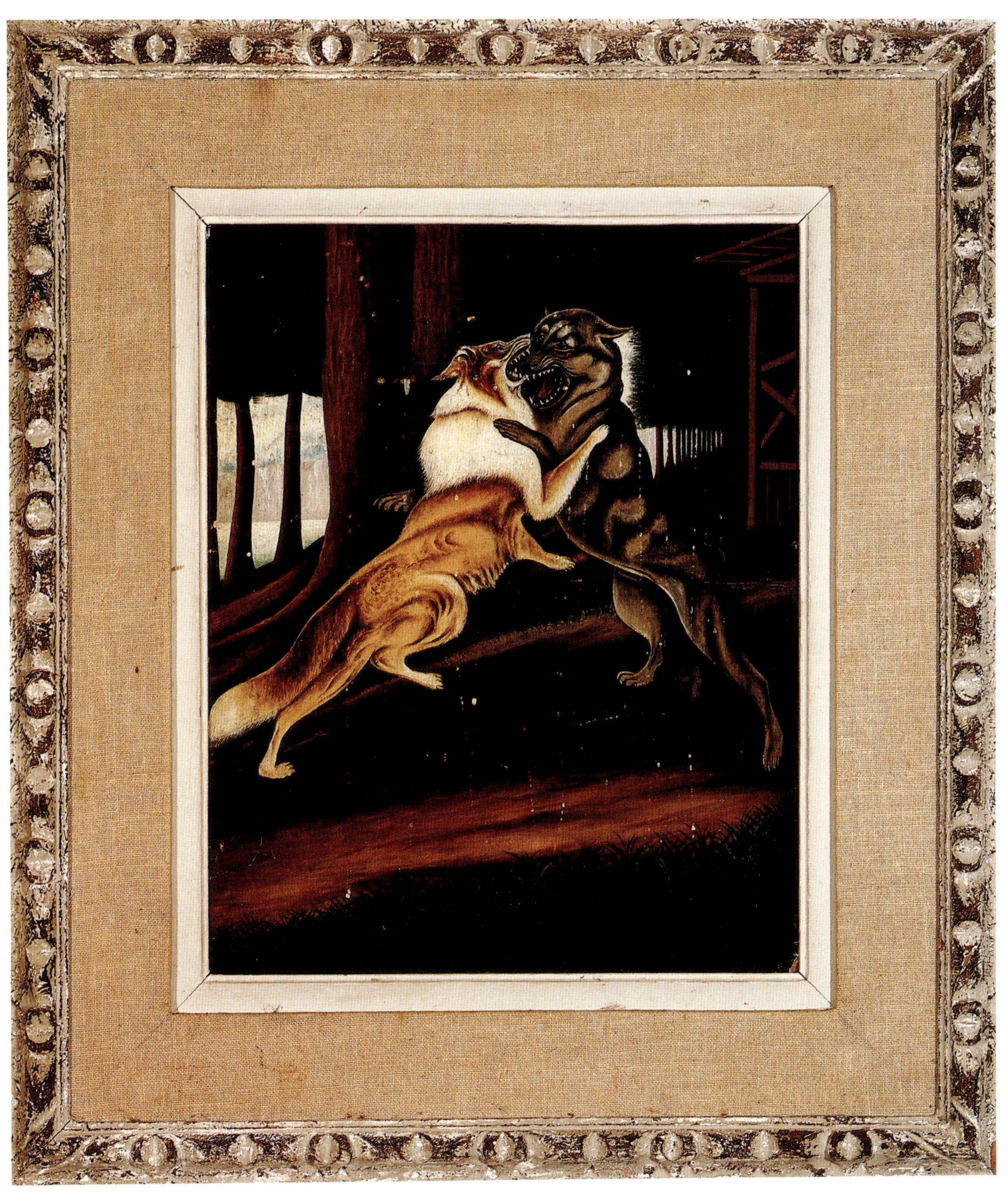

Two Dogs Fighting in Forest

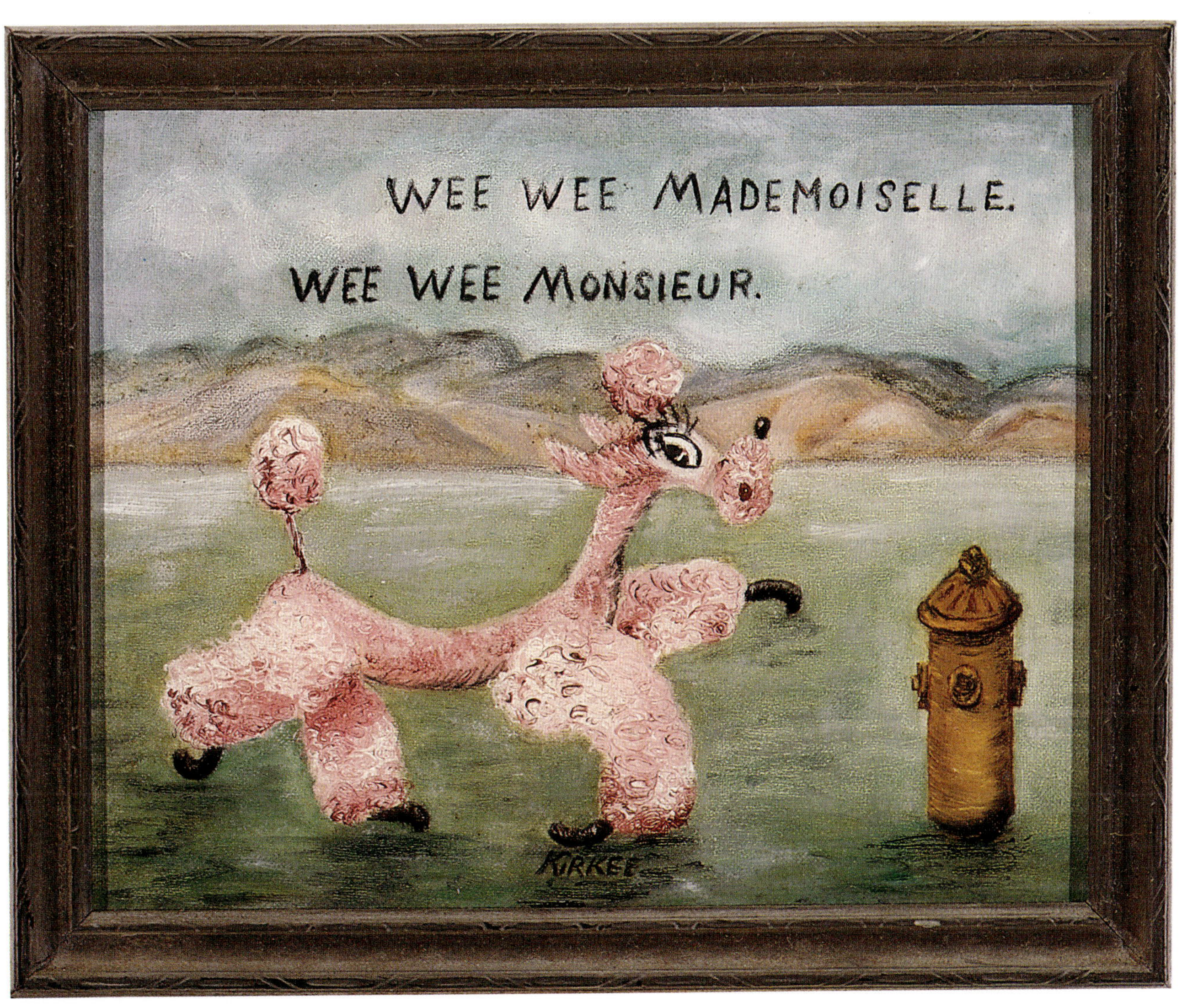

Pink Poodle and Hydrant with Text

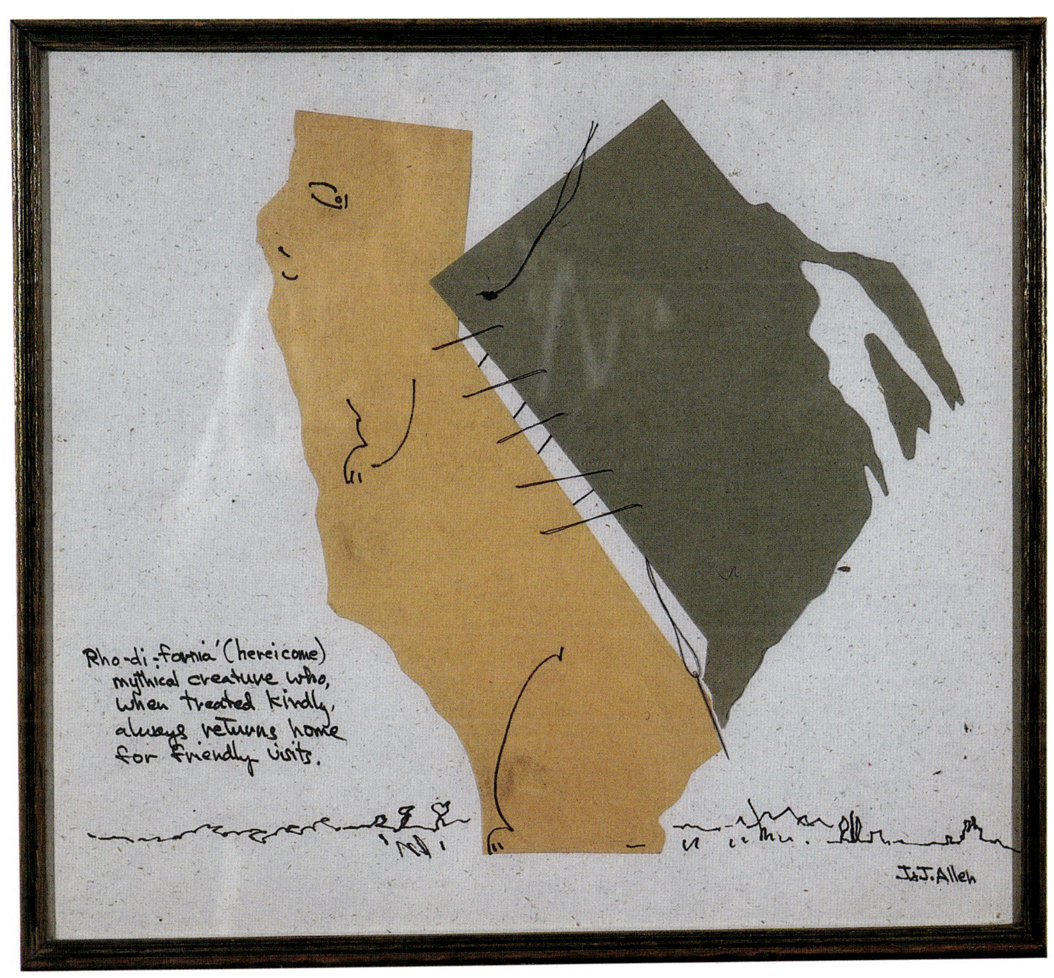

Strange Interstate Bondage Image

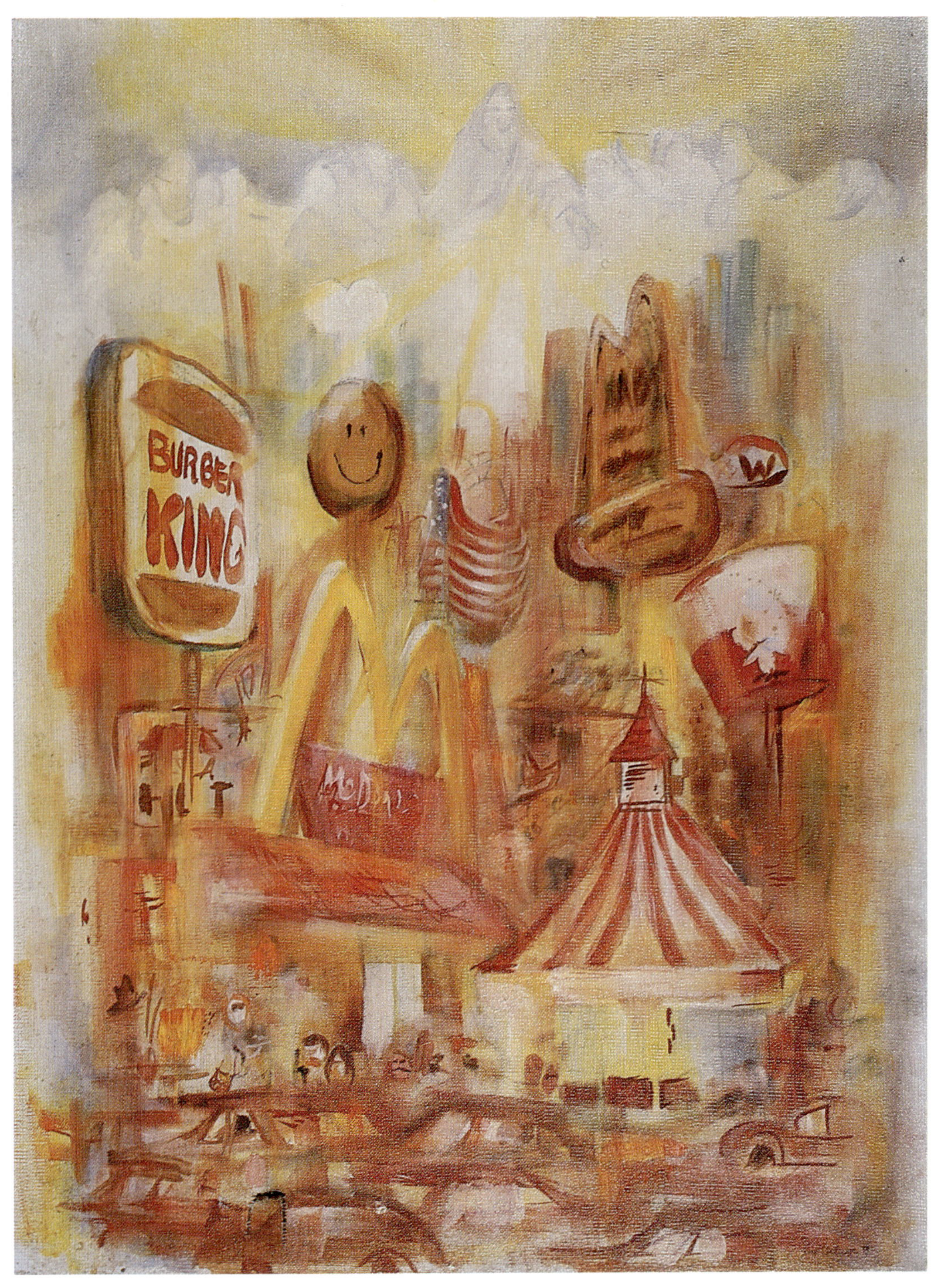

Fast Food Last Supper

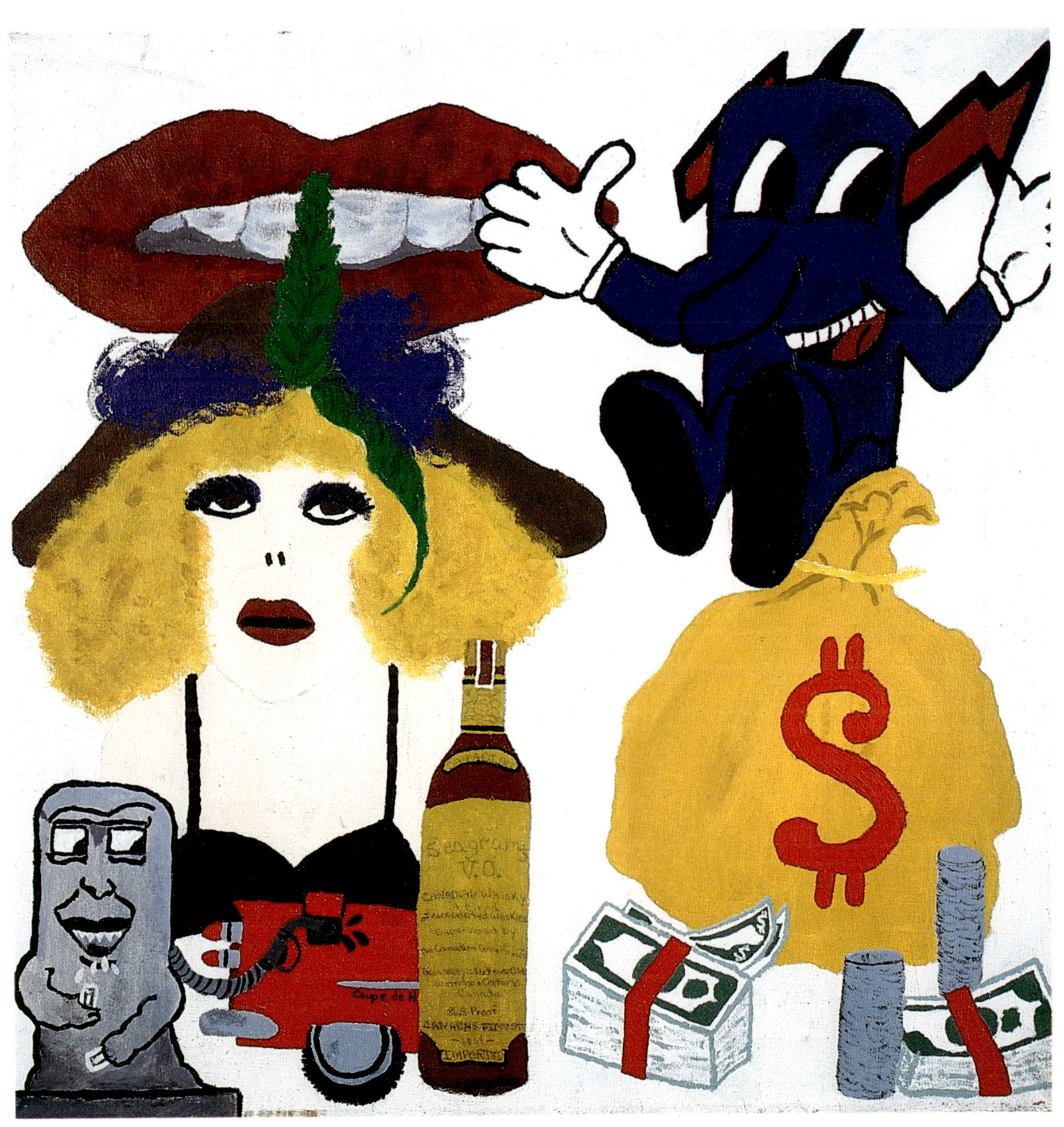

Pop Art with Gas Pump, Whiskey, Money, Mouth, Woman

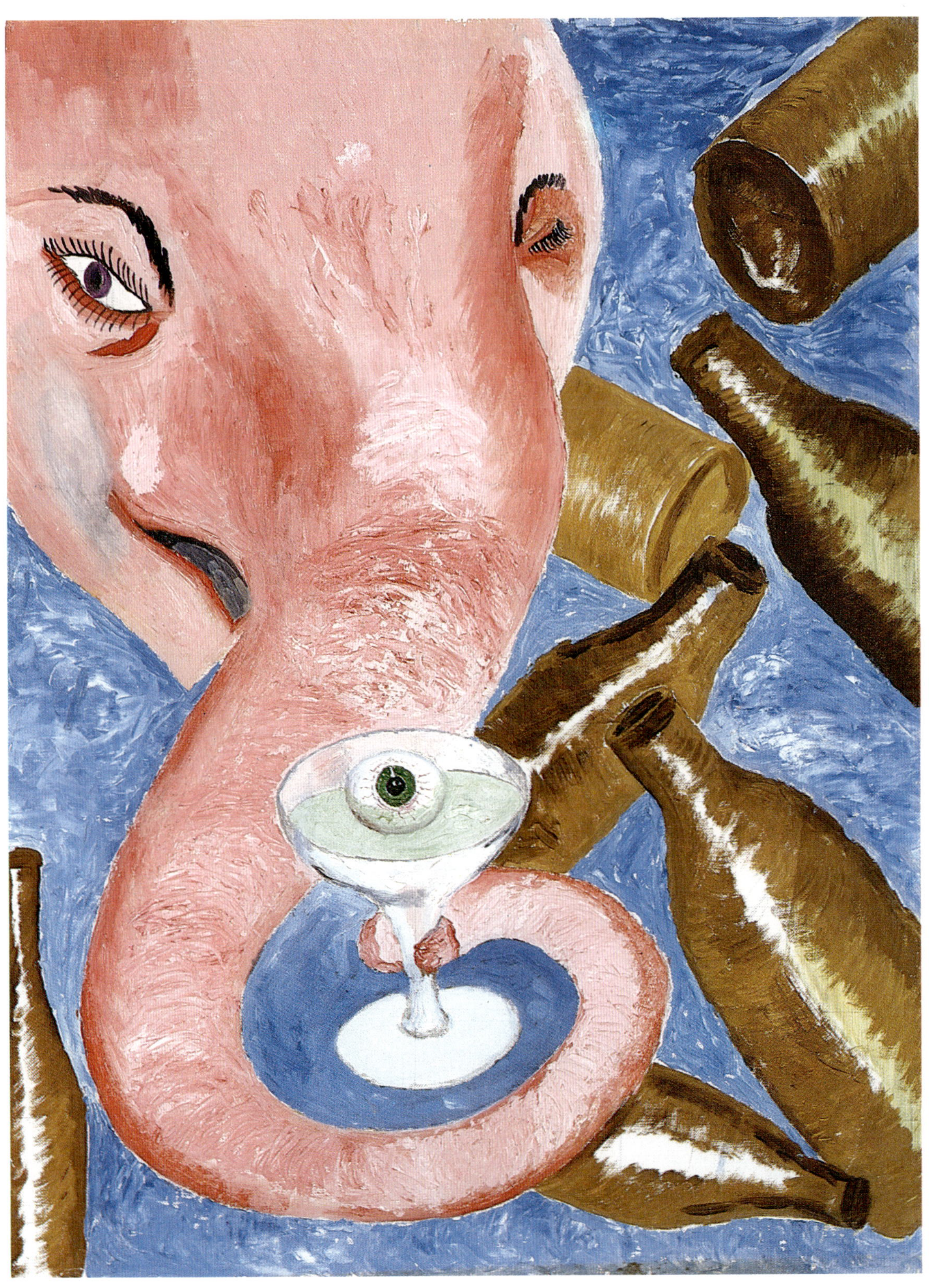

Pink Elephant with Bottles and Eye in Cocktail Glass

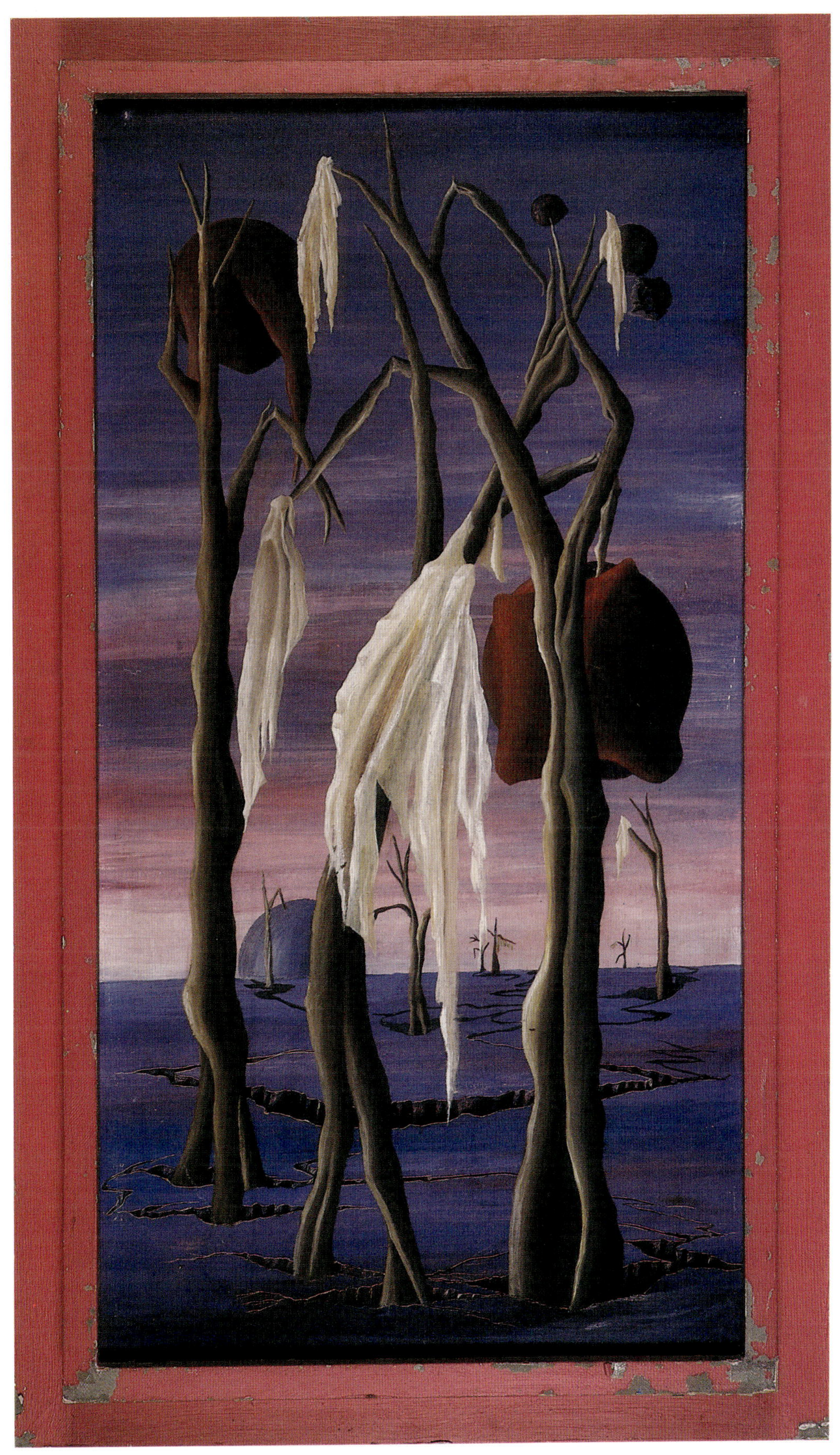

Purple Surrealist Landscape with Pink Frame

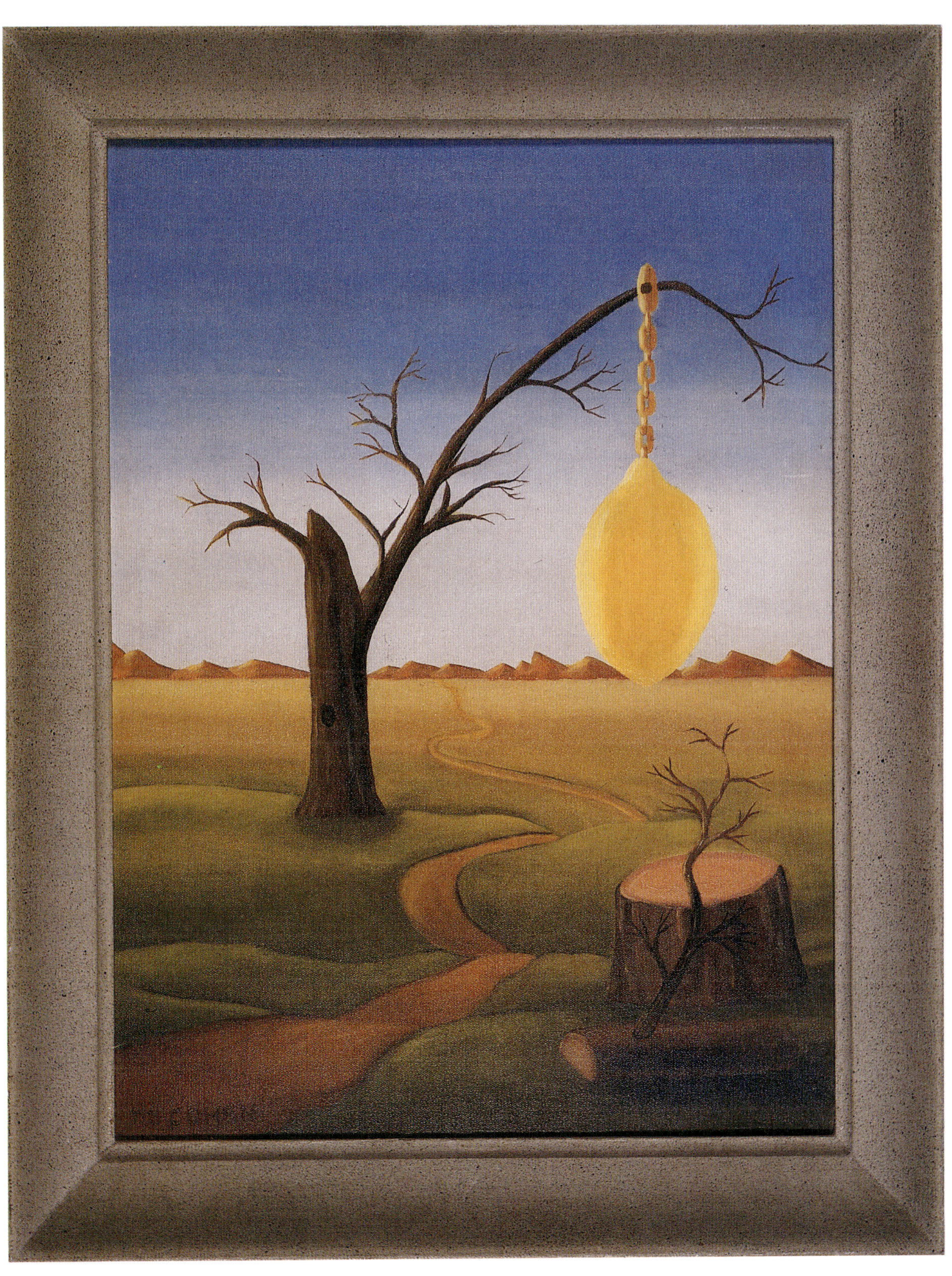

Dead Tree with Giant Lemon on Chain

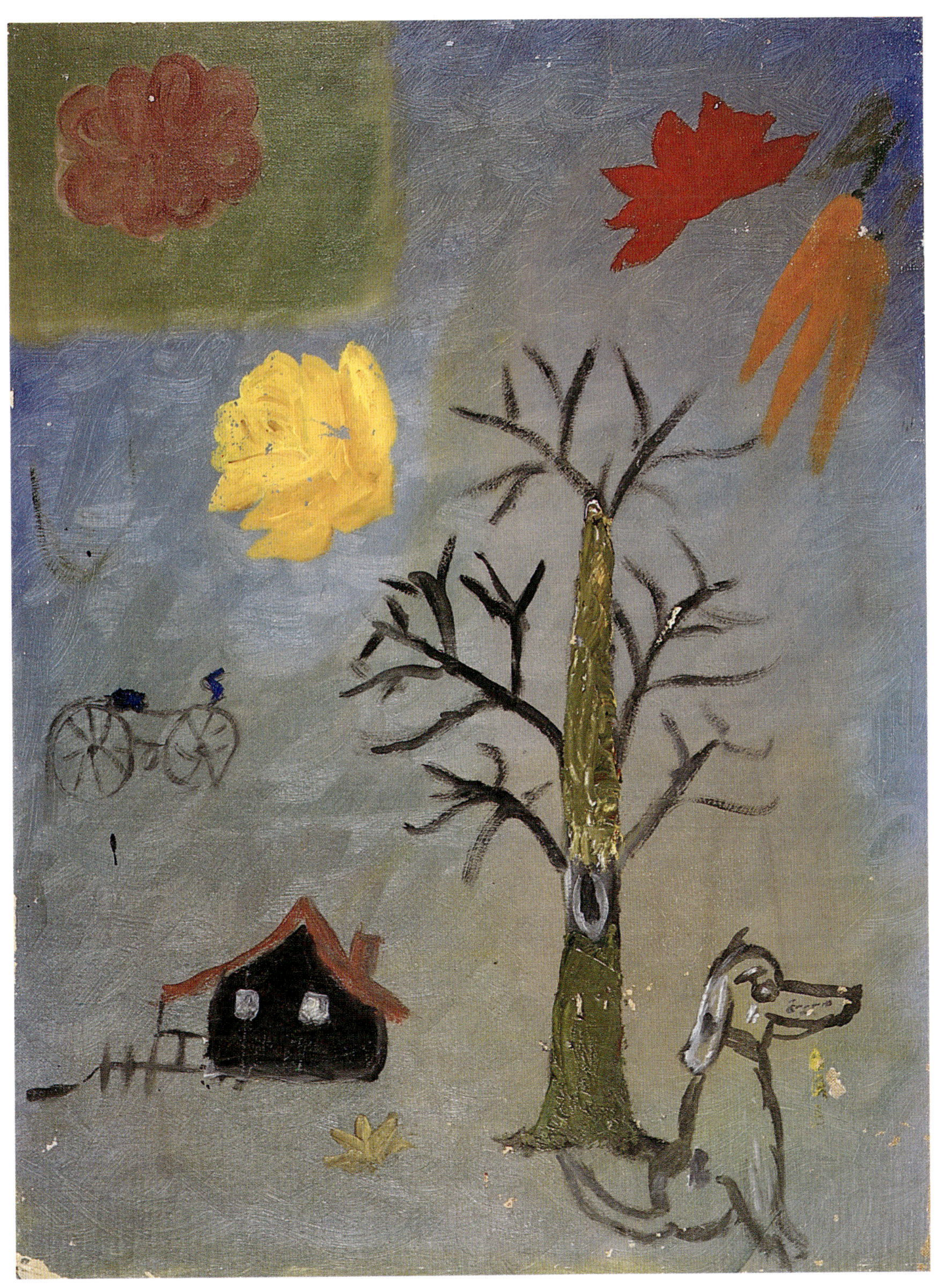

Blue Field with Dog, Tree, House, Flowers, Carrots, Bike

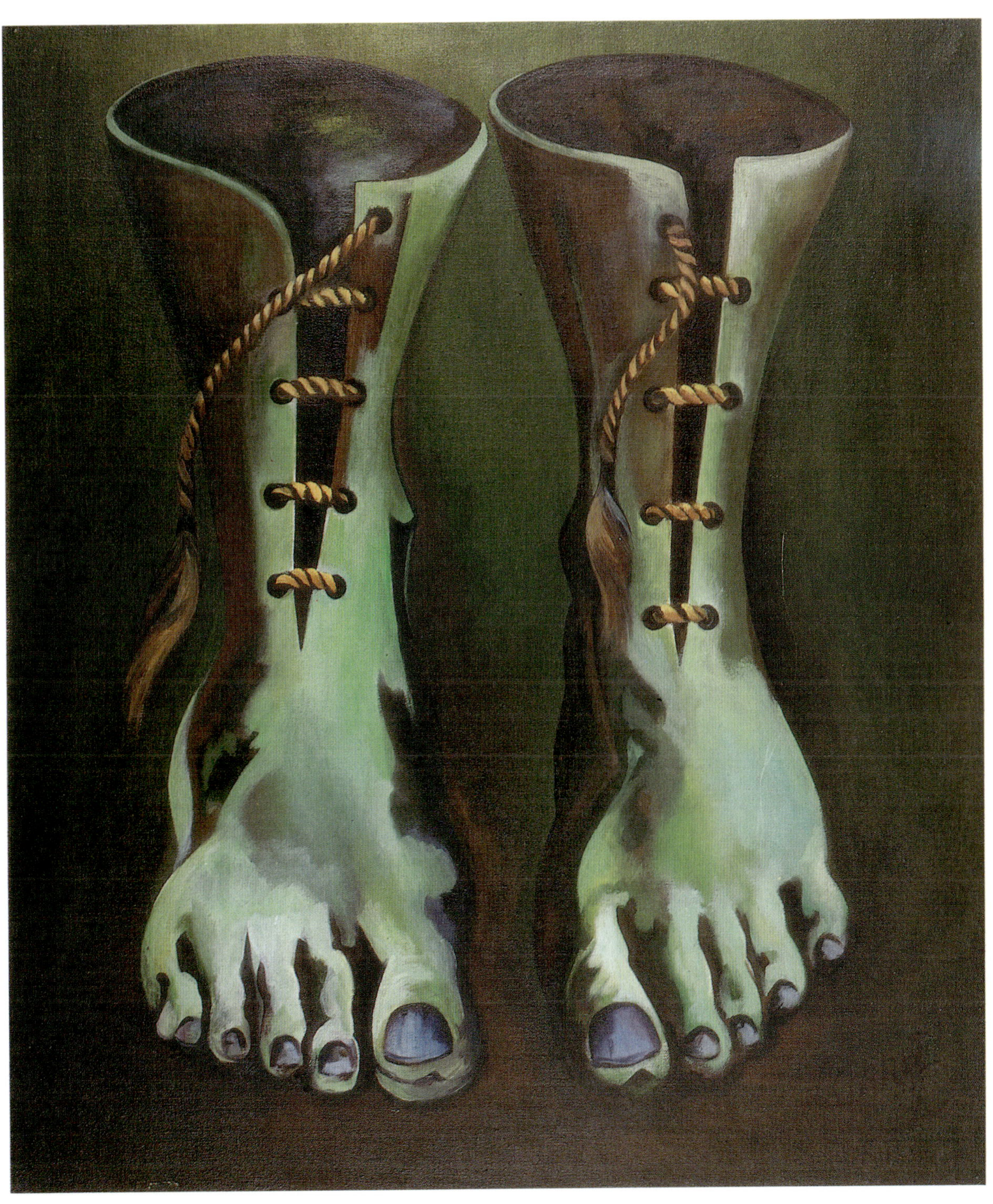

Frankenstein-Magritte Boots

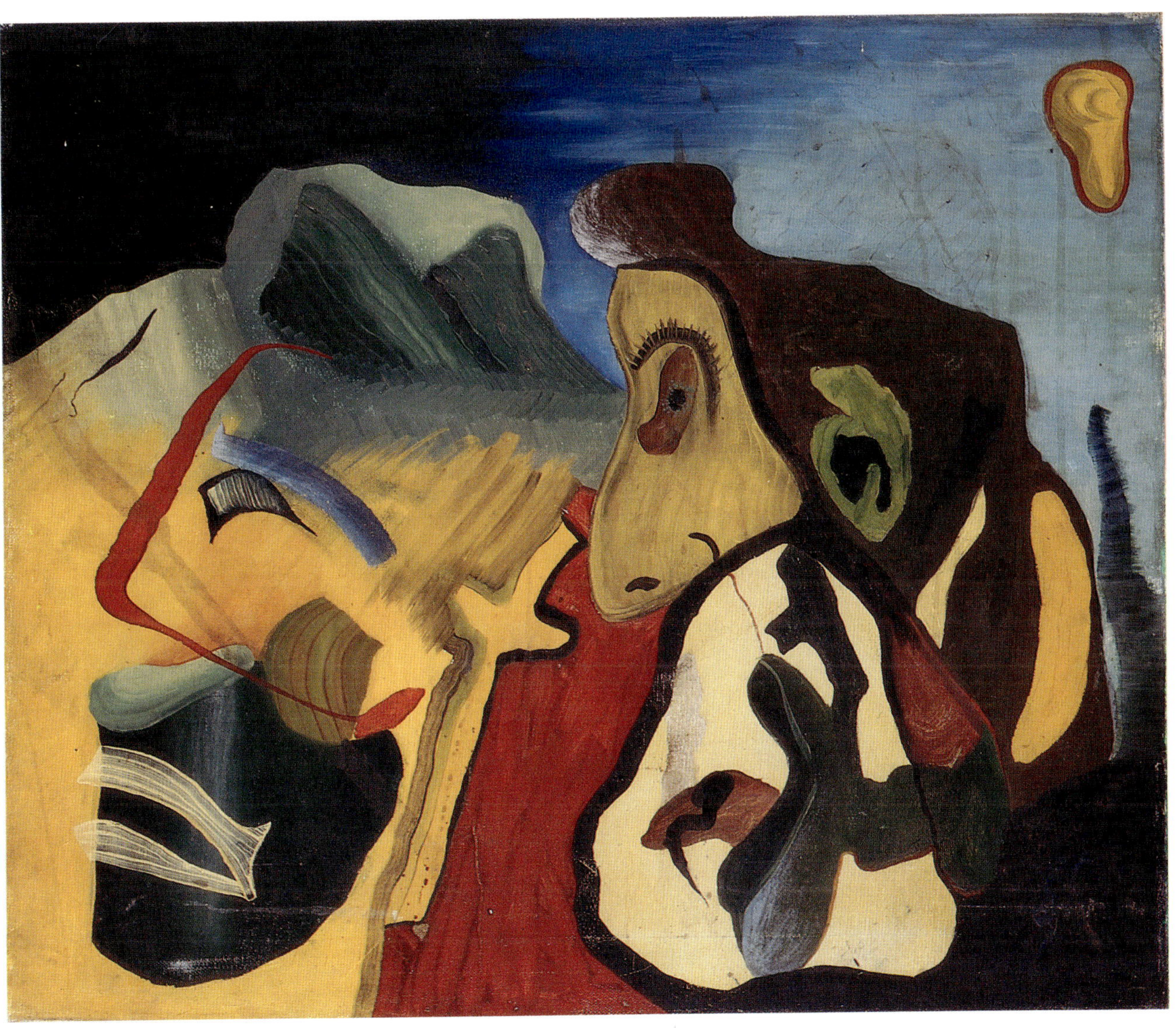

Two Surreal Heads in Landscape

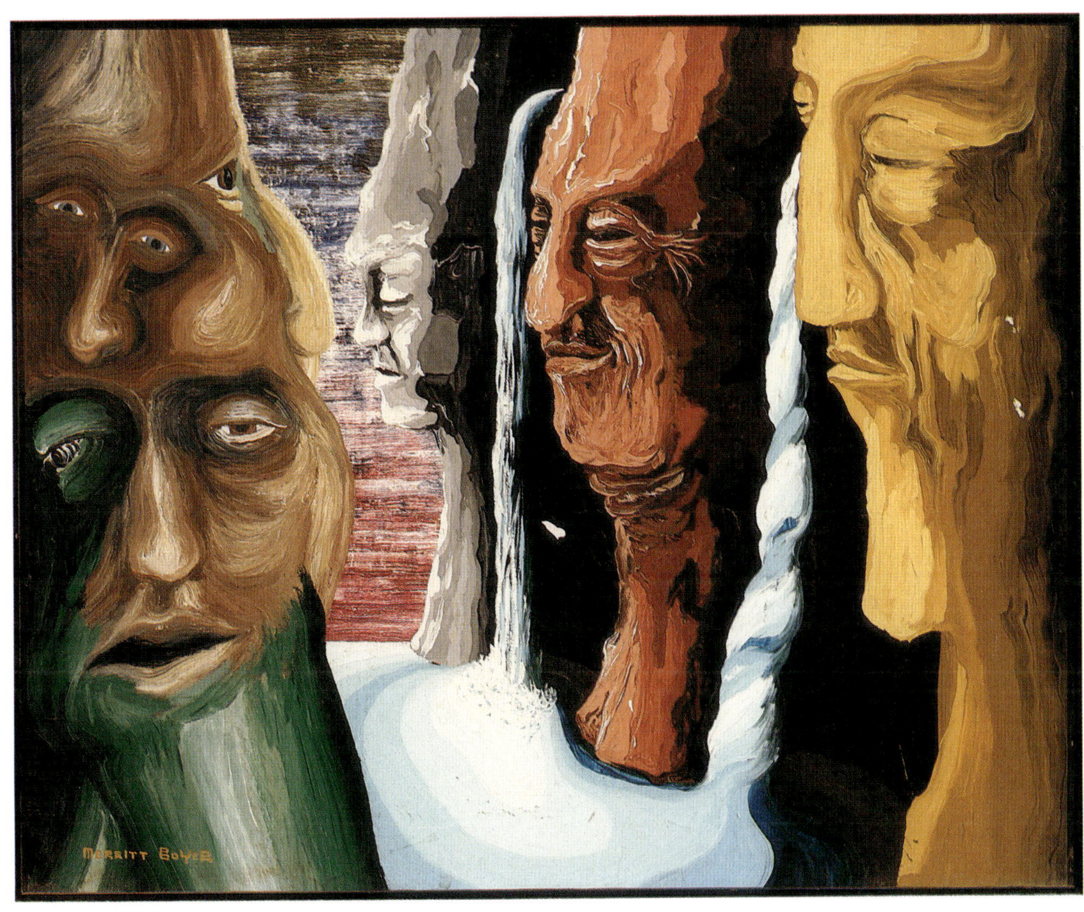

Many Faces Converge into Landscape

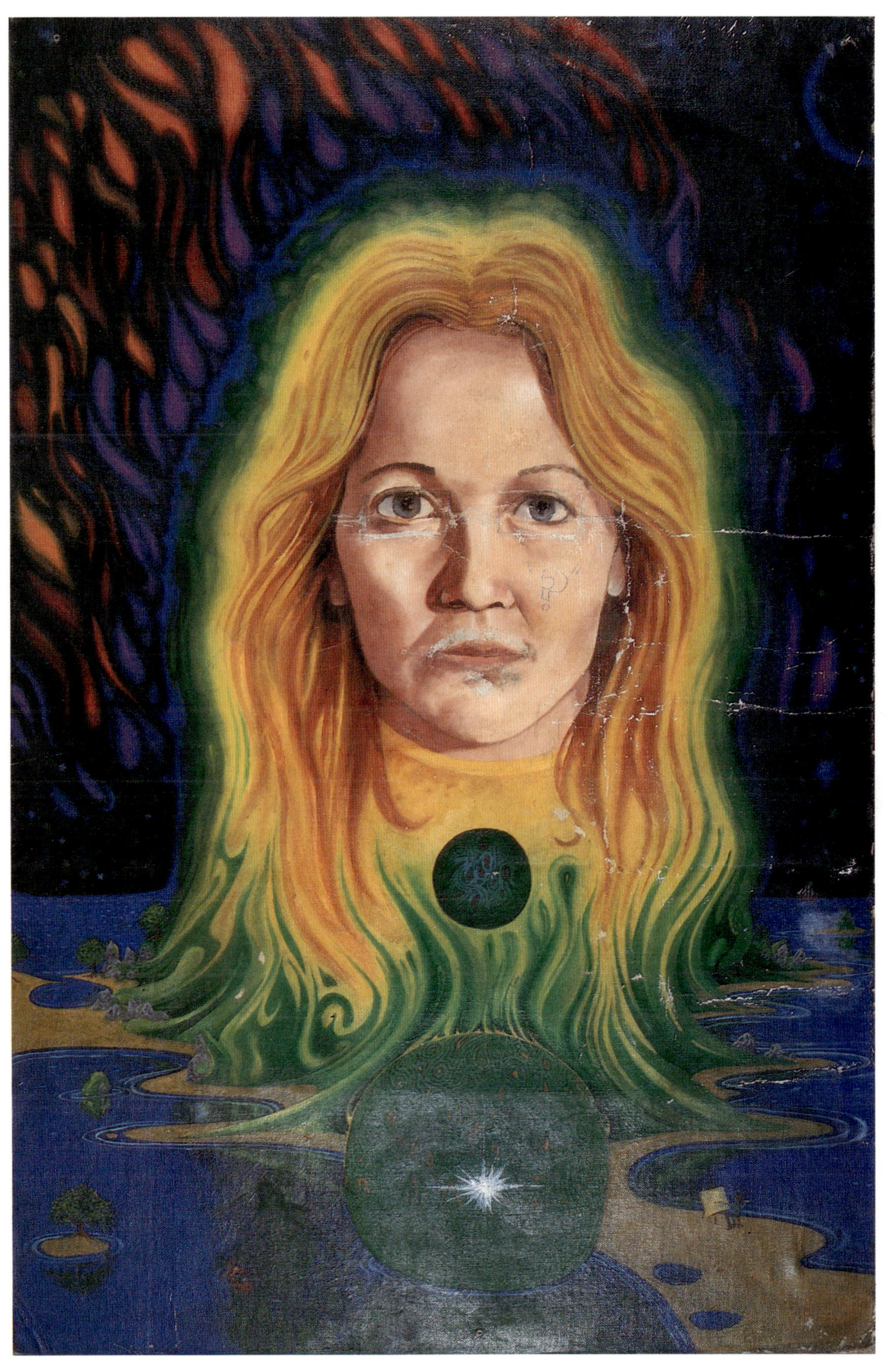

Cosmic Blonde Girl with Liquid Universe and Ball Point Defacing

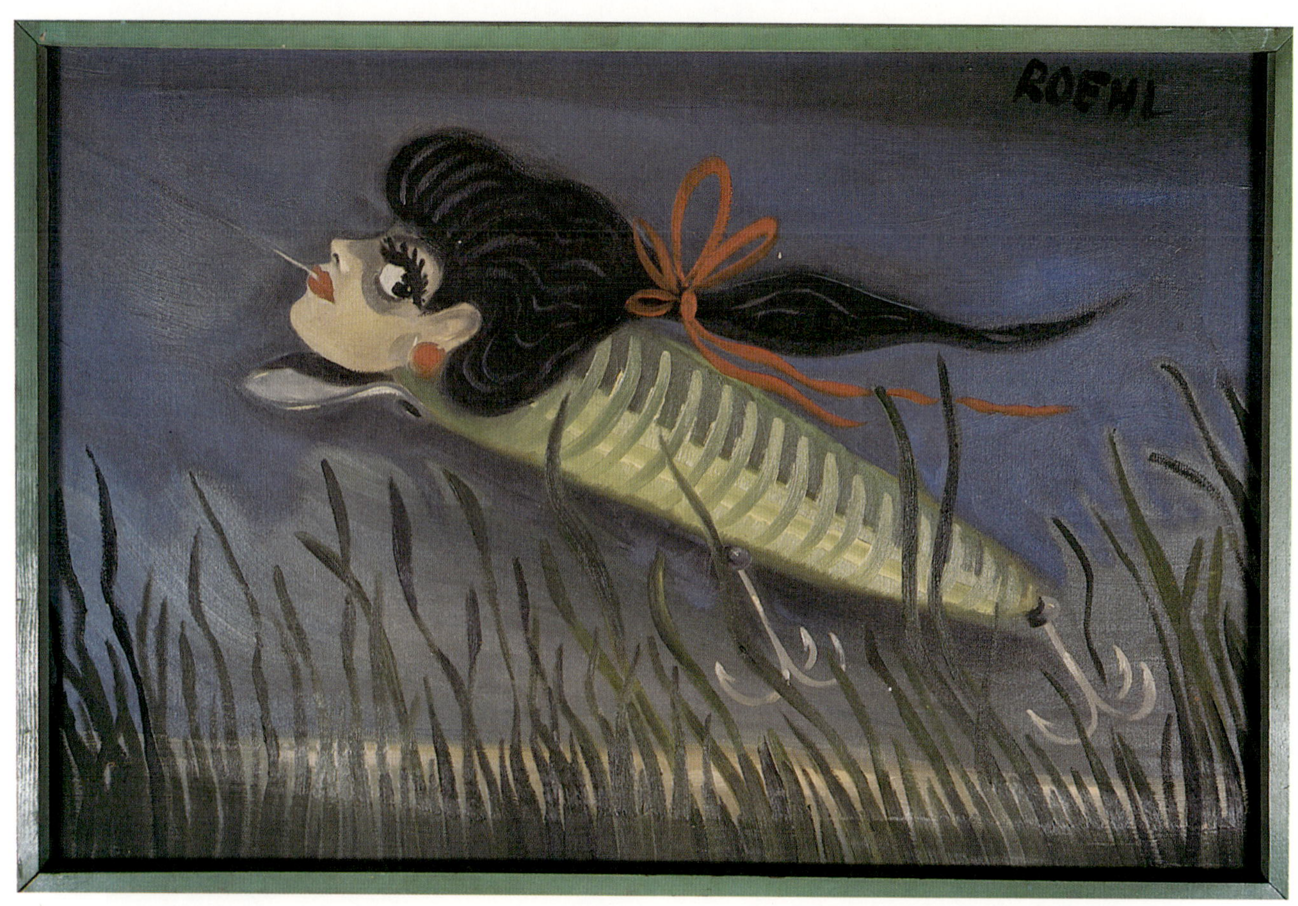

Fishing Lure with Woman's Head

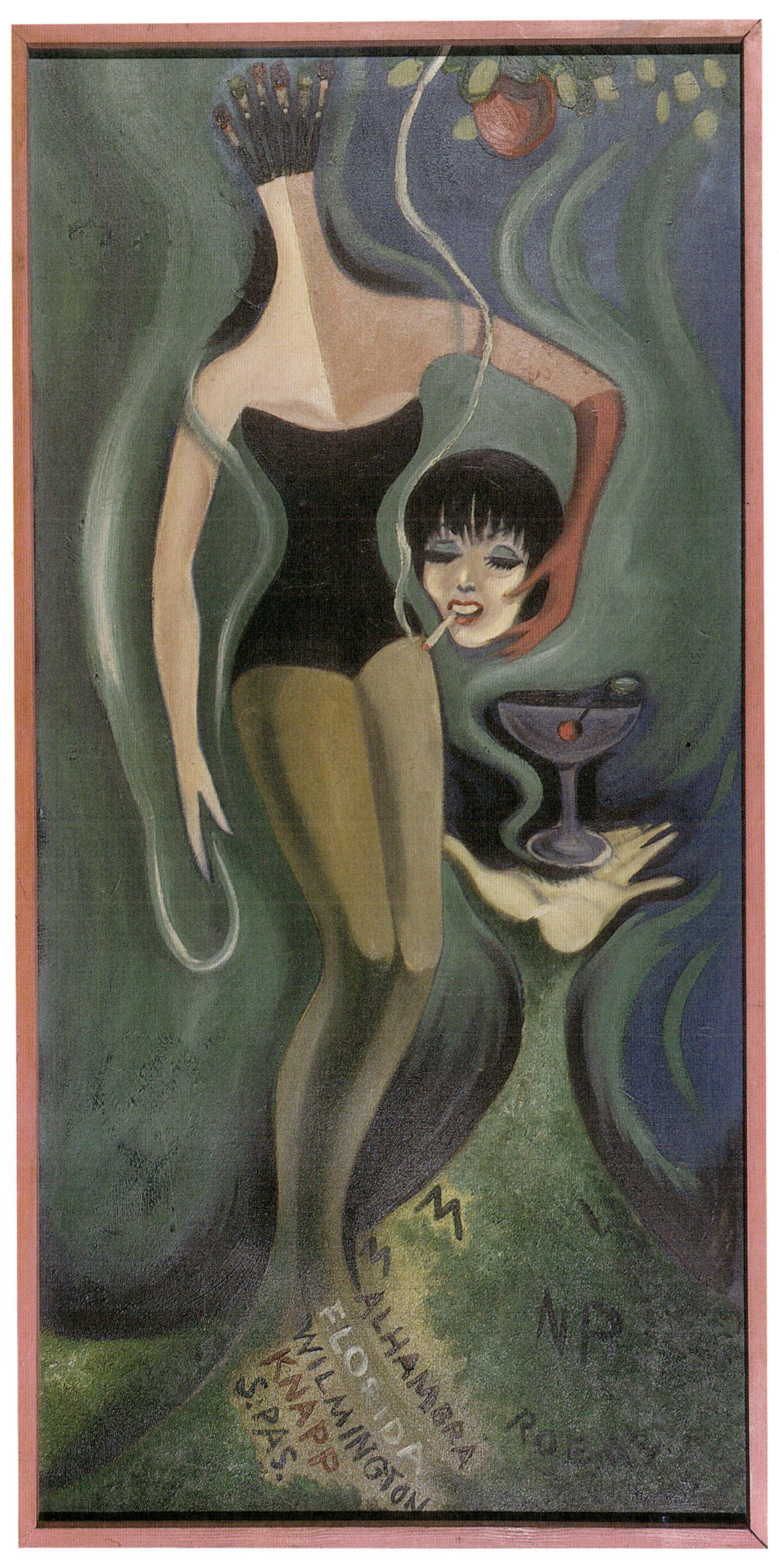

Headless Beat Girl with Text and Paint Brushes in Neck

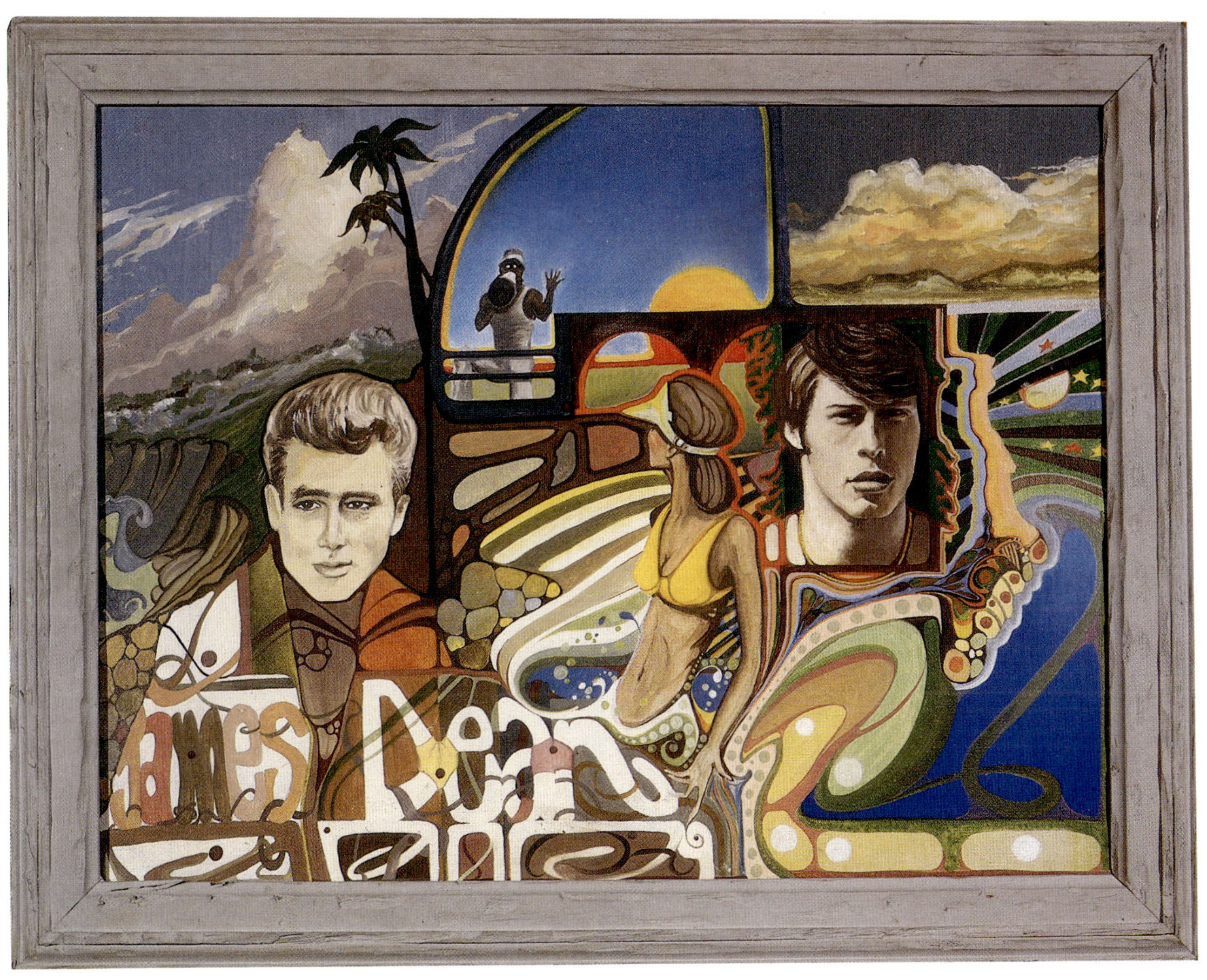

Psychedelic James Dean Portrait

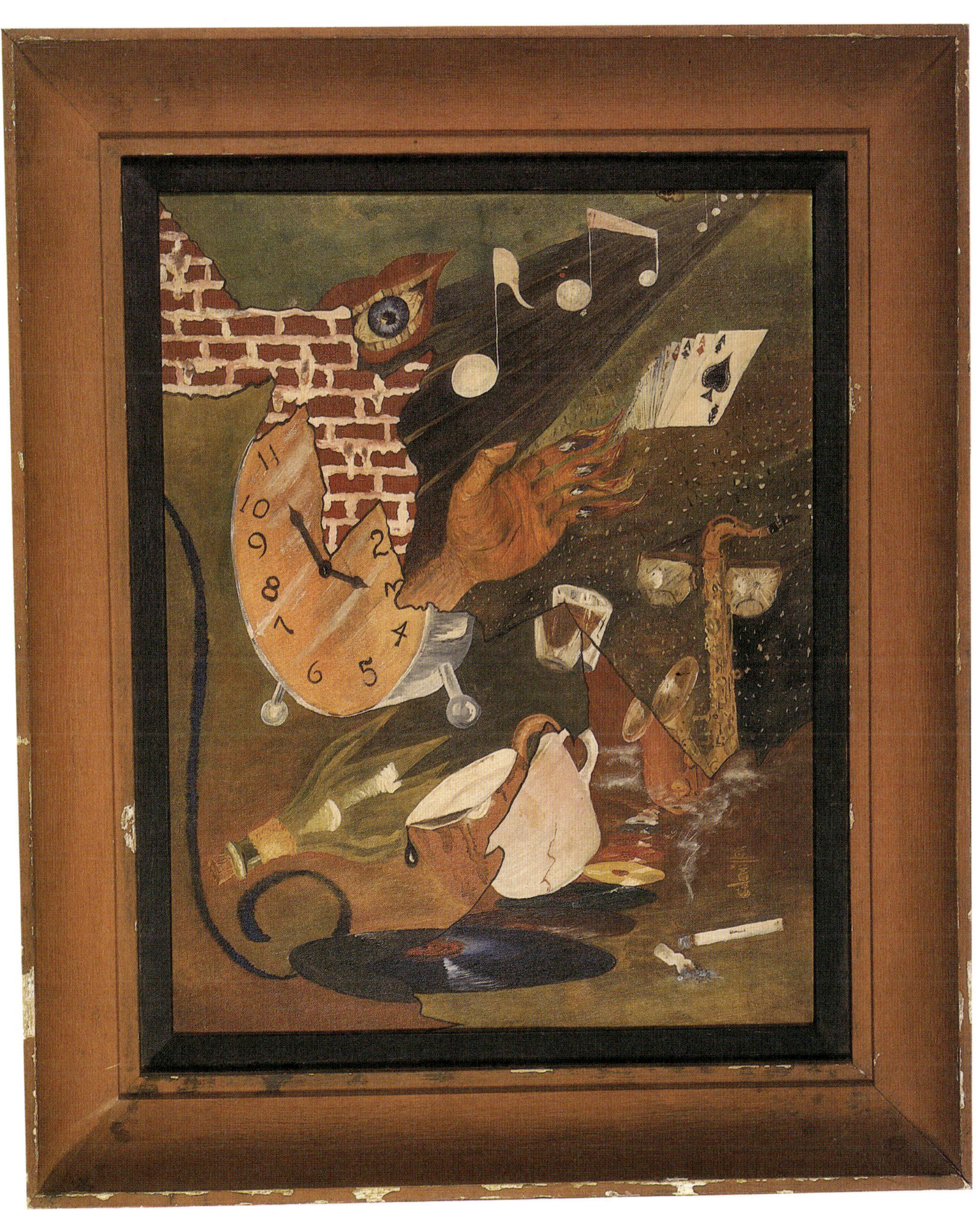

Cubist/Surrealist Piece with Saxophone, Clock, Mouth and Eye

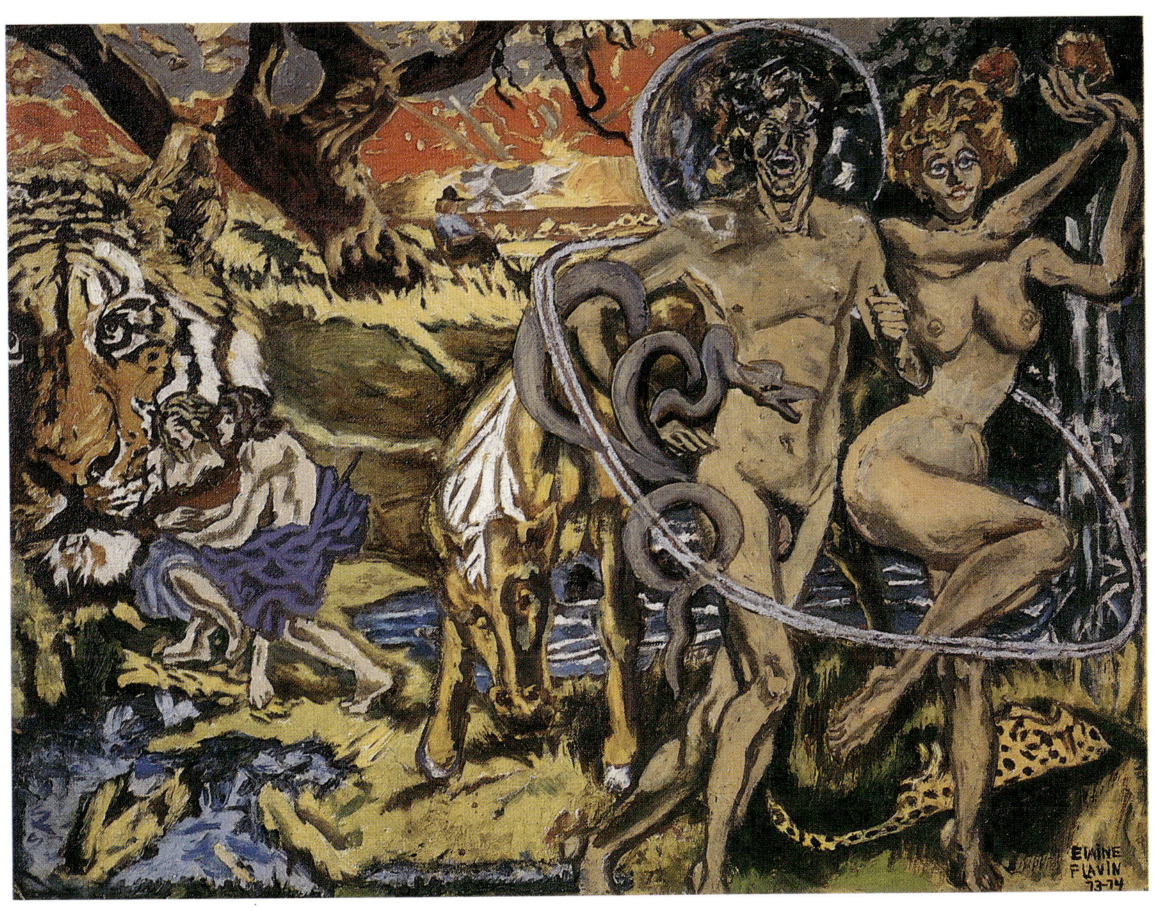

Weird Adam and Eve with Animals and Figures

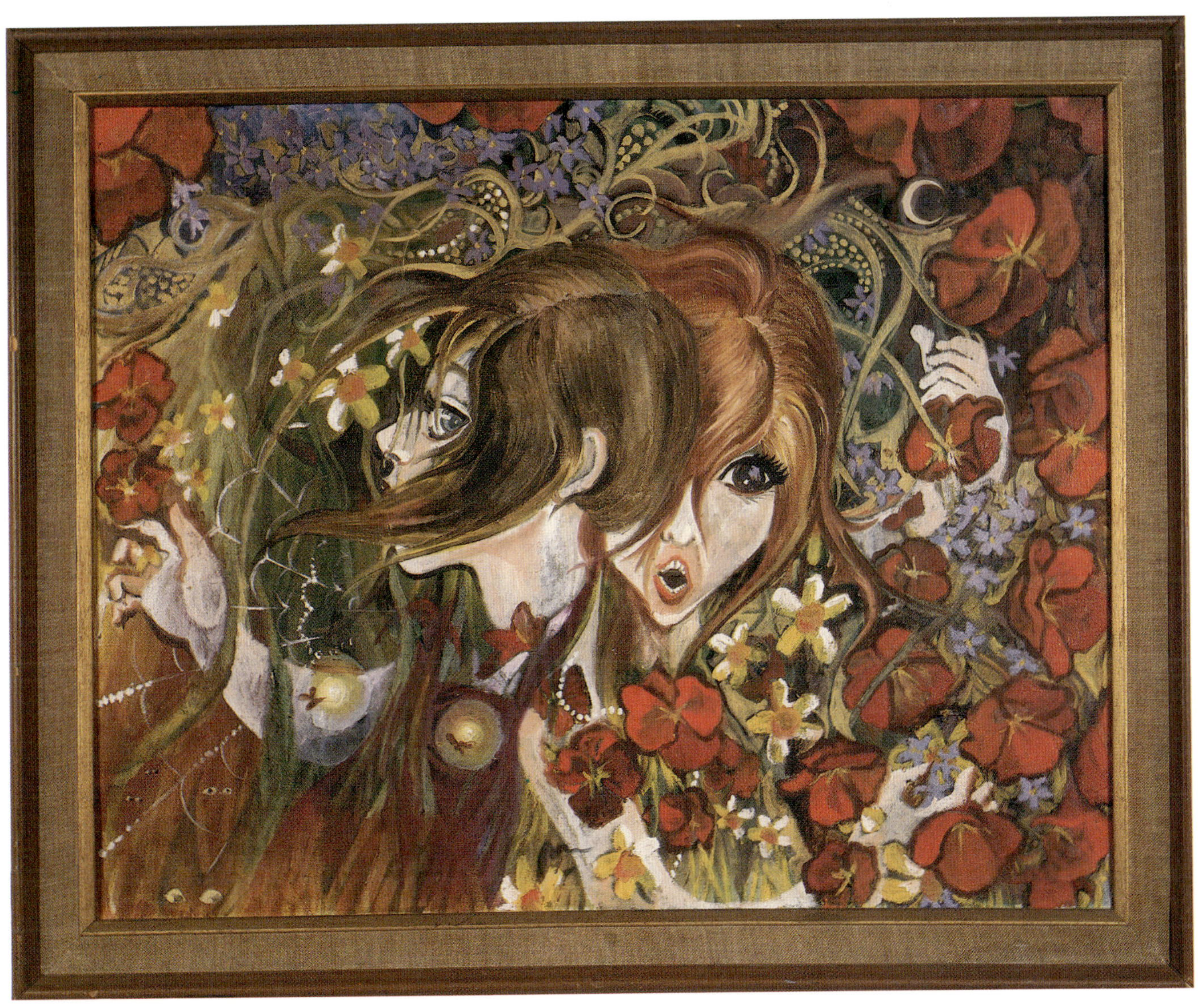

Two Girls Terrified in Garden

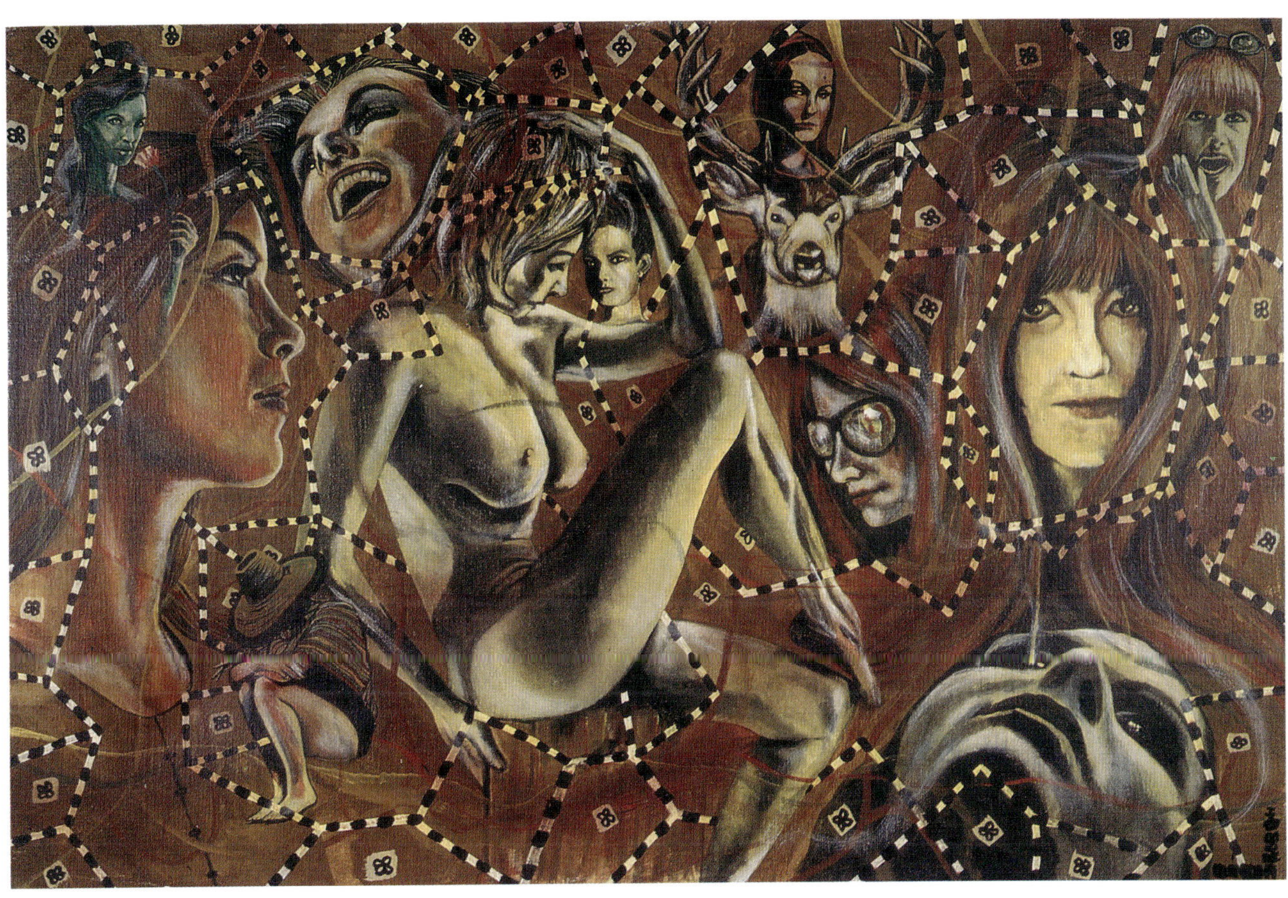

Nude, Deer Head, Many Women and Dotted Line

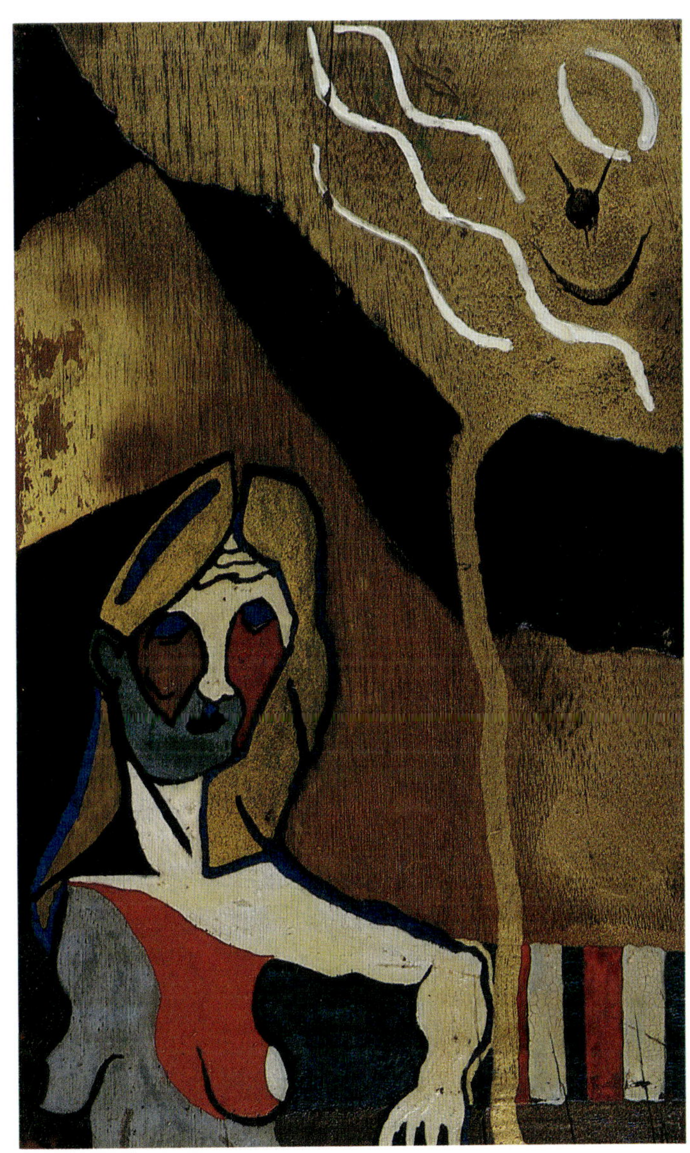

Psychedelic Tired-looking Woman

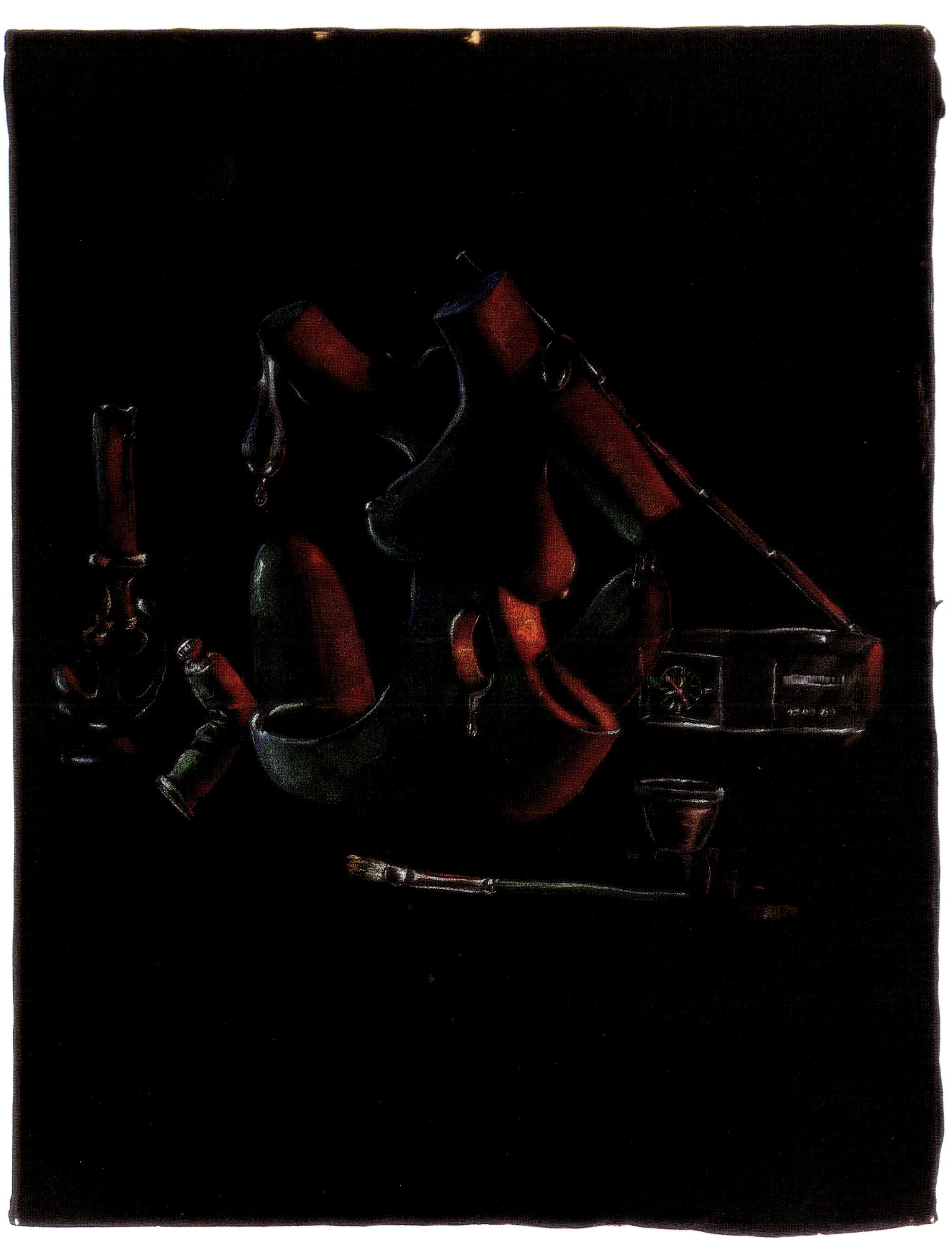

Black Velvet Woman's Torso with Phantom Limbs, Radio and Painter's Tools

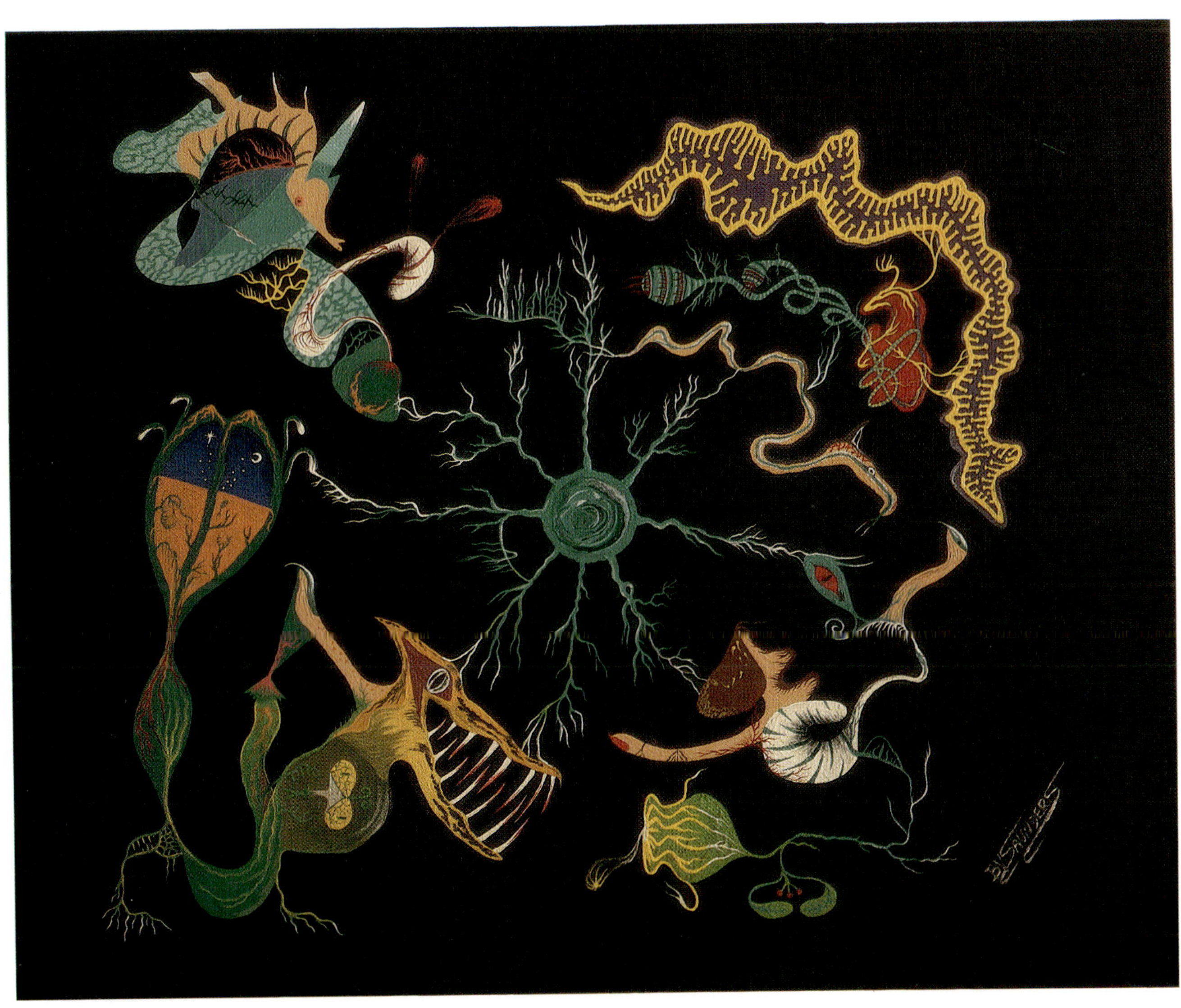

Psychedelic Organic Shapes on Black

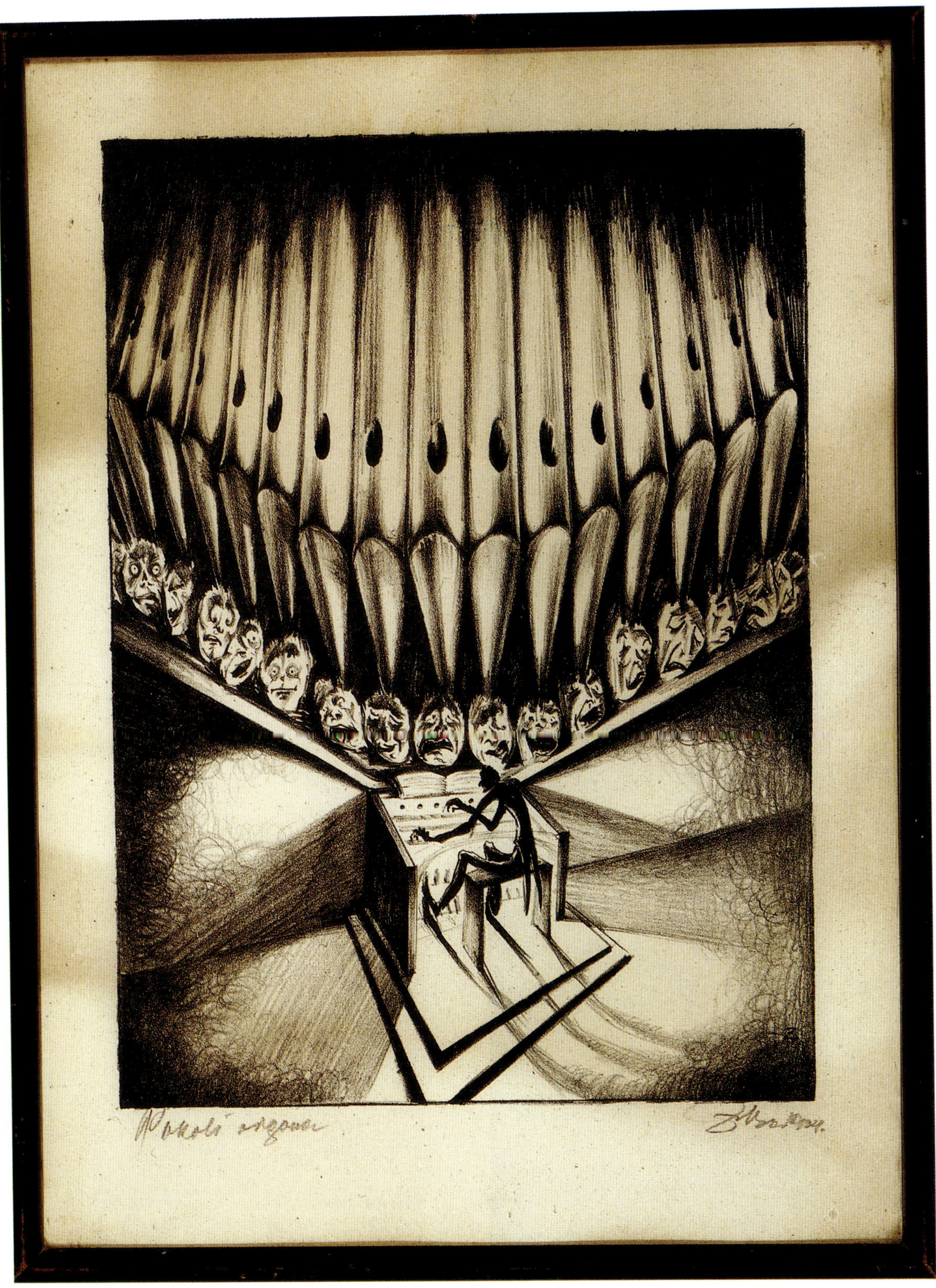

Fiendish Organ Player

Index

Page

Front Cover *Small Boy in Brown Room* 19 x 15″ (oil on board) by Clifford

7 *Man and Girl at Table in Gray & Cranberry* 18¼ x 22¼″ (oil on canvas) by Raul Gallery

9 *Ochre Baby Crawls on Man's Chest as Dog Looks On* 15 x 30″ (acrylic on canvas)

11 *Preacher at Blue Pulpit* 16 x 20″ (oil on canvas board) by Ruth B. Moore. Collection of Robert Lopez

13 *Still Life with Pipe, Cigarette, Banana, Champagne, etc.* 14¼ x 17¾″ (oil on canvas) by Erroll. Collection of Molly Cleator

15 *Purple Toilet Paper and Flower* 10 x 8″ (acrylic on canvas)

17 *Woman's Hand with Dark Red Ring, Fuzzy Sleeve* 16 x 20″ (acrylic on canvas) by Leon Dyer. Collection of Mike Kelley

19 *Hand on Bible* 15 x 12″ (oil on canvas) by Cora. Collection of Robert Lopez

21 *Woman by Table with Chinese Writing* 14 x 18″ (oil on canvas)

23 *Woman in Black Undies at Vanity Table* 19½ x 15½″ (oil on canvas)

25 *Blonde Woman with Large Necklace in Shadowy Theatre* 18 x 13½″ (oil on canvas) by Eugene Poinc. Collection of David Bradshaw

27 *Three Street Lights* 24 x 19½″ (oil on canvas)

29 *Small Boy in Brown Room* 19 x 15″ (oil on board) by Clifford

31 *Child's Elephant Lamp* 20 x 16″ (oil on canvas board). Collection of Jon Bok

33 *Drunken Clown, Blue with Red Dots* 20 x 16″ (oil on canvas) by Peggy Tucker. Collection of Jon Bok

35 *Bitter Clown, Sepia with Red Hair, Blue Collar* 20 x 16″ (acrylic on canvas board). Collection of Jon Bok

37 *Man at Piano* 18 x 12″ (acrylic on homosote). Collection of Ellen Kaufman

39 *Two Abstract Tiki-like Faces* 18 x 12″ (acrylic on homosote). Collection of Ellen Kaufman

41 *Couple with Candle in Black and Yellow* 36 x 24″ (acrylic on homosote) by Billie Gristle

43 *Woman on Ochre Background Comforts Gray-haired Person* 32¼ x 21⅝″ (oil on canvas) by J.G. Betkis

45 *Two Shoes with Faces* 29¼ x 21¼″ (oil on canvas) by De Rolf

47 *Two Kids with Farm in Background* 24 x 36″ (tempera on paper) by FMP. Collection of Michael Walker

49 *Man with No Crotch Sits Down with Girl* 22 x 29¾″ (oil on canvas) by Miller

51 *Dramatic Historical Scene* 22 x 29¾″ (oil on canvas) by Miller

53 *Maid Sprays Kids on Second Floor with Hose* 22¼ x 18¼″ (acrylic on canvas board) by Perry A. Sweter. Collection of Michael Walker

upper 55 *Robot Attacks Two Women* 18 x 30″ (gouache on illustration board) by Danny Hall

lower 55 *Robot Bursts Out of Crate* 18 x 30″ (gouache on illustration board) by Danny Hall

57 *Woman Made of Pillow, Wax Lips, Green Thing* 22 x 18″ (oil on canvas) by Vicki Torf

59 *Distorted Woman in Western Clothes with Grid* 24 x 19½″ (oil on canvas)

61 *Indian Woman and Papoose* 16 x 12″ (acrylic on canvas) by R. Gilbert. Collection of David Bradshaw

63 *Woman in Underwear Smiles at Photo by Pink Couch and Painting* 39⅛ x 29⅛″ (acrylic on board) by Roberto Garcia

65 *Nude Blonde Woman with Cigarette Holder* 33 x 42⅞″ (acrylic on cardboard)

67 *Platinum Blonde Woman in Red Dress in Blue Room* 48 x 24″ (acrylic on board) by Pena Ivar. Collection of Brad Dunning and Ann Magnuson

69 *Red-haired Woman in Blue Suit and Demon on Swing* 33 x 27″ (oil on canvas) by D. Richardson

upper left 70 *Unknown First Lady* 24 x 18″ (acrylic on canvas board)

upper right 70 *Mrs. Cleveland "1st Wedding in White House"* 24 x 18″ (acrylic on canvas board)

lower left 70 *Mrs. Monroe* 24 x 18″ (acrylic on canvas board)

lower right 70 *Grace Goodhue Coolidge* 24 x 18″ (acrylic on canvas board)

upper left 71 *Dolly Payne Todd Madison "Most Popular First Lady"* 24 x 18″ (acrylic on canvas board)

Page

upper right 71 *Frances Folsom Cleveland "First Lady to be Married"* 24 x 18″ (acrylic on canvas board)

lower left 71 *Lady Bird Johnson* 24 x 18″ (acrylic on canvas board)

lower right 71 *Jane Means Appleton Pierce "Reluctant First Lady"* 24 x 18″ (acrylic on canvas board)

73 *African Woman with Psychedelic Spider Web* 28½ x 24½″ (acrylic on canvas)

75 *Thin, White-haired Man* 38 x 13″ (oil on canvas) by Welsh

77 *Man with White Hair, Wide Shoulders* 20 x 16″ (oil on canvas) by Ike. Collection of Paul Ruscha

79 *Grandma with Blue Glasses and Brown Dress* 19¾ x 15¾″ (oil on board). Collection of Linda Cathcart

81 *Gas Station Owner* 12 x 9″ (acrylic on board) by Baker. Collection of Paul Ruscha

83 *Little Girl with Teeth* 21¼ x 18″ (acrylic on canvas) by Joan

85 *Girl Floating on Yellow Field* 15⅝ x 14″ (oil on board)

87 *Woman's Head in Blue Landscape* 22″ x 18″ (oil on board). Collection of Paul Ruscha

89 *Topless Woman's Portrait* 27 x 21″ (oil on canvas) by Kirk Miller. Collection of Byron Werner

91 *Bearded Black Man in White Shirt* 19¼ x 11″ (pastel on paper). Collection of Bianca Kovar

93 *Long-faced Man with Tie* 18 x 12″ (oil on board)

95 *Purple Man* 11⅜ x 8″ (oil on canvas)

97 *Black Man Mourning in Tones of Grey* 24 x 19″ (oil on canvas) by Milton. Collection of David Bradshaw

99 *Old Man with Zoroaster Book* 20 x 16″ (oil on board) by Michelangelo Selim Mickels

101 *Off-road Helmet Merges with Landscape* 18 x 24″ (oil on canvas)

103 *Old Man with Pipe* 15¼ x 12¼″ (oil on canvas). Collection of Bianca Kovar

105 *Blue Collar Worker* 16 x 18″ (oil on canvas) by Ike. Collection of Paul Ruscha

107 *Embossed Surrealist/Expressionist Cityscape* 26½ x 21″ (copper)

109 *Boy with Duck Toy Peers through Rusty Gates* 16 x 12″ (acrylic on canvas board). Collection of Helen Jewell

111 *Tiki God* 18 x 12″ (oil on canvas). Collection of Jon Bok

113 *Nude Woman Reclining on Orange Bed* 22 x 29″ (acrylic and pastel on canvas) by H. Berry

115 *Cleopatra with Cats and Tiled Floor* 26½ x 34″ (oil on canvas board) by R.M. Gullifer. Collection of Dahram Damama

117 *Nude Blonde Woman with Butterfly and Cherries* 17¼ x 15¼″ (oil on masonite) by J.V.. Collection of Byron Werner

119 *Woman in Barrel with Yellow Roses, Typewriter and Chair on Boxes* 41 x 30¾″ (oil on canvas) Alice Wesenen

121 *Indian Maidens Frolic in Bikinis* 24 x 34″ (oil on masonite) by J. Ray Stocks

123 *Neptune and Nymphs Astride Sea Mammals* 27½ x 34½″ (acrylic on board) by Edwin Lafferty. Collection of Michael Walker

125 *Man and Woman Emerge from Egg in Seascape* 24 x 36″ (acrylic on canvas) by Harris

127 *Yellow Surfer and Egg in Curl* 24 x 18″ (oil on canvas)

129 *Jesus and Babies Over Mountain Pool Landscape* 11½ x 17½″ (acrylic on board) by Matlock

131 *Loin-clothed Man Hanging by One Wrist* 14 x 10″ (oil on canvas) by C. Drie

133 *Bleeding Flaming Heart, Thorns and Caritas* 37¼ x 37¼″ (watercolor). Collection of Melissa Hoffs

135 *Girl with Calf* 19½ x 23½″ (oil on board) by J. Janzen. Collection of David Bradshaw

137 *Girl with Cigar-like Flute and Goats* 18½ x 14½″ (oil on linen) by Hus tel Avis. Collection of David Bradshaw

139 *Turtle in Hat with Cigar, Saying "Ybysaia (Baby)"* 19½ x 29½″ (pastel on paper) by Roger

141 *Leaves, Birds, Sky, Gold Leaf, Jupiter, etc.* 20 x 27½″ (acrylic and gold leaf on board) by Elmer D. Sandry. Collection of Michael Walker

143 *Elk's Head in Multiple Frames* 36½ x 30½″ (acrylic on board) by Elmer D. Sandry. Collection of Michael Walker

145 *Two Monkeys Hang from Tree* 28 x 22″ (acrylic on board) by Hodges. Collection of Ellen Kaufman

147 *Snarling Mountain Lion* 28 x 22″ (acrylic on canvas board) by Hodges. Collection of Ellen Kaufman

Page

149 *Pink Mountain Lion on Brown Background* 20 x 16″ (oil on board). Collection of Ellen Kaufman

151 *Two Chipmunks* 17¼ x 21¼″ (oil on canvas) by Luci. Collection of Mike Kelley

153 *Wolves Attacking Steer Carcass on Snowy Night* 14 x 18″ (acrylic on canvas board) by Vic Martin. Collection of Jon Bok

155 *Two Dogs Fighting in Forest* 27½ x 24⅛″ (oil on canvas) by Leo T. Parkhurst. Collection of Dahram Damama

157 *Pink Poodle and Hydrant with Text* 8½ x 10½″ (acrylic on masonite) by Kirkee. Collection of Robert Lopez

159 *Strange Interstate Bondage Image* 15½ x 17½″ (paper, thread, needle and ink) by J.J. Allen

161 *Fast Food Last Supper* 24 x 18″ (acrylic on canvas) by Dan Anderson

163 *Pop Art with Gas Pump, Whiskey, Money, Mouth, Woman* 22 x 21¾″ (acrylic on canvas)

165 *Pink Elephant with Bottles and Eye in Cocktail Glass* 24 x 18″ (acrylic on canvas board). Collection of Bryan Tucker

167 *Purple Surrealist Landscape with Pink Frame* 34 x 20¼″ (acrylic on board) by N. Prokos

169 *Dead Tree with Giant Lemon on Chain* 28 x 22″ (oil on canvas) by M. Cohen

171 *Blue Field with Dog, Tree, House, Flowers, Carrots, Bike* 24 x 18″ (oil on canvas board)

173 *Frankenstein-Magritte Boots* 30 x 26″ (oil on canvas) by L. Grace

175 *Two Surreal Heads in Landscape* 20 x 24″ (oil on canvas) by Louis Schorsch. Collection of Robert and Susanne Williams

177 *Many Faces Converge into Landscape* 20¼ x 24¼″ (acrylic on canvas) by Merit Boyer. Collection of Robert Lopez

179 *Cosmic Blonde Girl with Liquid Universe and Ball Point Defacing* 36 x 24″ (acrylic on canvas board)

180 *Fishing Lure with Woman's Head* 24⅝ x 36⅝″ (oil on canvas) by Roehl

181 *Headless Beat Girl with Text and Paint Brushes in Neck* 49 x 25″ (oil on canvas) by Roehl

183 *Psychedelic James Dean Portrait* 21 x 27″ (acrylic on canvas)

185 *Cubist/Surrealist Piece with Saxophone, Clock, Mouth and Eye* 25¾ x 21¾″ (oil on canvas)

187 *Weird Adam and Eve with Animals and Figures* 18 x 24″ (acrylic on canvas board) by Elaine Flavin. Collection of Ellen Kaufman

189 *Two Girls Terrified in Garden* 25⅜ x 31⅜″ (oil on canvas)

191 *Nude, Deer Head, Many Women and Dotted Line* 24 x 36″ (acrylic on canvas)

193 *Psychedelic Tired-looking Woman* 9¼ x 5¾″ (acrylic on wood)

195 *Black Velvet Woman's Torso with Phantom Limbs, Radio and Painter's Tools* 40 x 26″ (oil on velvet). Collection of Melissa Hoffs

197 *Psychedelic Organic Shapes on Black* 24 x 30″ (acrylic on canvas) by Saunders

199 *Fiendish Organ Player* 16½ x 12½″ (print) by Zitrel. Collection of Les Bernstein

Back Cover *Struggling Infant* 10 x 12″ (oil on canvas) by D. Sanford

All uncredited ownerships are from the collection of Jim Shaw.

All pieces from Jim Shaw, Ellen Kaufman and Paul Ruscha collections, photo credit Paul Ruscha.

All pieces from other collections, photo credit Fred Nilsen.

Special thanks to Cynthia Cleary, Joe Fuchs, Dick Bellanger and Lisa Blessing from the Brand Library, and all the artists represented in this book.